Majority World Theology Series

Series Editors

Gene L. Green, Stephen T. Pardue, and K. K. Yeo

The Majority World Theology series exists because of the seismic shifts in the makeup of world Christianity. At this moment in history, more Christians live in the Majority World than in Europe and North America. However, most theological literature does not reflect the rising tide of Christian reflection coming from these regions. The Majority World authors in this series seek to produce, collaboratively, biblical and theological textbooks that are about, from, and to the Majority World. By assembling scholars from around the globe who share a concern to do theology in light of Christian Scripture and in dialogue with Christian tradition coming from the Western church, this series offers readers the chance to listen in on insightful, productive, and unprecedented in-person conversations. Each volume pursues a specific theological topic and is designed to be accessible to students and scholars alike.

D1599444

The Spirit over the Earth

Pneumatology in the Majority World

Edited by

Gene L. Green, Stephen T. Pardue, K. K. Yeo

WILLIAM B. EERDMANS PUBLISHING COMPANY
GRAND RAPIDS, MICHIGAN

Wm. B. Eerdmans Publishing Co.
2140 Oak Industrial Drive NE, Grand Rapids, Michigan 49505
www.eerdmans.com

Published 2016
Printed in the United States of America

22 21 20 19 18 17 16   1 2 3 4 5 6 7

ISBN 978-0-8028-7273-9

Library of Congress Cataloging-in-Publication Data

A catalog record for this book is available from the Library of Congress

Contents

Contents

The Spirit over the Earth: Pneumatology in the Majority World

GENE L. GREEN

The Holy Spirit in Scripture and Christian Theology through History

"In the beginning God created the heavens and the earth. Now the earth was formless and empty, darkness was over the surface of the deep, and the Spirit of God was hovering over the waters" (Gen. 1:1, NIV). The biblical story begins with God. He is the Creator of all things and the divine Spirit is his active agent to bring order to chaos.[1] Throughout Scripture the biblical authors have also viewed the Holy Spirit as God's agent to empower human beings for work, especially as they become his prophets who express his will (Heb. 3:7–11; 1 Peter 1:10–12; 2 Peter 1:20–21). We learn from these authors that the Spirit empowered Jesus for his ministry in fulfillment of Isaiah's messianic prophecy (Luke 4:16–21; cf. Isa. 61:1–2). Upon his ascension, Jesus gave the church the Holy Spirit so that his people could carry out the work he ordained (Acts 1:6–8; 2:32–36). Scripture ascribes these and other roles to the Holy Spirit, and the church through the centuries has reflected on its teaching regarding the person and work of the Spirit of God.

1. Not all biblical commentators would identify the "Spirit of God" as the "Holy Spirit." While a context-sensitive exegesis of the passage may lead to the conclusion that the author of Genesis is speaking about the wind (*ruah*) of God, later Christian interpreters have read the passage within the context of the canon and Christian theology and so identify God's *ruah* (which may also be translated "Spirit") as the third person of the Trinity.

After the New Testament era, discussion about the Spirit continued in earnest as the church sought to articulate the nature of God and
the relationship between the Father, Son, and Holy Spirit. The Cappadocian fathers—Basil of Caesarea, Gregory of Nyssa, and Gregory of Nazianzus—vigorously defended the Spirit's divinity as they recognized
and described the Trinitarian foundation of Christian theology. The
Nicene Creed (325) affirmed the church's belief in the Holy Spirit as the
third member of the Trinity. The Council of Constantinople (381) reiterated Nicea's affirmation of the Spirit's divinity and then elaborated
on the nature and role of the Holy Spirit in this way:

> We believe in the Holy Spirit, the Lord, the Giver of Life,
> who proceeds from the Father and the Son.
> With the Father and the Son
> he is worshiped and glorified.
> He has spoken through the Prophets.

Although the Eastern and Western churches have debated the question
of whether the Spirit proceeds from both the Father and the Son, they
are in entire agreement that the Holy Spirit is divine and personal.
While the Western church's belief in the procession of the Spirit from
both the Father and the Son may seem to imply the subordination of
the Spirit to the other members of the Trinity, the church affirmed
that the Spirit's divinity was on par with that of the Son and the Father. The Holy Spirit and the Son are not "derived Deities" despite the
begetting of the Son and the procession of the Spirit.[2] Another way to
articulate this is to say that the Father, Son, and Holy Spirit are consub-
stantial, that is, of the same and not similar substance.

At the same time, Athanasius carefully distinguished the Spirit
from creation. In his *Letter to Serapion*, Athanasius celebrates the full
divinity of the Spirit, saying, "For as the Son, who is in the Father and
the Father in him, is not a creature but pertains to the essence of the
Father . . . so also it is not lawful to rank with the creatures the Spirit
who is in the Son, and the Son in him, nor to divide him from the
Word and reduce the Triad to imperfection" (1.21). The Holy Spirit is
not a creature but a full member of the divine Triad.

---

2. Thomas F. Torrance, *The Trinitarian Faith: The Evangelical Theology of the Ancient Catholic Church* (Edinburgh: T&T Clark, 1988), 112.

While the fathers were carefully working out the question of the being of the Spirit in relationship to the other members of the Trinity and creation, they also reflected on the Spirit's agency. Nicea states that he is the sovereign "Lord" and that all life has its source in him, "the Giver of Life." Moreover, "He has spoken through the Prophets." The Spirit has a particular role in revelation which, in the creed, is tied tightly to the prophets. Additionally, the creed points in the direction of the church since following the "third article" it confesses: "We believe in one holy catholic and apostolic church." Ecclesiology and pneumatology cannot be drawn asunder since it is through the Spirit's agency that Christ establishes his church.

With each succeeding generation the church's understanding of the person and work of the Holy Spirit has deepened and widened, becoming a great and powerful river at the end of the twentieth and the beginning of the twenty-first century.[3] Although the creed makes critical affirmations regarding the person and work of the Holy Spirit, it hardly reflects the whole of the biblical witness and does not answer many questions that have arisen in the church's long march up to this day. During the medieval period attention was drawn to the experience of the Holy Spirit. The mystics held the day but for them this experience was the privilege of those set apart for the religious life. We find, for example, Bernard of Clairvaux (1090–1153) in the monastery where he writes *Sermons on the Song of Songs* which promotes the devotional life, regarded as "a gift of the Holy Spirit."[4] Thomas Aquinas (1225–74) entered a Benedictine monastery and later became a member of the Dominican Order of Friars. In a life given over to theology and devotion he affirmed that the Holy Spirit is love, proceeds in love, and distributes his gifts accordingly.[5] With the dawn of the Reformation, however, Luther's understanding of the "priesthood of all believers" opened the door to understanding how the Spirit works for sanctification in every Christian, not just those devoted to the medieval conception of the spiritual life. The Reformers emphasized the Spirit's role in relation to the Word and sacraments, whereas some Radical Reformers

3. For the history of the doctrine of the Holy Spirit, see Anthony C. Thiselton, *The Holy Spirit—in Biblical Teaching, through the Centuries, and Today* (Grand Rapids: Eerdmans, 2013); Veli-Matti Kärkkäinen, *The Holy Spirit: A Guide to Christian Theology* (Louisville: Westminster John Knox, 2012).

4. Thiselton, *The Holy Spirit*, 234.

5. Thiselton, *The Holy Spirit*, 244.

turned to the Holy Spirit as the one who leads the believer, thereby decoupling the Spirit from Word and sacrament.

Contemporary Western and Majority World Developments in Pneumatology

Until recently, Western theology has focused more on Christology and less on the person and work of the Holy Spirit. A turning point came with the rise of Pentecostalism at the start of the twentieth century and Vatican II (1962–65). The renewed emphasis among Roman Catholics falls on the Spirit's work within the church. *Lumen gentium* begins its ecclesiological reflection stating, "Christ is the Light of nations. Because this is so, this Sacred Synod gathered together in the Holy Spirit eagerly desires, by proclaiming the Gospel to every creature, to bring the light of Christ to all men, a light brightly visible on the countenance of the Church." On the Protestant side, the rise of Pentecostalism in North America and globally has brought with it laser-focused attention on the empowerment that comes through the Spirit of God that enables the church to fulfill its role as witness in the world (Acts 1:8). Out of this movement arose a number of notable North Atlantic Pentecostal scholars, including Gordon Fee, Russell Spittler, and Frank Macchia, who emphasize God's presence and power through the Spirit.[6] Non-Pentecostal theologians, such as George-Yves Congar, Jürgen Moltmann, and Wolfhart Pannenberg, have also been deeply concerned with the Holy Spirit and ecclesiology, renewal, and especially life in all its forms.[7]

Unsurprisingly, the church in the Majority Word has begun renewed reflections on the role of the Holy Spirit in the church and in the world. The church in the Majority World is "self-theologizing." That is, it recognizes its responsibility as part of "one holy catholic and apostolic church" to make its own contribution to the universal or Catholic discussion about theology that has unfolded through the ages within the Western and Eastern churches. From within Africa, Christian theologians have embraced a theology of the Spirit that underscores the way he confronts other spiritual powers in the world.

---

6. Thiselton, *The Holy Spirit*, 373–93.
7. Thiselton, *The Holy Spirit*, 394–419.

The Holy Spirit is part of a power-encounter that finds few parallels in the West where the church has, at times, forgotten Paul's statement that "our struggle is not against flesh and blood, but against the rulers, against the authorities, against the powers of this dark world and against the spiritual forces of evil in the heavenly realms" (Eph. 6:12).

Within Asian theologies, the Holy Spirit is not separated from the material world as is common in Western theology but is the primary essence of reality. Instead of opposing dichotomies, the Spirit is not outside the world but is "the complementary pair of *yin* and *yang*" that organizes all things.[8] Questions about the role of the Holy Spirit within the complex of religions in Asia is another concern that occupies Asian theologians. In Latin American theology, the place of the Spirit in the community and the social implications of his presence are topics of concern. Although the role of the Spirit in personal transformation and empowerment for ministry receives prime attention within Latin American Pentecostalism, the social dimension of the Spirit's work receives attention among theologians who face the socioeconomic injustices of the region. The church in the Majority World is self-theologizing, and this is abundantly evident in the development of contemporary pneumatology.

Biblical and Theological Reflections in This Volume

The authors of this volume share a commitment to Scripture as God's Word and recognize that their reading is always from and to a particular place, time, and cultural matrix. Contextualization is inherent in the affirmation that Scripture is truly God's Word that is spoken in human words. The biblical scholars who speak in these pages—Zakali Shohe, Hua Wei, Samuel Ngewa, and René Padilla—all reflect on the biblical text in concert with their particular *Sitz im Leben* (situation in life), which gives rise to fresh questions and insights regarding the Spirit's work as witnessed in the Word. The theologians from the Majority World—Ivan Satyavrata, David Ngong, and Oscar García-Johnson—as well the Asian American scholar Amos Yong who is the author of the opening chapter, all attend to the theological heritage from the West

---

8. Veli-Matti Kärkkäinen, ed., *Holy Spirit and Salvation: The Sources of Christian Theology* (Louisville: Westminster John Knox, 2010), 420.

but recognize that the emphases and formulations developed there are not fully adequate to address the theological necessities of their communities. In other words, both the biblical scholars and theologians in this volume are connected deeply with Scripture and the tradition, but they also dialogue extensively with their context and their cultures. All theology, and all biblical studies, is contextual. We may embrace this fact without severing ourselves from Scripture or tradition. Indeed, the insights the authors present benefit the whole church since they are vital contributions to a genuinely catholic theology. Theology through the centuries has always been contextual. While we may read the ABCs of theology—Augustine, Barth, and Calvin—we always need to recognize that the theological alphabet ends with WYZ—Wei, Yong, and Zakali. And so it must be this side of the *eschaton* since now we know in part, awaiting that day when we will know even as we are fully known. Dimly reflected revelation will give way to face-to-face clarity (1 Cor. 13:9–12). Until that time we need one another, the voices of brothers and sisters through the centuries, and those that come to all of us from around the globe. We always get by with a little help from our friends. A few notes about each of the authors and chapters may help as you read along the grain of their concerns and questions that are related to the context of their reading and reflection.

Amos Yong is a familiar voice to anyone reading in the area of contemporary pneumatology. In his chapter he briefly surveys both the Western and Eastern Orthodox traditions regarding the Spirit before providing an overview of some Majority World pneumatology. The brilliance of Yong's chapter is that he ties the traditions together with global developments while, at the same time, reflecting on their connection with the Nicene Creed. Of particular interest is his emphasis on life through the Spirit and its implications for our understanding of God's agency in creation. He stands, along with Majority World theologians, in opposition to Enlightenment-inspired dualism that would want to preserve a sharp divide between spirit and matter. His concern is to show "the immanence of the divine breath within the fabric of created materiality." In this he speaks as an Asian American theologian.

Ivan Satyavrata brings us into the heart of pneumatological reflection from India. In a world where the influence of *advaitic* Hinduism is pervasive, he takes pains to underscore that the Holy Spirit should not be "confused with the human spirit," or be viewed as "an impersonal, immanent force." He closely links the Holy Spirit with Christ—he is the Spirit *of Christ*. The themes here are familiar to anyone reading the fathers, but the turn comes in his dialogue between the biblical witness and the "personalist *bhakti* strand within Hinduism," which he sees as offering "much more promise for Christian contextual engagement in India." In other words, he finds resonances between the early Christian emphasis on the personality of the Spirit and a devotional strain within Hinduism. As he says, "the Holy Spirit is a means by which God makes his personal presence felt among his people, the church, the community of the Spirit." He ties his argument up with Christology in stating, "the ultimate purpose of the Spirit's 'floodlight' ministry is to mediate the presence of the risen Christ, and to create and deepen an awareness of the reality of Jesus in human experience." His emphasis on personal relation and Christology melds historic theological orthodoxy with contextual insights. The seriousness with which he takes cultural influences derived from Hinduism in his theological reflection is characteristic of much Majority World theology. Cultural perspectives can be both critiqued and affirmed in this dance with Scripture and tradition.

Zakali Shohe writes from the Indian context as well, with special attention to Nagaland in Northeast India. She examines the role of the Spirit in Romans 8:14–17 from a relational perspective and draws out the significance of this passage for both Christians and society in India. The Spirit allows the believer to use the filial address "Abba Father," thus identifying all believers as co-heirs with Christ. For her, life in the Spirit is not about power but relationship. This Spirit-inspired relationship is a manifestation of the eschatological unity of God's people. Relationship and unity inspired by the Spirit lead to acceptance of the other. But Shohe is not content to stop at the doors of the church. While understanding that the church has not lived up to its full reality in the Spirit, she boldly states that, as unified community, "the church as an institution needs to be a model of openness by taking initiative in bridge building and creating platforms for meeting points." In other words, the church is an eschatological sign to the wider community and this relationality is part of Christian witness and social renewal. Shohe sees a much broader role for the Spirit than personal piety and powerful evangelistic campaigns. Social hopes are tied to the Spirit's work.

Wei Hua writes from a Chinese perspective on one of the enduring problems of Christianity in his country. How should Christians respond to the rites of ancestors and Confucius? After detailing the history of the controversy, Hua explains the meaning of these rites, understanding that they "have many dimensions, and these dimensions are clearly intertwined." He vigorously denies that due reverence is the same as idolatry, which both Confucius and he reject. The surprise in his chapter comes as he examines 1 Corinthians 8–10, where Paul reflects on the practice of eating meat offered to idols. May one participate in these rites? Hua proposes that the answer Paul gives is not a simple "Yes" or "No," as even a casual reading of 1 Corinthians reveals. This biblical reflection undergirds his discussion of the rites issue. Hua does not simply present a facile comparison between China and Corinth. He understands within Christian practice, both then and now, a fulfillment and renewal of culture. Thus, he concludes, "Just as the Jewish law had been fulfilled in the power of the Spirit by Gentile Christians, and the Roman customs had been renewed in Paul's time, so also the Chinese commemorating rights can be renewed and obeyed by Chinese Christians as 'humanizing' etiquette (*li*) in the power of the Holy Spirit, who moves and works through all believers." Hua, as other Majority World biblical scholars and theologians, is struggling and thinking deeply about how Christianity and culture can critically coexist so that the gospel becomes truly contextualized and is not seen as a foreign entity but as the fulfillment of hopes. His desire in the end is expressed in the final prayer: "May the Spirit of God help the global church in China not to be 'Christianity *in China*,' but to be *Chinese* Christianity." He is able to get to this point because he understands that Christian identity is wrapped around the reception of the Holy Spirit. Christian *koinonia* is possible within a diverse community, one that includes Jews, Gentiles, and Chinese, without the dissolution of their cultures.

Samuel M. Ngewa brings his biblical expertise to bear on the work of the Holy Spirit in Acts 2, 8, 10, and 19. Like Shohe, he focuses on inclusion as he discusses the Spirit's work among Samaritans, Gentiles, and those who reside in the ends of the earth. "What God seems to be doing in the book of Acts" is "bringing people of all races and nations under the same umbrella." In Acts that inclusion is not tied with ethnicity—Jews, Samaritans, and Gentiles all gather together due to the work of the Spirit. While he celebrates the way that the Spirit brings together those of different ethnicities, Ngewa asks why it was that the location of the East African Revival, Rwanda, succumbed to genocide. "The unfortunate thing," he says, "is that even persons who claimed to be Christians were involved in such killings. These serve as examples of many such conflicts all over the continent of Africa and beyond. Even within the church itself, there have been deep conflicts, with some of them centering on such matters as speaking in tongues and other such dramatic gifts of the Holy Spirit." Ngewa's essay is a realistic plea for the church to model and live the realities of its faith: one God for all the races of the world, one Savior, the same Spirit, and one family of God. And so he concludes, "All divisions on the basis of race, tribe, or the like have no place in the church of Christ." He understands that perceptions must be changed by God. The Spirit's presence should break down prejudice wherever it occurs.

David Tonghou Ngong traces the development of a Christian theology of the Spirit in Africa, beginning with the North African theologians. He, along with other African Christians, wants the global church to remember that the most significant trinitarian reflection came out of North Africa. He urges that the African church move beyond simply emphasizing the function of the Holy Spirit to examining the place of the Spirit in the Trinity, as did the early North African theologians. Ngong reflects on the Pentecostalization of African Christianity with its concomitant emphasis on pneumatology. He wants to draw together Nicea and contemporary African theology while at the same time rejecting Western Enlightenment rationalism. As part of this concern, Ngong notes that African cosmology is not otherworldly but deeply connected with life as it is lived here and now. For him, theology is worked out on the road of life but this does not divorce him from the Nicene Creed. In his discussion of African spirituality, he focuses on experience through the power of the Spirit and the transformative function of the Spirit. He emphasizes the belief in the existence of spirits and notes that it is not a superstition but rather a reality that can only be confronted via the power of the Spirit through Jesus Christ. Moreover, spirituality is not simply a question of the believer's individual life but for the community and, indeed, the whole of society. Human flourishing that comes through the Spirit is communal and is connected to threats to its survival. His chapter ends with a question about religious pluralism in Africa, a theme taken up by García-Johnson as well.

Oscar García-Johnson pens what will be, for many readers of this volume, one of the most challenging chapters. Western theology commonly reflects on general and special revelation, with its overriding emphasis being on God's revelation through Christ and Scripture. But the affirmation of general revelation brings with it entailments not often discussed in the West. Within African Christianity the question often arises: "Did God bring the missionaries to Africa, or did the missionaries bring God?" If we respond that God brought the missionaries to Africa, the question becomes: "Where, then, was God before the missionaries came?" García-Johnson presses the question within the frame of colonial theology. Was there a presence of the Spirit in the Americas before the colonial era? In answering the question, he moves toward seeing the Spirit outside the gate and, in doing so, wishes to uncover an indigenous theology of the Spirit. He reminds us of Melchizedek, Abraham, Balaam, and Paul's quotation of a Greek poet at the Athenian Areopagus (Acts 17) as he tries to trace out the "pneumatological continuity" between the pre-conquest and post-conquest communities of the Americas.

García-Johnson takes a journey into ancestral folk traditions in the Americas. While he does not examine theological trends within contemporary indigenous communities in Central and South America, this could well be a further stage of reflection. While objecting to the West being the *locus theologicus* par excellence, he affirms the Nicene Creed since "early Christian teachers emphasize the Spirit as a Revealer and Giver of Life." The concern expressed here is one every reader needs to take with the utmost seriousness. Does the gospel come into culture as an alien entity, or has God prepared the way, given perspectives, and raised expectations, which are then fulfilled in the gospel? The colonial mentality is one that see the gospel as a conquering and pulverizing force over indigenous peoples and beliefs. The consequence of this perspective has been the devastation of indigenous communities across the Americas, which lost life, land, and culture due to misconceived notions of Christian mission. García-Johnson, as a Central American, pushes back against that heritage and attempts to re-envisage the wideness of God's agency while not losing hold of Christ and his centrality.

The final chapter of this anthology comes from one of the senior statesmen of Majority World theology, C. René Padilla. Since the first Lausanne Conference in 1974, Padilla has been a leader in the development of Latin American evangelical theology. That theology, which developed parallel to and is not derivative from liberation theology, places special emphasis on *misión integral* (integral mission). The gospel of Christ is the in-breaking of the kingdom, or the rule of God through both word and deed. As such, the gospel is transformative not only for the life of the individual or the gathered community of believers, but also for society as a whole. In his chapter, Padilla emphasizes the work of the Spirit "as the source of power for life and hope, especially among the poor." The experience of the Spirit in Latin America, mostly among Pentecostals, occurs in the midst of deep poverty and social oppression. "The mission of the Messiah in the power of the Spirit," Padilla states, "is oriented toward the most vulnerable persons in society: the poor, the prisoners, the blind, the oppressed." So radical was Jesus's ministry among these people that the socioeconomic changes were big enough to be regarded as signs of "the coming of a new era of justice and peace—'the year of the Lord's favor,' the Jubilee year (cf. Leviticus 25)—a metaphor of the messianic era initiated in history by Jesus Christ." Those who are swept up by the wind of the Spirit become part of an "empowered, transnational, multilinguistic, intercultural movement for justice." The Spirit empowers the church and allows it "to experience the kingdom of God as a present reality." The values of the kingdom are here present in history in anticipation of that final day when all will be complete.

The authors of these chapters take us on the journey of the Spirit whose workings are wider than the individual heart. Issues of community and relationality are paramount, often stemming from the relational dimension of the Trinity. The community where the Spirit works is not only the church but also the wider society, both before and after the coming of the gospel. The Holy Spirit is not antithetical to culture, as he both critiques and affirms. Each of these authors deeply appreciates the heritage of Nicea but understands that the Spirit is restless. There is work to be done in the world, healing and redemptive work, that began in the first moments of creation and continues in the present out to the *eschaton*. The Spirit was, and is, and will be over all the earth.

*   *   *

This book, along with the other volumes in the Majority World Theology series, is the product of a strong community effort to facilitate the discussion about emerging Majority World perspectives in biblical studies and theology. We want to thank the authors for their literary contribution and for their willingness to gather in San Diego in November 2014 for the annual meetings of the Evangelical Theological Society and the Institute for Biblical Research (unfortunately, Ngewa and Satyavrata were unable to attend). We are all indebted to the Rivendell Steward's Trust, ScholarLeaders International, and the SEED Research Institute for their financial support and tremendous encouragement. Many of the scholars could not have attended these gatherings without the gracious help these agencies offered. Thanks also goes out to the leadership of the Evangelical Theological Society and the Institute for Biblical Research for creating space for this important discussion about pneumatology. Michael Thomson of Eerdmans has been an indefatigable supporter and counselor all along the way, and, once again, we tip our hats to him. Thanks are also due to Langham Partnership International and Langham Literature for supporting the global publication and distribution of the Majority World Theology series. Pieter Kwant of Langham Literature has been an energetic ally and we offer him our thanks. Jessica Hawthorne, teaching assistant extraordinaire, prepared the indices. We are all indebted to her. And, as always, we are grateful to God for his answers to prayers so that this global project could move forward. *Soli Deo gloria!*

CHAPTER 1

I Believe in the Holy Spirit:
From the Ends of the Earth to the Ends of Time

AMOS YONG

ABSTRACT

The first section of this chapter provides an overview of the broad spectrum of the Christian tradition and highlights the diversity of its pneumatological thinking, especially in the Eastern Orthodox tradition, Majority World theologies of the past century, and modern pentecostal-charismatic movements. Building on such foundations, the second section of the chapter revisits the third article of the Nicene Creed and suggests how such global perspectives can enrich contemporary pneumatological resourcement even as the latter might be disciplined in light of historic Christian commitments.

The doctrine of the Holy Spirit—pneumatology—is experiencing a contemporary renaissance that promises to correct its relative neglect by the classical tradition.[1] Yet the claim that the Spirit historically has

---

1. See Veli-Matti Kärkkäinen, *Pneumatology: The Holy Spirit in Ecumenical, International, and Contextual Perspective* (Grand Rapids: Baker Academic, 2002), 9.

Thanks to Steve Pardue, K. K. Yeo, and Gene Green for their invitation to participate in the "Scripture and Theology in Global Context" joint consultation of the Evangelical Theological Society and Institute for Biblical Research, San Diego, California, November 20–24, 2014; the original version of this chapter was presented there and revised based on helpful feedback from the audience. I am grateful also to my graduate assistant Ryan Seow for his feedback on a prior version of this chapter.

been the "shy" or "hidden" member of the Trinity[2] tells us only half the story when assessed in a world Christian context. This chapter revisits the broad spectrum of the Christian tradition and highlights the diversity of its pneumatological thinking, especially in the past century. Such pneumatological pluralism reflects both the many ways in which the divine breath[3] encounters people across space and time and the various modalities through which understanding of such occurs. Contemporary "third article theology"—which refers to the theology of the Spirit (pneumatology) and theology informed by a Spirit-oriented approach (pneumatological theology)[4]—retrieves and elaborates on the third article of the creed both by being anchored in the revelation of God in Christ and by being open to wherever and however the wind of God blows.

This chapter begins descriptively with an overview of pneumatology in a global historical context, and then shifts toward a constructive theology of the Spirit that is simultaneously a theology inspired by the Spirit (pneumatological theology). As a pentecostal theologian,[5] I find inspiration from the New Testament book of Acts, especially in a number of phrases in the early chapters. The narration of Luke, the author, about Peter's Day of Pentecost sermon—quoting from the prophet Joel: "God declares, . . . I will pour out my Spirit upon all flesh" (2:17)[6]—invites consideration of the global character of Christian pneumatological reflection, especially non-Western voices and perspectives.

2. Frederick Dale Bruner and William Hordern, *Holy Spirit: Shy Member of the Trinity* (Minneapolis: Augsburg, 1984).

3. Nomenclature for the Spirit based on the Hebrew *ruah*—literally "wind" or "breath"—preferred and introduced by Donald L. Gelpi, *The Divine Mother: A Trinitarian Theology of the Holy Spirit* (Lanham: University Press of America, 1984).

4. See Myk Habets, ed., *The Spirit of Truth: Reading Scripture and Constructing Theology with the Holy Spirit* (Eugene: Pickwick, 2010).

5. Especially relevant for the following is Amos Yong, *The Spirit Poured Out on All Flesh: Pentecostalism and the Possibility of Global Theology* (Grand Rapids: Baker Academic, 2005), among a number of other works that will be cited in due course.

6. Unless otherwise noted, all Scripture quotations will be from the NRSV. Although perhaps controversial, I believe that the "all flesh" reference includes not only all classes regardless of gender, age, or social status (2:17b–18) but also, potentially and eschatologically, all cultural-linguistic groups (following Acts 2:8–11); for discussion, see my commentary, with Anh Vince Le, "Acts 2," in *Global Bible Commentary Online* (2013), ed. Michael J. McClymond, http://www.globalbiblecommentary.org/index.html?book=Acts&chapter=2.

Even before this, Luke records Jesus telling the disciples that they will receive the empowerment of the Spirit to be his witnesses "to the ends of the earth" (1:8b). The Greek in this case, *eschatou tēs gēs*, refers not only to the spatial breadth of the earth but more technically to its temporal ends as well, the ends of the times of the earth, in fact.[7] Both aspects of the Spirit's outpouring—the spatial and the temporal—are reiterated at the end of Peter's Day of Pentecost homily where the gift of the Spirit is promised "for you, for your children, and for all who are far away, everyone whom the Lord our God calls to him" (2:39b).[8] So if the first part of this chapter attempts to document the breadth of pneumatological reflection "upon all flesh," the second section seeks to think creatively with the historical and dynamic deposit of faith, particularly with the Nicene confession about the Spirit, in ways appropriate to the third-millennium global context and beyond.

Poured Out on All Flesh:
Pneumatology in Global Historical Perspective

This initial mapping proceeds along three lines. I begin with Eastern Christian understandings of the Spirit in order to ensure that this important historic stream is not neglected in any constructive pneumatology for the present time, move on to more recent Majority World perspectives, and conclude with developments in pentecostal-charismatic and renewal theology. Throughout I highlight minority reports on theology of the Spirit in order to gain traction and momentum vis-à-vis the dominant Western pneumatological tradition for when we turn to the second part of this chapter.

Eastern Christian Pneumatology

There is no doubt that the achievement of a fully trinitarian orthodoxy, one that speaks not just to the Son's relationship with the Father

---

7. See Vitor Westhelle, *Eschatology and Space: The Lost Dimension in Theology Past and Present* (New York: Palgrave Macmillan, 2012), 132.

8. This line of pneumatological thinking is further exemplified in another of my books: *Who Is the Holy Spirit? A Walk with the Apostles* (Brewster: Paraclete, 2011).

but also includes the Spirit, would not have been secured apart from the efforts of theologians in the Eastern, or Greek-speaking, church in the fourth century. The Cappadocian fathers—Basil of Caesarea, Gregory of Nyssa, and Gregory of Nazianzus—each played crucial roles in arguing against those who did not believe the Spirit to be divine as the Son and the Father.[9] Against these so-called Spirit-fighters (Greek *pneumatomachians*) from the region of Macedonia,[10] these champions of trinitarian faith followed out the theological logic of the church's hallowed practices of baptism into the triune name and of prayer and worship offered to the Spirit, and insisted that such liturgical commitments sustained over centuries would be invalid apart from the implicit recognition of the Spirit's divine essence and character. Their efforts not only secured creedal elaboration on the deity of the Spirit (at the Council of Constantinople in 381) but also have profoundly impacted the main lines of Christian pneumatological reflection even in the Western tradition.

For our purposes, however, it would be a mistake to overlook the distinctive features of early Syriac pneumatology given their shaping of Cappadocian thinking about the Spirit. Second- and third-century Syriac sources clearly delineate the role of the Spirit in the process of Christian initiation.[11] The Spirit is invoked in the pre-baptismal anointing of new catechumens, is present to generate faith and active in healing, cleansing, and purifying them through their new birth of baptism in water, and enables their reception of the Messiah in their first Eucharist, thus accompanying their initiation from death to eternal life. While numerous biblical symbols for the Spirit are prevalent in these sources (e.g., the Spirit as fire, dove, or oil), it is the regenerative work of the Spirit that is prominent: to indwell believers, to

---

9. For example, Basil the Great, *On the Holy Spirit*, trans. David Anderson (Crestwood: St. Vladimir's Seminary Press, 1980), and Gregory of Nyssa, "On the Holy Spirit," §§19–26, in *Gregory of Nyssa*, ed. Anthony Meredith (London: Routledge, 1999), 35–45.

10. For a brief overview of the "pneumatomachian" position, see Stuart George Hall, *Doctrine and Practice in the Early Church* (Grand Rapids: Eerdmans, 1992), 153–54.

11. See especially the insightful studies of Joseph Chalassery, *The Holy Spirit and Christian Initiation in the East Syrian Tradition* (Rome: Mar Thomas Yogam and St. Thomas Christian Fellowship, 1995); Emmanuel Kaniyamparampil, *The Spirit of Life: A Study of the Holy Spirit in the Early Syriac Tradition* (Kerala: Oriental Institute of Religious Studies, 2003); and Sebastian P. Brock, *The Holy Spirit in the Syrian Baptismal Tradition*, 3rd ed., Gorgias Liturgical Studies 4 (Piscataway: Gorgias, 2008).

catalyze new birth and sonship, to sanctify and bring about union with God. For these early Syriac pastors and leaders, then, this life-giving Spirit stimulated symbolic reflection about a divine motherhood that nurtured, refreshed, and purified human creatures in order that they might participate in the divine nature.[12]

The Eastern emphasis on salvation as union with God and deification has given rise to a distinctive spiritual tradition across the Orthodox world. In this framework the life-giving work of the Spirit includes first and foremost the sanctifying formation of saints, and Pentecost becomes a symbol, then, of a community devoted to the spiritual path of disciplined ascent to the divine presence from the mundane and fallen world of creaturely passions.[13] Yet this tradition of contemplative praxis has also, when explicated with certain intellectual resources informed by philosophical idealism and even gnosticism, opened up to controversial theological developments. The pneumatology of Russian Orthodox thinker Sergei Bulgakov (1871–1944), for instance, set against the backdrop of his Christian divine-humanity and Neoplatonic sophiology (philosophy of divine wisdom), led to charges of heresy that, although eventually formally absolved, marked his views as at least disconcerting, if not flawed and aberrant.[14] Yet some of Bulgakov's central notions, such as the kenosis of Spirit in creation and the Spirit's gift of love being made available as a continuing Pentecost, resonate with important pneumatological themes both East and West, even as they are both consistent with and arguably intrinsic to Orthodox sensibilities and spiritual life. If Orthodox theologians have by and large prided themselves on retrieving the patristic tradition rather than reconstructing what has been received and handed down from the ecumenical church of the first millennium, Bulgakov is exemplary of those within this Eastern Christian milieu that have attempted to

12. Brock, *The Holy Spirit*, 176, notes that "in the earliest literature up to about AD 400 the Holy Spirit is always treated grammatically as feminine," and that this applies also to liturgical prayers (i.e., a Trinity of Father, Mother, and Son); this begins to change so that after about the sixth century, *ruah* as masculine predominates except in liturgical and poetic texts.

13. A Russian Orthodox account is that of I. M. Kontzevitch, *The Acquisition of the Holy Spirit in Ancient Russia*, trans. Olga Koshansky, ed. Abbot Herman (Plantina: St. Herman of Alaska Brotherhood, 1988).

14. Sergius Bulgakov, *The Comforter*, trans. Boris Jakim (Grand Rapids: Eerdmans, 2004).

creatively reappropriate inherited resources according to the pneumatological dynamic of a continuing Pentecost.

Nevertheless, Orthodox pneumatology remains largely scriptural in foundation, liturgical in orientation, and poetic in expression. Contemporary Orthodox pneumatologies generally draw from the patristic heritage and attempt biblical articulation in ecumenically relevant categories.[15] Over time, then, the main lines of Orthodox thinking about the Spirit have permeated Latin traditions and contemporary Western theologies so much so that it almost goes without saying that efforts to formulate a pneumatology relevant for the twenty-first-century global context will be deeply shaped by Eastern thought in essential respects.[16] Yet it is important not to take for granted these Orthodox resources that remind us about the feminine dimension of pneumatology as well as the intimate and irrevocable connection between theological ideas and spiritual praxis.

Contemporary Trends in the Majority World

If Orthodoxy has contributed distinctively to the texture of pneumatological reflection throughout the Christian tradition, then the emergence of Christianity as a world religion in the twentieth century has extended reflection on the Holy Spirit to the Majority World. The following in no way exhaustively summarizes the state of the discussion—the many gaps of which the rest of this book fills in—but rather highlights a few developments relevant to the constructive task ahead of us. What we will see is that Asian, African, and Latin American developments have the capacity to enrich if not complicate pneumatological thinking for the present time.[17]

---

15. Two examples from diverse Orthodox communions include Fr. Tadros Y. Malaty, *The Gift of the Holy Spirit*, The Coptic Orthodox Church and the Dogmas 7 (Cairo: Anba Reuiss, and Alexandria: St. Mark and Pope Peter Church, 1991), and John Oliver, *Giver of Life: The Holy Spirit in Orthodox Tradition* (Brewster: Paraclete, 2011).

16. See, for example, the work of Stanley M. Burgess, whose material in his earlier *The Holy Spirit: Eastern Christian Traditions* (Peabody: Hendrickson, 1989) is incorporated within and effortlessly interwoven into his later *Christian Peoples of the Spirit: A Documentary History of Pentecostal Spirituality from the Early Church to the Present* (New York: New York University Press, 2011).

17. Note that the following is not intended to be reductionistic in its treatment of

The Asian context of course defies summarization, even when it comes to developments in pneumatology. It is not just that there is a diversity of thinking about the Holy Spirit across the Asian continent but also a reconsideration of what vehicles—for example, storytelling, dance, music, drama—best mediate and communicate the Spirit's presence and activity.[18] Nevertheless, the scope of form and content is commensurate: different modalities of experiencing the Spirit lead to a range of pneumatological reflection. Limiting our focus to the Indian subcontinent at this juncture, we can see a spectrum of thinking about the Spirit, from a more traditionalist approach on the one side to more distinctively Indian versions on the other.

On the one hand, more evangelical approaches tend to parallel Western pneumatologies, both in the use of primary biblical and doctrinal categories and in concerns about overemphasis on indigenous sources believed to tend toward syncretism.[19] On the other hand, the search has been under way for more than a century for an authentic Indian theological paradigm and this has included thinking about matters pneumatological as well. At the forefront of at least this latter trajectory have been Indian theologians like Aiyadurai Jesudasen Appasamy (1891–1975), Pandipeddi Chenchiah (1886–1959), and Vengal Chakkarai Chettiar (1880–1958), each of whom has attempted to articulate pneumatological realities according to categories derived from Indian cultural, philosophical, and even religious traditions.[20] If the

---

Majority World contributions; the selectivity of what follows cannot be justified apart from the anticipated project in the second part of this chapter. For other equally selective but no less helpful overviews of global South pneumatological developments, see Kärkkäinen, *Pneumatology*, chap. 6, and Veli-Matti Kärkkäinen, ed., *Holy Spirit and Salvation: The Sources of Christian Theology* (Louisville: Westminster John Knox, 2010), chaps. 15–17.

18. See John C. England and Alan J. Torrance, eds., *Doing Theology with the Spirit's Movement in Asia*, ATESEA Occasional Papers 11 (Singapore: ATESEA, 1991).

19. See Indian pentecostal theologian Ivan Satyavrata, *The Holy Spirit: Lord and Life-Giver* (Downers Grove: InterVarsity Academic, 2009), including his guarded reaction (in chap. 4) to the by now infamous invocation of Korean spirits of *han* by Chung Hyun Kyung at the opening ceremony of the World Council of Churches General Assembly in 1991. For the text of Chung's speech, see her "Come Holy Spirit, Renew the Whole Creation," in *The Ecumenical Movement: An Anthology of Key Texts and Voices*, ed. Michael Kinnamon and Brian E. Cope (Grand Rapids: Eerdmans, 1996), 231–37.

20. P. V. Joseph, *Indian Interpretation of the Holy Spirit: An Appraisal of the Pneumatology of Appasamy, Chenchiah, and Chakkarai* (Delhi: New Theological College–ISPCK, 2007).

bhakti spirituality lends itself to understanding the Holy Spirit in terms of *antaryamin*, referring to the immanent and indwelling divine presence, especially in the soul (Appasamy), then yogic praxis is suggestive of the Spirit as the spiritual power, "supra-mind," and cosmic energy of the new creation (Chenchiah), and the Vedic tradition emphasizes the relationship between the human spirit and the Holy Spirit using *Brahman* notions of *paramatman-atman* (Chakkarai). The latter runs parallel to the efforts of Indian feminist theologians to think about the Spirit in terms of power and of the Vedic *sakti*, the material dimension of *Brahman*, symbolized in *Devi*.[21] The challenge in the Indian context is the monistic underpinnings of Hindu philosophical and contemplative traditions that blur the distinction not only between divine and creaturely spiritual realities but also between the Spirit of the historical Jesus of Nazareth and the more ambiguous spirit of the cosmic (dis- or pre-incarnate) Christ. So while there is ongoing debate about whether Christian theology in India ought to be Hinduized, the open question persists about the need for specifically Indianized features to be articulated.[22]

The way forward has to be a dialectical conversation between the received historic tradition of orthodox Christianity and Indian thought forms.[23] Approached carefully, *atman*, *antaryamin*, and *sakti* can be understood as "analogous to the Spirit," and in the long run, these notions can potentially "throw light on our understanding of the Holy Spirit and evoke certain hidden aspects of Christ and the Spirit."[24] The discussion has to proceed deliberately and be engaged patiently, however. Theological advances are usually not made overnight.[25]

The call for a more dialogical approach applies not only along the East-West axis, but also along the North-South axis. One difference when thinking about African theology in general and pneumatology in particular is that the legacies of Tertullian of Carthage and Augustine

21. T. Mercy Rani, *Assailants of the Spirit and Upholders of 'Sakti': An Indian Feminist Assessment of the Holy Spirit* (Bangalore: South Asia Theological Research Institute, 2003).

22. Joseph, *Indian Interpretation of the Holy Spirit*, 130; cf. Kirsteen Kim, *Mission in the Spirit: The Holy Spirit in Indian Christian Theologies* (Delhi: ISPCK, 2003).

23. An example is Christina Manohar, *Spirit Christology: An Indian Christian Perspective* (Delhi: ISPCK, 2009), who interacts with both Western and Indian voices.

24. Manohar, *Spirit Christology*, 295.

25. For further discussion of the state of pneumatology in the Indian context, see Ivan Satyavrata's essay in this volume.

of Hippo inform both traditions.[26] The former's time with the charismatic Montanist movement may be of new relevance in the contemporary African context since what is most pressing on this front is the combination of indigenous spirit-type churches over the past century alongside, amid, and against pentecostal-charismatic movements.[27] Across the continent, then, the kind of Christianity that is most vibrant is pneumatic in sensibility, orientation, and praxis, with manifestations of miracles, exorcism and deliverance, signs and wonders, healings, and other Spirit-related phenomena. Alongside concomitant emphases on being "born again" prevalent in especially pentecostal and charismatic churches, however, there are also extensive concerns about witchcraft, the practice of which is sustained by the African cosmology and worldview. Anxieties about witchcraft hence persist across the spectrum of African Christianity, wherever a pneumatic spirituality is prominent.[28]

If evil spirits remain to haunt the living because of tragic or untimely deaths, the Holy Spirit has been suggested as the "grant ancestor"—alongside the Father as the "proto-ancestor" and the Son as the "great ancestor"—that is, as the "source of a new life, and the fountainhead of Christian living . . . [who] sustains the entire line of humanity by embracing the beginning as well as the end of human spiritual destiny."[29] This is "a kind of pneumatology from below" wherein the divine Spirit retains consanguinity with the living and mediates communication between the human and celestial domains through prayers, rituals, and periodic visitations (i.e., dreams, visions), but yet remains distinct from other ancestor spirits in being eternal in nature (rather than subject to death), in residing within, not just existing

26. Tertullian is a major resource for A. Okechukwu Ogbonnaya, *On Communitarian Divinity: An African Interpretation of the Trinity* (St. Paul: Paragon, 1998).

27. Both types are delineated and discussed in Allan H. Anderson, *African Reformation: African Initiated Christianity in the Twentieth Century* (Trenton: Africa World, 2001); cf. Cecil M. Robeck Jr., *Prophecy at Carthage: Perpetua, Tertullian, and Cyprian* (Cleveland: Pilgrim, 1992).

28. This includes within the charismatic renewal in African Roman Catholicism; see the discussion of witchcraft, for instance, in Clement Chinkambako Abenguni Majawa, *The Holy Spirit and Charismatic Renewal in Africa and Beyond* (Nairobi: Catholic University of Eastern Africa, 2007), chap. 19.

29. Caleb Oluremi Oladipo, *The Development of the Doctrine of the Holy Spirit in the Yoruba (African) Indigenous Christian Movement*, American University Studies VII, Theology and Religion 185 (New York: Peter Lang, 1996), 107.

external to, human beings, and in sanctifying and enabling the fruit of everlasting life in the image of the "great" and "proto" ancestors.[30] Nevertheless if Western thought spiritualizes, soteriologizes, and eschatologizes the work of the Holy Spirit, African thought focuses on the material, physical, and socioeconomic work of the Spirit as an extension of the blessings of Christ in the present life.

Parallels between African and Latin American pneumatologies derive at least in part from the slave trade. African spirituality arrived in the New World through forced migration, and slave religion merged with indigenous traditions over the next few centuries. Against the backdrop of Roman Catholic saints, a range of ancestor spirits appeared, some more distant from but others more accessible to and engaged with the living.[31] But if African pneumatology has remained this-worldly in the material and existential sense, Latin American thinking about the Spirit has been this-worldly in the sociopolitical sense, especially in the hands of liberation theologians. The latter's spirituality of the poor is, of course, also concerned with the materiality of salvation, but its liberative praxis seeks to change the world and its social, political, and economic structures in cooperation with the divine Spirit, "the start of creation's road back to the Father."[32]

Pneumatology across the Global Renewal Movement

We must also briefly survey pneumatological thinking inspired by the emergence of the global pentecostal and charismatic renewal movement in the twentieth century. If the classical pentecostal theology insisted on a sharp dualism between the good Holy Spirit and demonic local or indigenous spiritual entities,[33] contemporary pentecostal and

---

30. Oladipo, *The Development of the Doctrine of the Holy Spirit*, 108.

31. See Joseph M. Murphy, *Working the Spirit: Ceremonies of the African Diaspora* (Boston: Beacon, 1996); cf. Claude F. Jacobs and Andrew Jonathan Kaslow, *The Spiritual Churches of New Orleans: Origins, Beliefs, and Rituals of an African-American Religion* (Knoxville: University of Tennessee Press, 1991), and Samuel Cruz, *Masked Africanisms: Puerto Rican Pentecostalism* (Dubuque: Kendell Hunt, 2005).

32. José Comblin, *The Holy Spirit and Liberation*, trans. Paul Burns (Maryknoll: Orbis, 1989), 186.

33. This is arguably of one cloth with "colonial pneumatology," a view of the spirit-world shaped by Enlightenment and Western presuppositions about Majority

charismatic thought is more nuanced. Led by the recognized dean of pentecostal studies Walter J. Hollenweger,[34] there is much greater awareness that the effectiveness of Pentecostalism as a religion of the Majority World derives at least in part from a spirituality that is contextualizable among indigenous cultures, cosmologies, and world-views.[35] If there is a distinct gulf between the Holy Spirit and other spirits in pentecostal theology, the lines are much more blurred in practice, as the "principalities and powers" are never unambiguously good or bad so that healings, miracles, signs and wonders, glossolalia, or manifestations of other so-called spiritual gifts have to be discerned on a case-by-case basis.[36]

Two distinct trajectories of pentecostal pneumatology are note-worthy for our purposes: those crafted by Hispanic theologians and those in search of a global pneumatological theology. The former have engaged, not surprisingly, with liberation theological themes, urging attentiveness to how pentecostal spirituality and perspective is conducive not only for other-worldly foci but also for this-worldly soteriological concerns.[37] In each case, substantive attention is placed on socioeconomic realities, albeit the approach is informed by a deeply pentecostal and Latino(a)-Hispanic spirituality, one that is affectively

World cultures; see, for example, J. W. Westgarth, *The Holy Spirit and the Primitive Mind: A Remarkable Account of a Spiritual Awakening in Darkest Africa* (London: Victory, 1946).

34. On Hollenweger's stature in pentecostal studies, see Lynne Price, *Theology Out of Place: A Theological Autobiography of Walter J. Hollenweger* (London: Sheffield Academic, 2002).

35. Walter J. Hollenweger, *The Pentecostals: The Charismatic Movement in the Churches* (Minneapolis: Augsburg, 1972), and *Pentecostalism: Origins and Developments Worldwide* (Peabody: Hendrickson, 1997); cf. Harvey G. Cox, *Fire from Heaven: The Rise of Pentecostal Spirituality and the Reshaping of Religion in the 21st Century* (Reading: Addison-Wesley, 1995).

36. See Allan Anderson, *Moya: The Holy Spirit in an African Context* (Pretoria: University of South Africa Press, 1991); Wilma Davies, *The Embattled but Empowered Community: Comparing Understandings of Spiritual Power in Argentine Popular and Pentecostal Cosmologies* (Leiden: Brill, 2010); and Opoku Onyinah, *Pentecostal Exorcism: Witchcraft and Demonology in Ghana* (Blandford Forum: Deo, 2011). On the importance of spiritual discernment, see Kirsteen Kim, *The Holy Spirit in the World: A Global Conversation* (Maryknoll: Orbis, and London: SPCK, 2007), chap. 7.

37. Leading the way are Eldin Villafañe, *The Liberating Spirit: Toward an Hispanic American Pentecostal Social Ethic* (Grand Rapids: Eerdmans, 1993), and Samuel Solivan, *Spirit, Pathos and Liberation: Toward an Hispanic Pentecostal Theology* (London: Bloomsbury–T&T Clark, 1998).

shaped and that motivates a distinctive pentecostal orthopathy and or-
thopraxy. The goal here is not only to theorize or theologize about the
Spirit, but also to nurture a pentecostal "social spirituality" through
which the divine breath can transform the world.[38]

Asian and African pentecostal pneumatologies are still on the horizon. However, the quest for a global pentecostal theology is well under
way, and the major developments along this line are robustly pneumatological in orientation.[39] The emphases here are not only on formulating or extending discussion on the Christian doctrine of the Holy
Spirit, but on rethinking Christian theology itself, as well as its constitutive doctrines, from a pneumatological perspective. Hence pneumatological themes are woven into other theological loci, resulting oftentimes in new insight on established doctrines and formulations.[40]
The intuition driving these explorations is that the pentecostal and
charismatic encounter with the Spirit inspires not only theologies of
the Spirit (pneumatology) but also has the capacity to expand thinking
toward a more vigorously articulated trinitarian theology.

To the Ends (of the Times) of the Earth:
Toward a Third Article Theology

This section seeks to press forward in part by looking backward. The
goal is to contribute toward a global theology that both builds on the
preceding and thinks pneumatologically with the early church,[41] in

---

38. On "social spirituality," see Villafañe, *The Liberating Spirit*, chap. 4.

39. For example, Yong, *The Spirit Poured Out on All Flesh*; see also volumes in the
Pentecostal Manifestos series published by Eerdmans: Frank D. Macchia, *Justified in the
Spirit: Creation, Redemption and the Triune God* (2010), Wolfgang Vondey, *Beyond Pentecos-
talism: The Crisis of Global Christianity and the Renewal of the Theological Agenda* (2010), and
Nimi Wariboko, *The Pentecostal Principle: Ethical Methodology in New Spirit* (2011).

40. Leading the way in North America has been charismatic Baptist theologian
Clark H. Pinnock, *Flame of Love: A Theology of the Holy Spirit* (Downers Grove: InterVar-
sity, 1996), and charting a similar path in the eastern hemisphere is mainline Korean
Methodist theologian Jong Chun Park, *Crawl with God, Dance in the Spirit: A Creative
Formation of Korean Theology of the Spirit* (Nashville: Abingdon, 1998).

41. In this respect, the theological methodology at work here resonates with that
of Oscar García-Johnson's transoccidentalist approach (see his chapter in this volume)
that seeks to bring non-Western voices into the wider theological conversation so far
dominated by Western perspectives, but in a way that neither merely displaces the

particular the third article of the Nicene Creed: "We believe in the Holy Spirit, the Lord and Giver of life, who proceeds from the Father, who with the Father and the Son together is worshiped and glorified, who spoke by the prophets."[42] Each clause of this affirmation will serve as a springboard for engagement with non-Western and Majority World resources in order to sketch the contours of a historically rooted pneumatological theology that is nevertheless relevant for the twenty-first-century world context.

The Lord, the Giver of Life

That the divine wind is the Spirit of life is clear from the scriptural witness to its bringing forth and sustaining animal and human creaturely breath (Gen. 1:30; 2:7; Job 34:14–15; Ps. 104:29–30).[43] Yet these ancient Hebraic reflections on the breath of YHWH remain pertinent for Majority World theologians. Amid rapid social change, poverty, injustice, and environmental degradation, the communal-forming, health-giving, interpersonally harmonizing, and ecologically nurturing work of the Spirit is potent, if not actually salvific.[44] Even if some forms of pentecostal and charismatic emphasis on prosperity theology are unbalanced and the expectation that the Spirit will bring about maximal material health and wealth is unsound, the cries and prayers of the faithful for divine blessing and favor in the present life are both instinctive and in accord with the biblical testimony.[45] The point is that the work of the

---

latter nor gives only lip service to the former. As should be clear in what follows, my own proposal involves retrieval of the Western canon within a global context even as I seek to engage with global (non-Western) perspectives from outside the Western theological tradition. The key is to respect the alterity of each even while forging not a third way (which would inappropriately synthesize or syncretize both) but a more enriched harmony of diverse, disparate, and sometimes not altogether coherent accounts.

42. An exemplary model in this regard is Joel C. Elowsky, ed., *Ancient Christian Doctrine*, vol. 4, *We Believe in the Holy Spirit* (Downers Grove: InterVarsity Academic, 2009).

43. See also David H. Jensen, ed., *Lord and Giver of Life: Perspectives on Constructive Pneumatology* (Louisville: Westminster John Knox, 2008); cf. Jürgen Moltmann, *The Spirit of Life: A Universal Affirmation*, trans. Margaret Kohl (Minneapolis: Fortress, 1992).

44. Paul Murray, Diego Irarrázaval, and Maria Clara Bingemer, eds., *Lord and Life-Giver: Spirit Today* (London: SCM, 2011).

45. See Katherine Attanasi and Amos Yong, eds., *Pentecostalism and Prosperity: The*

life-giving Spirit has been understood perennially as having implications for human material well-being and flourishing.

Two theological points are worth noting in this regard. First, the divine Spirit bestows not only new (everlasting, eternal) life but also historical (material, fleshly) life. The life-giving Spirit thereby imbues both spiritual and creaturely vivacity. In contradistinction to the dualism between spirit and matter bequeathed by modern Enlightenment assumptions, Anglican theologian Eugene Rogers has in recent times accentuated just this material dimension of the Spirit's character and work, in conversation with Eastern Christian theological resources.[46] The strength of Rogers's thesis is to highlight the working and resting of the Spirit on bodies, including the materiality of the Spirit's primary modus operandi in the life of Christ: his annunciation, conception, baptism, transfiguration, resurrection, and ascension. Rogers's material pneumatology is thus not materialistic but Christological: the identity of the Spirit in the light of Christ is not ethereal but palpable, tangible, and historical. Such a pneumatological construct—informed not only by the biblical witness but also by the early Syriac emphases on the feminine features of the Spirit—undermines the modernist binary of spirit as opposed to matter and illuminates the immanence of the divine breath within the fabric of created materiality.[47]

The second point to be noted is that the prominence of the Spirit as material and creaturely life-giver begs reconsideration of the relationship between the Spirit of creation and the Spirit of Pentecost. Classical Reformed pneumatology presumes a sharper distinction between the Spirit that gives life and the Spirit who births new life—through justification and especially sanctification—in Christ. This is consistent with the Protestant scholastic *ordo salutis* (order of salvation) that also separates common grace from saving grace, or general revelation from

---

Socioeconomics of the Global Charismatic Movement, Christianities of the World 1 (New York: Palgrave Macmillan, 2012).

46. Eugene F. Rogers Jr., ed., *After the Spirit: A Constructive Pneumatology from Resources outside the Modern West* (Grand Rapids: Eerdmans, 2005).

47. The wider scheme of Rogers's agenda includes a theology of sexuality that seeks to move beyond a rigid male-female distinction. One can appreciate the proposed pneumatology without having to agree that male-female is just another type of modernist duality. The way forward is to recognize the biblical normativity of male and female but develop a range of pastoral strategies that are discerning about the challenges attending to the differentiations of human sexuality in the present time.

special revelation. Yet even if the regenerative work of the Spirit is not denied, identification of the Spirit as life-giver undermines notions of creaturely life as being bereft of the divine breath.[48] Again, the goal is not to equate the Spirit of creation and of re-creation or Pentecost, but to acknowledge that any hard and fast bifurcation between the two goes beyond the scriptural witness.[49] Acknowledgment of the continuity, rather than discontinuity, between the Hebraic wind of YHWH and the apostolic Spirit of Jesus reopens old questions and raises new ones about the relationship between the older and newer covenants, testaments, and peoples of God.

Among a number of other tasks, then, a theology of the third article includes a theology of creation. More precisely, what opens up is a pneumatology of creation, even a pneumatology (rather than just theology) of nature itself,[50] since the work of the Spirit rests not only on material bodies but also animates the very dust of the ground if not the stardust of the cosmos. Such a pneumatological and theological vision, however, is not just theoretical, but also potentially practical. The liberative, transformative, and salvific work of the life-giving Spirit in this case is not limited to the practice of spiritual disciplines but also includes the deployment of scientific, political, and socioeconomic rationalities in order to effect change and bring about the common good.[51] Hence, when assessed as the Spirit of life, pneumatology opens up to theology's interface with the broad scope of the scientific and

48. This is the argument also of John R. Levison, *Filled with the Spirit* (Grand Rapids: Eerdmans, 2009).

49. As clearly articulated also a generation ago by C. F. D. Moule, *The Holy Spirit* (Grand Rapids: Eerdmans, 1978), 7–12.

50. For example, Amos Yong, *The Spirit of Creation: Modern Science and Divine Action in the Pentecostal-Charismatic Imagination*, Pentecostal Manifestos 4 (Grand Rapids: Eerdmans, 2011); cf. Native North American theologians like Randy Woodley, *Shalom and the Community of Creation: An Indigenous Vision* (Grand Rapids: Eerdmans, 2012), and Terry LeBlanc, "New Old Perspectives: Theological Observations Reflecting Indigenous Worldviews," in *Global Theology in Evangelical Perspective: Exploring the Contextual Nature of Theology and Mission*, ed. Jeffrey Greenman and Gene L. Green (Downers Grove: InterVarsity, 2012), 165–79.

51. David Tonghou Ngong, *The Holy Spirit and Salvation in African Christian Theology*, Bible and Theology in Africa 8 (New York: Peter Lang, 2010), makes this argument in the African context, especially vis-à-vis pentecostal churches, urging embrace of spiritual, material, and scientific means to respond to the poverty widespread across the African continent. See also his chapter in this volume for a briefer treatment of pneumatology in an African context.

anthropological disciplines. Theology of life as an inter- and multidisciplinary undertaking is here fundamentally pneumatological.[52]

Who Proceeds from the Father

It is well known that the addition of the *filioque* clause (the Spirit proceeds not only from the Father but also from the Son)[53] by the Roman Church has been a perennial source of dogmatic division between East and West. While there are many implications that follow from retention, or not, of the *filioque*, for our purposes one important question for pneumatology in the global context relates to how to understand the economies of the Son and the Spirit in relationship to the religious traditions of the world. On one reading, assertion of the *filioque* subordinates the economy of the Spirit to that of the Son and, concomitantly, defines the soteriological work of the triune God ecclesiologically (the church being the body of Christ); in this case, then, any consideration of the religions would either be ecclesiological (subsuming the diversity of religions within the sphere of the church), or without theological warrant altogether. An alternative approach, apart from the *filioque*, insists on the economies of Son and Spirit as related and yet distinct, as the two hands of the Father, to use Irenaeus's metaphor; following this line of thought, if the religions were to be understood in relationship to this pneumatological economy, then their domain would be related to but yet also distinct from that of the church, defined Christologically.[54] The need to attend to the world religions on their own terms, not just understand them according to Christological or even ecclesiological categories, is what motivates this proposal. Simultaneously, application of the Irenaean metaphor of the two hands of the Father to the theology of religions not only risks bifurcation of the economies of the Son and the Spirit but also, from an Orthodox perspective, fails to secure the interconnections between (a pneumatologically rich) trini-

52. See Wolfgang Vondey, ed., *The Holy Spirit and the Christian Life: Historical, Interdisciplinary, and Renewal Perspectives*, CHARIS: Christianity and Renewal—Interdisciplinary Perspectives 1 (New York: Palgrave Macmillan, 2014).

53. The classic defense of the *filioque* is Photios, *The Mystagogy of the Holy Spirit*, trans. Joseph P. Farrell (Brookline: Holy Cross Orthodox Press, 1987).

54. I have summarized these issues in my *Beyond the Impasse: Toward a Pneumatological Theology of Religions* (Grand Rapids: Baker Academic, 2003), chap. 4.

tarian theology and ecclesiology.[55] The problem, of course, is that to ask about whether the religions are salvific in Christian terms is a non-starter since the religions invoke neither Christ nor the biblical way of salvation—that is precisely why they are *non-Christian* traditions; yet defining them in relationship to Christ (as needing to be fulfilled by Christ or as lacking Christ's saving power, for instance) misrepresents the religious other in defining them negatively, precisely what Christians hope to avoid in terms of their own representation to people of other faiths.

Any pneumatological and trinitarian theology of religions will need to give both a Christological and an ecclesiological account as part of a comprehensive approach. The latter locus related to the church will need to resist triumphalism while also empowering appropriate Christian missional praxis. Toward this end, a pentecostal theology of hospitality, based on the outpouring of the Spirit on all flesh, empowers members of the church to be hosts of those in other faiths amid the presence of the welcoming Father even while enabling them to be guests of religious others just as Christ sojourned in a far country and was received by strangers.[56] This involves bearing witness from out of Christian commitment even as it discerningly welcomes the gifts of others as potentially enriching and even transforming Christian self-understanding. Such a pneumatological praxis may also have the capacity to reconcile all people—indeed, "everyone whom the Lord our God calls to him" (Acts 2:39b)—to the Father according to the image of the Son even if the trinitarian identity of God is not clearly perceived by those in other faiths not fully or formally initiated into the Christian church.

55. For an Orthodox response, see Paraskevè (Eve) Tibbs, "A Distinct Economy of the Spirit? Amos Yong, Pentecostalism and Eastern Orthodoxy," in *The Theology of Amos Yong and the New Face of Pentecostal Scholarship*, ed. Wolfgang Vondey and Martin W. Mittelstadt, Global Pentecostal and Charismatic Studies 14 (Leiden: Brill, 2013), 221–38. On the dualism that may be threatening the incarnational and pentecostal missions, see Gerald R. McDermott and Harold A. Netland, *A Trinitarian Theology of Religions: An Evangelical Proposal* (Oxford: Oxford University Press, 2014), chap. 2, esp. 53–57; my response to McDermott and Netland is published as "Toward a Trinitarian Theology of Religions: A Pentecostal-Evangelical and Missiological Elaboration," *International Bulletin of Mission Research* 40, no. 1 (2016): 1–12.

56. For details regarding such a hospitality praxis vis-à-vis people in other faith traditions, see Amos Yong, *Hospitality and the Other: Pentecost, Christian Practices, and the Neighbor*, Faith Meets Faith series (Maryknoll: Orbis, 2008).

That the life-giving Spirit also proceeds from the Father thus invites consideration of how the world's religious traditions, insofar as they are life-giving conduits of goodness and holiness,[57] are also related to the primordial source of all living creatures. Pentecostal theologian Koo Yun thus pneumatologically reframes the classical doctrine of general revelation in dialogue with East Asian philosophical and religious sources (particularly the classic *I Ching*).[58] Distinguishing the formal dimension of the Spirit of God as being present and active in all cultures and even religious traditions from the material aspect of the Spirit of Christ (and the church and its missional arm), Yun suggests what he calls a chialogical pneumatology and theology—following the East Asian cultural, philosophical, and religious concept of *chi*, which is at least semantically parallel to the Hebrew *ruah* or the English "wind" or "breath"—whereby the cosmic Spirit is generally revelatory of the divine even in the world religions. Others have forayed in similar directions, albeit seeking not only theological but also sociopolitical cache in observing how points of contact between Christian pneumatology and East Asian notions of *chi* are suggestive for reconfiguring democratic public spaces that are egalitarian, liberative, and life-giving.[59] While these efforts remain distinctive on multiple fronts and precipitate new perspectives, insights, and questions—not to mention precipitate questions that heretofore have not yet garnered answers agreed on across the ecumenical spectrum—each seeks to think theologically in conversation with East Asian religious and philosophical sources via a pneumatological bridge and demonstrates the potential for rethinking the procession of the Spirit from the Father in our late modern and pluralistic global context.[60]

57. Here I follow the church fathers at Vatican II, who affirmed: "The Catholic Church rejects nothing of what is true and holy in these religions"; see *Nostra aetate* §2 ("Declaration on the Relation of the Church to Non-Christian Religions," in *Vatican II: The Conciliar and Post-Conciliar Documents*, ed. Austin Flannery, OP, new rev. ed. (Boston: St. Paul's Books and Media, 1992), 738–43, at 739.

58. Koo Dong Yun, *The Holy Spirit and Ch'i (Qi): A Chialogical Approach to Pneumatology* (Eugene: Pickwick, 2012).

59. For example, Grace Ji-Sun Kim, *The Holy Spirit, Chi, and the Other: A Model of Global and Intercultural Pneumatology* (New York: Palgrave Macmillan, 2011), and Hyo-Dong Lee, *Spirit, Qi, and the Multitude: A Comparative Theology for the Democracy of Creation* (New York: Fordham University Press, 2014); cf. Jung Young Lee, *The Trinity in Asian Perspective* (Nashville: Abingdon, 1996), chap. 5, for more on the Holy Spirit and *chi*.

60. For another foray at this intersection of pneumatology and world religions,

Who with the Father and the Son Together Is Worshiped and Glorified

Yet even if the original Nicene-Constantinopolitan Creed did not include the *filioque*, the following clause leaves no doubt that the Spirit is worshiped and glorified together with—neither more nor less than—the Son. Hence there can be no pneumatomonism (as if focused only on the Spirit) even as there cannot be a Spirit-Father binitarianism that neglects the Spirit or the Spirit's relationship with the Father and the Son. Any theology of the third article as well as pneumatological theology, then, will have to include both a Spirit Christology and a pneumatologically configured trinitarian theology.[61]

Classical Spirit Christologies regularly treated pneumatology as an appendix to the person and work of the Son. But what if Christological reflection not only began with but also understood the Spirit as essential to the identity and achievements of the Son?[62] On the one hand, there is no doubt that the Spirit is understood as the Spirit of Jesus and the Spirit of Christ, and that the Day of Pentecost sending of the Spirit was by the Son from the right hand of the Father (Acts 2:33). On the other hand, the Word is incarnate by the Spirit and Jesus of Nazareth is the anointed Messiah—the Christ—through the empowering Spirit. Further, there is also no recognition of the Son apart from the Spirit (cf. 1 Cor. 12:3), so that authentic acknowledgment of the Son is always and already pneumatically mediated. Last but not least, even any initial confession of the Son awaits both moral and behavioral confirmation, usually related to manifestations of the fruit of the Spirit, and final or eschatological verification (Matt. 7:21–23). For all of these reasons, besides others, any Spirit Christology must proceed at least

---

but this time on an aesthetic register, see Jonathan A. Anderson and Amos Yong, "Painting Pentecost: The Spirit-Filled Painting of Sawai Chinnawong," *Christian Century* (May 28, 2014): 30–33.

61. Such a third article theological project that begins with the work of the Spirit is well under way—for example, Myk Habets, ed., *The Spirit of Truth: Reading Scripture and Constructing Theology with the Holy Spirit* (Eugene: Wipf and Stock, 2010), and Amos Yong, with Jonathan A. Anderson, *Renewing Christian Theology: Systematics for a Global Christianity* (Waco: Baylor University Press, 2014).

62. Suggestive is Sammy Alfaro, *Divino Compañero: Toward a Hispanic Pentecostal Christology* (Eugene: Wipf and Stock, 2010); see also Roman Catholic theologian Ralph Del Colle, *Christ and the Spirit: Spirit-Christology in Trinitarian Perspective* (Oxford: Oxford University Press, 1994), and Baptist theologian Myk Habets, *The Anointed Son: A Trinitarian Spirit Christology* (Eugene: Wipf and Stock, 2010).

methodologically as if both hands of the Father were equally defini-
tive. Put alternatively, a Spirit Christology is the flip side of a Christological pneumatology, with both approaches mutually and variously
informing each other.[63]

Finally, for present purposes, if the Spirit is worshiped and glorified together with the Son and the Father, then the Spirit is not only
the culmination of the doctrine of the Trinity but also constitutive of
trinitarian confession.[64] If so, then the triune nature of the Christian
God is simultaneously patrological, Christological, and pneumatological. Anything less than a fully articulated pneumatology—whatever is
possible within present horizons—will be deficiently trinitarian. More
weightily, if the Spirit is the eschatological horizon through which all
creation is reconciled in the Son to the Father, then there is also a
fundamental sense in which "now we see in a mirror, dimly" (1 Cor.
13:12a), not only because of epistemological constraints but because
the full glory of the triune God is yet to be revealed, if not achieved.
Christian pneumatology thus charts new trajectories for trinitarian
theology, and does so, as can be seen through this exploratory essay,
by inviting reassessment of Christology, the theology of religions and
of interfaith encounter, the theology of creation, and global theology,
among other traditional and newly emerging theological loci.[65]

Interim Conclusion—Who Spoke by the Prophets

The concluding clause to the third article is that the ancient prophets spoke through the Holy Spirit. The question left for consideration

---

63. I develop these points in my essay "Christological Constants in Shifting Con-
texts: Jesus Christ, Prophetic Dialogue, and the *Missio Spiritus* in a Pluralistic World," in
Mission on the Road to Emmaus: Constants, Contexts, and Prophetic Dialogue, ed. Stephen B.
Bevans and Cathy Ross (London: SCM; Maryknoll: Orbis, 2015), 19—33; see also Amos
Yong, *The Missiological Spirit: Christian Mission Theology for the Third Millennium Global Con-
text* (Eugene: Cascade, 2014), pt. 4.

64. Pentecostal theologians are leading the way in this discussion: Steven M.
Studebaker, *From Pentecost to the Triune God: A Pentecostal Trinitarian Theology* (Grand Rap-
ids: Eerdmans, 2012), and William P. Atkinson, *Trinity after Pentecost* (Eugene: Wipf and
Stock, 2013); see also Aaron T. Smith, *A Theology of the Third Article: Karl Barth and the
Spirit of the Word* (Minneapolis: Fortress, 2014).

65. See my *Spirit of Love: A Trinitarian Theology of Grace* (Waco: Baylor University
Press, 2012).

is whether the Spirit's speaking through the prophets was merely a thing of the (ancient Hebrew) past. This specific confession is itself drawn from the apostolic witness (2 Peter 1:21), so it must be assumed at least that the Spirit continued to speak through the followers of Jesus the Messiah, beyond the prophets of ancient Israel. If so, then by extension, in a post-apostolic context, does the Spirit speak similarly and perhaps in an ongoing way through the church? Orthodox Christians urge that there is a sense in which the earliest ecumenical councils were vehicles of the Spirit even as the Roman Catholic magisterium suggests there are limited albeit no less real occasions in which the Spirit has spoken and continues to speak through the ecclesial hierarchy. Contemporary pentecostal and charismatic movements insist on *sola scriptura* (with the Reformers against Catholic and Orthodox emphases on the tradition of the church) and on the ongoing manifestations of the gifts of the Spirit (here in opposition to dispensationalist theologies which argue that such ceased with the apostolic period). For theology, not just pneumatology, in a global context that engages with Majority World voices and perspectives, one senses that this question will continue to be debated, even if part of an affirmative "answer" to it consists in arguments such as those found in this chapter and book.

Further Reading

Congar, Yves. *I Believe in the Holy Spirit*. Trans. David Smith. 3 vols. in 1. New York: Crossroad, 1997.

Kim, Kirsteen. *Joining in with the Spirit: Connecting World Church and Local Mission*. London: Epworth, 2009.

Macchia, Frank D. *Baptized in the Spirit: A Global Pentecostal Theology*. Grand Rapids: Zondervan, 2006.

Rasmussen, Ane Marie Bak. *Modern African Spirituality: The Independent Holy Spirit Churches in East Africa*. London: I. B. Tauris, 2009.

Rogers, Eugene F., Jr., ed. *The Holy Spirit: Classic and Contemporary Readings*. Chichester: Wiley-Blackwell, 2009.

Thiselton, Anthony C. *The Holy Spirit—in Biblical Teaching, through the Centuries, and Today*. Grand Rapids: Eerdmans, 2013.

Yong, Amos. *Pneumatology and the Christian-Buddhist Dialogue: Does the Spirit Blow through the Middle Way?* Studies in Systematic Theology 11. Leiden: Brill, 2012.

CHAPTER 2

The Spirit Blows Where It Wills: The Holy Spirit's Personhood in Indian Christian Thought

IVAN SATYAVRATA

ABSTRACT

A critical survey exposes the significant influence of *advaitic* (non-dualist) Hinduism on Indian Christian pneumatology. The Holy Spirit's personhood is consequently undermined and even denied in Indian Christian thought. The personalist *bhakti* Hindu tradition offers more positive prospects for constructive engagement with and meaningful contextualization of the Christian faith in India.

In his discourse on the nature and importance of the new birth in John 3, Jesus uses the metaphor of the wind in illustrating to Nicodemus the mysterious and sovereign nature of the Holy Spirit's workings: "The wind blows where it wills. You hear its sound, but you cannot tell where it comes from or where it is going" (v. 8). These words of Jesus offer real hope and promise to a generation that seeks reality beyond the world of cold logic, deductive reasoning, and academic analysis. All around us we see evidence of a hunger for spiritual experience and an upsurge of interest in spirituality. Daoism, Tibetan and Zen Buddhism, Spiritualism, Kabbalism, Yoga, New Age spirituality, and various forms of Eastern mysticism are all an integral part of Western culture today. People in our world are perhaps more aware and accepting of the realm of the spirits today than ever before in recent history.

But is this openness to the world of religious experience essentially healthy or detrimental to the future of biblical Christian faith? This chapter is an attempt to draw from the Indian experience of the gospel-culture encounter in addressing this question, and to help us see both the pitfalls and possibilities of relating the Christian conception of God as Spirit to notions of spirit (or Spirit) within non-Christian cultural traditions. The Indian experience is helpful in this regard because the subject of the Holy Spirit occupies a place of natural prominence in India due to the ancient tradition of spirituality in the subcontinent. Indians thus naturally tend to think of God as spirit (or Spirit). This positive orientation to spirituality within the dominant religious culture presents the Christian witness in India with potential opportunities and challenges.

My principal concern in this chapter is to clarify the biblical account of the Holy Spirit in the context of myriad prevailing conceptions of "spirit" in India, some of which overlap, while others compete with, the biblical notion. How does the Christian understanding of the Holy Spirit relate to other ideas of spirit, such as *Brahman, atman,* or *sakti* in Hinduism? Must we always view the Holy Spirit in essentially personal terms, or can we look beyond the personalist language and regard the Spirit as an impersonal, abstract force? Can we accommodate the traditional understanding of the Holy Spirit with impersonalist conceptions of spirit (or Spirit) in other faiths in the interest of affirming common ground in interreligious dialogue?

We will see that relating the Christian idea of the Holy Spirit with prevailing notions of spirit in other religious traditions and cultures does have some serious pitfalls. But are there any prospects for positive engagement with Hindu spirituality that could provide stepping stones to dialogue and potential enrichment of traditional Christian understandings of the Spirit? Perhaps an even more pressing existential question, as increasing numbers of people of other faiths move into the neighborhood, into our shrinking global village, is the following: is the Spirit at work among people of other faiths and cultures? Some Christians find it easy to offer a glib, unqualified "No" to this question. At the other extreme, we have those who say a simple "Yes," and have no difficulty accepting that the Spirit is present and at work everywhere in the same way as he is among the believing community.

The Bible does teach that the Spirit is present and active everywhere in creation. But is God's omnipresence and spiritual immanence simply to be equated with the active, dynamic influence of the Holy Spirit poured out upon the church on the Day of Pentecost? The New Testament describes the Holy Spirit, the Spirit of God, as preeminently the Spirit of Jesus: the one who was promised by Jesus, who was bestowed by Jesus, and who imparts life, based on the redemptive work of Jesus. Our search for points of contact between Christian and other notions of Spirit (or spirit) will thus have to take into account the normativity of Christ as a crucial yardstick. A balanced approach will thus affirm the distinctiveness of the Christ-centered presence and activity of the Spirit within the community of faith, while also exploring Christocentric criteria for identifying and discerning the Spirit's work in the world in the midst of people of other faiths and no faith.

As a prelude to my survey of Indian pneumatological reflections I briefly compare Christian and Hindu notions of spirit (or Spirit). The main body of the chapter is devoted to a critical survey of representative Indian pneumatological contributions. I conclude with a summary evaluation of the extent to which the Holy Spirit's personhood has been adequately affirmed in the Indian Christian tradition, and offer a positive critique indicating prospects for constructive engagement.

The "Spirit" in India: Christian and Hindu Conceptions

Christian theology has found it necessary since its inception to express itself in categories relevant to its missional context. The church, which was born and initially nurtured in the cultural environment of Palestinian Judaism, eventually had to adopt the ideas and vocabulary of Greek culture as a result of its encounter with the Greco-Roman world. In a similar vein, since the nineteenth century, Christian thinkers in India have attempted to meaningfully engage the majority Hindu culture by seeking to relate Christian truth to Hindu thought forms and terminology. An approach to pneumatology that is sensitive and critical seems essential for effective contextualization of the gospel in India, given the pronounced "spirit" orientation within Hindu culture.

The importance of pneumatology to the Indian tradition is highlighted in the following observation by one of India's most creative and stimulating Christian thinkers, P. D. Chenchiah: "The future of Christianity will ultimately depend upon the discovery of the Indian Church of the tremendous importance of the Holy Spirit and of its capacity to communicate that spirit to the Hindu."[1] This observation

---

1. D. A. Thangasamy, *The Theology of Chenchiah* (Bangalore: Christian Institute for the Study of Religion and Society, 1966), 218.

is based on the fact that Indians tend to think of God as spirit. One indication of this is that the Hindu philosophical language, Sanskrit, is rich with "spirit" terminology such as *atman* (spirit, soul) and its cognates *paramatman* (supreme spirit), *antaratman* (inner spirit), *jivatman* (human spirit), *antaryamin* (inner ruler), *sakti* (power), and *adhyatmikta* (spirituality). Inasmuch as *Brahman* (ultimate reality) is identified with the *paramatman* (supreme spirit), ultimate reality is understood in essentially spiritual terms. Much of Hindu religion focuses on the relation of the *atman* to the *paramatman*. Spirituality pervades all of Hindu philosophy and culture.

This positive orientation to spirituality within Hindu thought has, however, presented the Christian witness in India with some potentially serious pitfalls in its task of contextualization. The danger arises largely due to the fundamental difference between the Christian view of God as a tri-personal being and the veiled agnosticism within the Hindu conception of God. Although there are primarily two traditions in classical Hindu thought—one that speaks of the Absolute as an impersonal Spirit and the other of a personal God—the latter has tended to be eclipsed by the former.

Neo-Hinduism has tried to bridge the divergent tendencies in one of two ways. Most frequently, the personalist strand is subordinated to the traditional *advaita* (non-dualism) view, as an essentially inferior conception, a concession to the popular devotion of the untutored masses. Alternatively, the absolutist and personalist ideas of God are treated as complementary truths, culturally conditioned expressions of the same ultimate mystery, and the personalist conception is subsumed within the dominant *advaitic* view.[2] The Absolute is thus viewed as beyond all conceptions of personality and impersonality. Where personality is ascribed to God, it is treated merely as a symbol, as the highest category to which human beings are able to relate.

The crucial question for Christian theism then is: Does the biblical personalist language about God have an ontological reference? More specifically, is there an adequate biblical basis for the Christian notion of the Holy Spirit's personhood?

The identity and activity of the Holy Spirit in the New Testament

2. For the views of two of the most influential modern Hindu philosophers, S. Radhakrishnan and Sri Aurobindo, see M. Braybrooke, *Together to the Truth* (Madras: Christian Literature Society, 1971), 49–52.

is always intrinsically bound up with the person and work of Jesus Christ.[3] The Spirit's bestowal upon people is clearly linked to the ministry of Jesus (Matt. 3:11; Mark 1:8; Luke 3:16) and, more specifically, to his glorification (John 7:37–39). It is, thus, in the ministry of the Spirit, especially in relation to the person and work of Christ, that the personhood of the Spirit is most clearly disclosed in the New Testament.

The strongest evidence for the personhood of the Spirit in the Gospels comes to us in two authentic sayings of Jesus. In the first of these (Mark 3:29; cf. Matt. 12:31; Luke 12:10) Jesus warns his hearers of the serious consequences of blaspheming against the Holy Spirit. In the second instance (Mark 13:11; cf. Matt. 10:20; Luke 12:12) Jesus assures his disciples that the Spirit will help them by speaking through them when they are called to testify during times of persecution. Thus, Jesus clearly regarded the Holy Spirit as a personal being who could be blasphemed against, and on occasion, could speak through people.

The book of Acts is filled with references to various personal activities of the Holy Spirit. On several occasions in Acts the Spirit is said to speak (1:16; 8:29; 10:19; 11:12; 13:2; 28:25). He is also one who forbids (6:6), thinks about what is good (15:28), appoints (20:28), sends (13:4), bears witness (5:32; 20:23), snatches (8:39), and prevents (16:7), and he can be lied to (5:3), tempted (5:9), and resisted (7:51). The evidence for Paul's belief in the personal character of the Spirit is also convincing. The Spirit, according to Paul, testifies (Rom. 8:16), intercedes (Rom. 8:26), knows (1 Cor. 2:11), teaches (1 Cor. 2:13), determines (1 Cor. 12:11), gives life (2 Cor. 3:6), calls out (Gal. 4:6), and can be grieved (Eph. 4:30).

The Gospel of John, too, refers to the Spirit in clearly personal terms. The Spirit variously teaches and reminds (14:26), testifies (15:26), and guides and speaks (16:13). When Jesus refers to the Spirit (who has come from the Father) as *allos paraclētos* (another Advocate; NRSV) in 14:16, he clearly implies that he himself is the present *paraclētos* (Advocate). The Spirit was thus regarded as a person in the same sense that Jesus was. Similar personal references to the Holy Spirit may be found in other parts of the New Testament as well. The Spirit is described as speaking (1 Tim. 4:1), predicting the future (1 Peter 1:11), and addressing

3. The treatment of the New Testament material in the following paragraphs is largely based on Ivan Satyavrata, *The Holy Spirit: Lord and Life-Giver* (Nottingham: Inter-Varsity, 2009), 72–74.

God's people in the writings of the Old Testament (Heb. 3:7). The book of Revelation records a number of instances when the Spirit is said to speak (2:7, 11, 17, 29; 3:6, 13, 22; 14:13).

Christians who take the authority of the Bible seriously have thus always insisted that, despite the limitations of human language, in speaking of God the Spirit as personal they are speaking of him as he really is. The language is not merely figurative or anthropomorphic, nor is it meant to reflect some subordinate aspect of God's nature. While one of the central affirmations of Christianity is that God, the ultimate reality, is personal, the highest conception of God in Hinduism is that of the impersonal absolute, *Brahman*. We turn now to a critical survey of the pneumatological reflections of select Indian Christian thinkers and see how they deal with this fundamental theological divergence in their attempts to meaningfully correlate Christian and Hindu notions of "spirit."

A Critical Survey of the Holy Spirit's
Personhood in Select Indian Thinkers

The first Indians to have reflected seriously on Christian theological themes were, ironically, not Christians, but pioneers of the Hindu Renaissance in India: Ram Mohan Roy, who founded the Brahmo Samaj, and one of his successors in the movement, Keshab Chandra Sen.[4]

Ram Mohan Roy devoted much of his life to a polemic against Hindu polytheism and idolatry. Consequently, he vehemently opposed the Christian doctrine of the Trinity, favoring the Arian view of the person of Christ, and rejecting totally any idea of the Holy Spirit's personality. He devotes an entire chapter of one of his writings to "The Impersonality of the Holy Spirit."[5] He regards the Spirit as merely the holy influence and power of God; he is neither self-existent nor is he a distinct personality. This influence or power was instrumental in the virginal conception of Jesus, and is also the means by which men are guided in the path of righteousness.[6]

---

4. Ram Mohan Roy is widely regarded as the first Indian to have engaged in serious scholarly interaction with the Christian faith. See Robin Boyd, *An Introduction to Indian Christian Theology* (Delhi: ISPCK, 1991), 19.

5. Boyd, *An Introduction*, 24.

6. B. J. Christie Kumar, "An Indian Christian Appreciation of the Doctrine of the

Keshab Chandra Sen is a crucial figure in the development of Indian Christian thought. As Boyd observes, "many of the conceptions and categories which have become familiar in the writings of later Indian theologians were first stated by Sen."[7] The highest point of Sen's theological creativity is, perhaps, his exposition of the Trinity in terms of the Vedanta concept of *Saccidananda*. He seems to have been the first to draw on this concept in interpreting the Trinity in the Indian context. The nature and expression of his thought are such as to leave it open to conflicting interpretation, making his teaching the subject of much theological controversy.

In his famous lecture, "That Marvellous Mystery—the Trinity," Sen explains the correspondence between *Saccidananda* and the Trinity:

> The Trinity of Christian theology corresponds strikingly with the Sachchidananda of Hinduism. You have three conditions, three manifestations of Divinity. Yet, there is one God, one substance, amid three phenomena. . . . Whether alone, or manifest in the Son, or quickening humanity as the Holy Spirit, it is the same God, the same identical Deity, whose unity continues indivisible amid multiplicity of manifestations . . . the true Trinity is not three persons, but three functions of the same Person.[8]

There is a tendency toward modalism in Sen's trinitarian thinking. In fact, Sen seems to have regarded the Trinity as only a symbol, with the three members, Father, Son, and Holy Spirit, simply pointing to the reality of God in different ways. In his careful study, Pape notes the importance of the Holy Spirit in Sen's Christology. He compares Sen's approach to a Spirit-Christology, which views Christ as an incarnation of the Holy Spirit.[9] Thus, the Holy Spirit is the presence and activity of God focused in Jesus Christ, the "transforming" activity of God, the "Sanctifier" and "Savior." Pape thus concludes that in Sen's thought

Holy Spirit: A Search into the Religious Heritage of the Indian Christian," *Indian Journal of Theology* 30, no. 1 (1981): 29.

7. Boyd, *An Introduction*, 27.

8. Keshub Chunder Sen, *Lectures in India*, vol. 2 (London: Cassell and Co., 1904), 16–18.

9. W. Roy Pape, "Keshub Chunder Sen's Doctrine of Christ and the Trinity: A Rehabilitation," *Religion and Society* 11, no. 3 (1964): 65.

"the Holy Spirit is God personally and powerfully at work in Christ the Son and in all who follow Christ."[10]

The problem, however, arises when one considers Sen's fondness for personification and dramatic imagery. One thus detects a certain ambiguity in Sen's thought when he speaks of the Spirit in terms of a "divine enthusiasm" or "a pervading passion," or in language such as the following: "In one favoured spot on earth is the Eternal Sun reflected; thence the concentrated rays of heaven's light are diffused by the inspiration of the Holy Spirit . . . already the Holy Ghost has shaken the foundations of our carnal nature, and brought Christ into us as a living force. The storm-wave of inspiration has touched us, bringing Christ into us all."[11]

Sen leaves us in little doubt as to the basic *advaita* orientation of his conception of God when he declares: "Lo! Within Jesus is concealed the Holy Spirit, and as you go deep into the Holy Spirit you discover at last the Invisible Supreme Essence. . . . In the inmost recesses of every man's soul is the Supreme God."[12]

Nehemiah Goreh has justly been regarded as the most deeply versed in Hindu learning of all Indian Christians. Also one of the most conservative Indian Christian theologians, Goreh affirms the orthodox view of the Spirit's personhood: the Holy Spirit is for him the Spirit of God and the third person of the Trinity. He uses the Gospel of John as his principal source in what is essentially an exegetical defense of the orthodox position. According to Goreh, the language of Scripture clearly shows that the Holy Spirit is God and not merely a creature. John's use of the pronoun *ekeinos* (that) in the masculine gender, as well as the title *ho paraclētos* (the Advocate) in referring to the Spirit are among the arguments he uses to establish that the Holy Spirit is "a Person, and not a quality or power, in the abstract sense of the word."[13]

Brahmabandhab Upadhyaya is a striking example of a Hindu who found the bridge to an indigenous form of Christianity in the teachings of K. C. Sen. Upadhyaya had a passionate concern for the formulation of a "Hindu" expression of Christian faith and life in India, and was convinced that the Vedanta philosophy must be made to render

10. Pape, "Keshub Chunder Sen's Doctrine," 69.

11. Sen, *Lectures*, 42–43.

12. Sen, *Lectures*, 35.

13. A. M. Balwant Paradkar, *The Theology of Goreh* (Madras: Christian Literature Society, 1969), 82.

the same service to the Catholic faith in India as to the Greek philosophy in Europe. A fair portion of his theology consists of an exposition of some of Sen's creative insights from a somewhat more orthodox perspective.

A devout Roman Catholic, Upadhyaya sought to combine the Thomist idea of God as pure Being with the Vedanta conception of *Brahman*. His teaching on the Holy Spirit comes in the context of his exposition of the Trinity: "God comprehends Himself by one act of eternal knowledge. The knowing self is the Father, the known self or the self-begotten by His knowledge is the Son; and the Holy Ghost is the Spirit of reciprocal love proceeding from the Father and the Son."[14]

Upadhyaya elaborates Sen's interpretation of the Trinity as *Saccidananda* in a classic Sanskrit hymn of devotion. The Father is described as *Sat* (Being), the Son as *Cit* (Consciousness or Intelligence), and the Spirit, which proceeds out of the union of Sat and Cit, as *Ananda* (Bliss). The verse describing the Holy Spirit says: "Proceeding from the union of Sat and Cit, gracious Spirit, pure Ananda Sanctifier, Inspirer, revealing the Word, our Life-giver!"[15]

At first glance the language of this hymn seems to point toward an orthodox understanding of the Spirit's person. But inasmuch as *Ananda* (Bliss, Joy) is grounded in the impersonalist monism of *advaita*, it merely denotes an abstract attribute—at best an aspect of *Brahman*. As Christie Kumar is careful to note, "here the very idea of the Christian Trinity as persons is missing."[16]

In fairness to Upadhyaya it must be observed that he was convinced that the conception of God in *advaita* Vedanta is not impersonal. His own definition of personality as "self-knowledge" would, strictly speaking, only apply to his interpretation of *Cit* (Intelligence) as the second person of the Trinity. He thus still comes short of adequately affirming the personhood of the Spirit.

Aiyadurai Jesudasen Appasamy, in contrast to Upadhyaya, turns to the personalist theistic tradition of *bhakti* as an instrument for formulating an Indian Christian theology. He uses the word *antaryamin* (inner ruler) to denote the Holy Spirit—the immanent God dwelling

14. Brahmabandhab Upadhyaya, "Hinduism and Christianity as Compared by Mrs. Besant," *Sophia* 4 (February 1897): 8.

15. Brahmabandhab Upadhyaya, "Our Personality," *Sophia* 5, no. 10 (October 1898): 146-47.

16. Christie Kumar, "An Indian Christian Appreciation," 33.

by nature in all people. There is, however, a certain ambiguity about Appasamy's use of *antaryamin*, for he also occasionally uses the term in referring to the immanence of Christ in the preexistent Logos. Appasamy's interpretation and use of this term does suggest a concern to affirm the Spirit's personhood.

Despite Appasamy's adoption of the *bhakti* philosophical framework and his consequent rejection of the *advaitic* conception of God in his approach to Christian mysticism, he is clearly attracted to it. He thus discerned with positive appreciation both personal and impersonal aspects in the Johannine conception of God. Boyd observes that this accommodation to *advaitic* mysticism may be prompted by "the uncomfortable feeling . . . that for the millions in India the conception of God as *nirguna Brahman* will always rank as higher than that of any kind of personal revelation."[17]

Pandipeddi Chenchiah was one of the most original and radical Indian thinkers. He was convinced that pneumatology would play a decisive role in shaping Christian thought in India, and would, in fact, "become the cornerstone of Indian Christian theology."[18] Chenchiah rejected both the absolute monism of *advaita* as well as the personal mysticism of *bhakti*, opting instead for Sri Aurobindo's modern but indigenous evolutionary line of thought.

Chenchiah used the Sanskrit terms *mahasakti* (great power) and *sakti* (power) in referring to the Holy Spirit. The word *sakti* in Hinduism is associated with an extraordinary power. Christie Kumar comments: "It [*sakti*] is an energy coming into individuals by means of which people are able to do unique things and utter certain predictions."[19] Furthermore, *sakti* is often personified as the goddess of power in popular Hinduism. Chenchiah believed that the traditional Hindu understanding of *sakti* as personalized divine energy prepares the way for a fresh interpretation of the Holy Spirit that is at the same time both Christian and distinctly Indian. He found the idea of an external power of *sakti* coming in and transforming humanity from within extremely appealing, foreign as it is to the traditional (*advaitic* and *bhakti*) forms of Hindu spirituality. His teaching was that as *mahasakti*, the Holy Spirit

17. Boyd, *An Introduction*, 129–30.
18. D. M. Devasahayam and A. N. Sudarisanam, eds., *Rethinking Christianity in India* (Madras: Hogarth, 1938), 161.
19. Christie Kumar, "An Indian Christian Appreciation," 29.

introduces new life and power into the lives of believers and is the dynamic means by which the entire cosmos is being transformed and incorporated into Christ as the new creation.[20]

In Chenchiah, we observe again the common tendency in Indian Christian theology to confuse the identities of Christ and the Holy Spirit: "the Holy Spirit is the Universal Jesus," and, "the Holy Spirit is the power that descended vertically in the human stream in Jesus." His description of the Holy Spirit as "the new cosmic energy" and statements such as "the Holy Spirit is the energy beyond Creation which as Christ has flowed into the world" make us doubt the extent to which he accepted the personhood of the Spirit as an ontological reality.[21]

Vengal Chakkarai, of all Indian Christian thinkers, makes the most extensive use of Hindu terminology, although his theological reflections display no specific philosophical affiliation. The Holy Spirit occupies a vital place in his thought and is, in fact, the starting point of his Christology: "it is from the Holy Spirit our *antaryamin*, the Indweller, that we start our enquiry concerning the nature of the person of Jesus."[22] The relation between Jesus and the Spirit, according to Chakkarai, is simply one of identification: "the Holy Spirit is Jesus Christ in the human personality . . . the Holy Spirit is Jesus Christ himself taking his abode with us . . . the Holy Spirit is Jesus Himself."[23] He identifies the Holy Spirit with the risen, living Christ at work in the world today, and thus sees his work as a continuing part of the incarnation, or *avatara*.

When it comes to the question of the Spirit's personhood, Chakkarai seeks to preserve what he regards as scriptural ambiguity. He perceives a tension within the New Testament between the representation of the Spirit in personalist terms in John's Gospel and Luke's description of the Spirit in Acts as a kind of influence or force. He thus concludes that "the Spirit is evidently in its nature both personal and impersonal."[24] While he does sometimes refer to the Holy Spirit in personal terms, a close perusal of his writings seems to reveal a basic conception of God that is essentially *advaitic* in nature. He totally rejects, for instance, the idea of personality in God—on the grounds

---

20. Thangasamy, *The Theology of Chenchiah*, 217–18.
21. Devasahayam and Sudarisanam, *Rethinking Christianity*, 55.
22. V. Chakkarai, "Jesus the Avatar," in *Vengal Chakkarai*, ed. P. T. Thomas, vol. 1 (Madras: CLS, 1981), 123.
23. Chakkarai, "Jesus the Avatar," 124–25.
24. Chakkarai, "Jesus the Avatar," 153.

that it is a "Western" concept—supporting instead the common *advaitic* claim that *aham* (ego or personality) is in some way a limitation on universality. Consistent with this line of thinking is his belief that the "Christ of experience" whom we now worship and who lives in our hearts is a "universal spirit" who is outside the realm of mere human personality. It seems evident that for Chakkarai personality is a human and historical constraint that must not be applied to pure divinity.

In the concluding paragraphs of his discussion of the Spirit's functions, Chakkarai distinguishes between our unrestricted worship of the Father and the Son and our somewhat "mysterious" relationship with the Spirit. A deeper understanding of the latter, he believes, "leads us to the heart of religion as we have known it in one of its most powerful manifestations in India."[25] The *advaitic* orientation is unmistakable, especially when in his subsequent concluding explanation we read: "He [the person who has the Spirit] stands in the tumultous [sic] ocean as a beholder, alone and without a second, he whose world is the Brahman . . . *in his own self only he beholds the self, he beholds all as self* . . . he becomes a Brahmana, he whose world is the Brahman."[26] Thus, Chakkarai's attempt to formulate a "Christology of the Spirit" without adequate grounding in the New Testament historical account leads him to an *advaitic* view of Christ that negates the Holy Spirit's personhood.

The tradition inaugurated by Brahmabandhab Upadhyaya of seeking a positive relationship between Christianity and *advaita* philosophy has remained very much alive within Roman Catholic theology in India. Its popularity and influence has increased considerably in recent years, in some measure due to the blessing and support extended to the interreligious dialogue movement by Vatican II. We consider briefly the views of three representatives of this school of thought: Jules Monchanin, Swami Abhishiktananda (Henri Le Saux), and Raimundo Panikkar.

Jules Monchanin was a French Benedictine missionary whose work represents, in some ways, the fulfillment of Upadhyaya's highest aspirations. He assumed the Sanskrit name *Parama Arubi Anandam*, testifying to his special devotion to the Holy Spirit, the Supreme (*Parama*), Formless (*Arubi*), Bliss (*Anandam*). Along with Swami Abhishiktananda, Monchanin founded the *Saccidananda* Ashram, a monastery devoted

---

25. Chakkarai, "Jesus the Avatar," 156.
26. Chakkarai, "Jesus the Avatar," 157; emphasis added.

to the adoration and contemplation of the Trinity. It was in his understanding of the Trinity as *Saccidananda* that Monchanin carried forward the work of Upadhyaya, perceiving in the Christian doctrine of
the Trinity the solution to some of the common antinomies in Hindu
thought.

The Spirit occupies an important place in Monchanin's thought.
He often insists that it is the third person of the Trinity that India
"awaits" with special eagerness: "the Divine Spirit, the 'uncircum-
scribed' Person, who appears only under fluid forms, breath, water . . .
fire . . . the mysterious immanence of all in every one and of every one
in all. He is the very one whom India is awaiting."[27]

Thus, the Spirit, according to Monchanin, is the all-pervasive "Indwelling God"—who is the least circumscribed in his manifestation, the
least anthropomorphic, and the most spiritual—at the meeting point of
India's quest for the personal God and the impersonal Absolute.[28] Regarding the question of divine personhood, like Upadhyaya, Monchanin
seems to begin with the assumption that personality can be attributed
to the *nirguna Brahman* of *advaita* philosophy. He then goes on to speak
of the Trinity as constituting three "centers of personality": "For us God
is neither the impersonal nor the unimpersonal. In his intimate life he
is Three persons. . . . He is Sat, he is Cit, he is Ananda, Being, Consciousness, Bliss—in such a manner that he constitutes three centres of personality, each one polarised by the other two."[29]

In spite of this seemingly clear affirmation of trinitarian personalism, however, elsewhere Monchanin seems to be groping for a fresh,
"non-anthropomorphic" notion of divine personhood that might more
easily be accommodated within the *advaitic* framework: "Perhaps the
notion of person also has to be reshaped since the person in God is
relationship itself." He thus maintains that "the constitutive element
of the divine person is co-esse: each is a Person only by his relation to
the other."[30]

27. Jules Monchanin, *Swami Parama Arubi Anandam: [Fr. J Monchanin], 1895–1957: A Memorial* (Tiruchirapalli: United Printers, 1959), 103.
28. Joseph Mattam, "Modern Catholic Attempts at Presenting Christ to India," *Indian Journal of Theology* 23, no. 4 (1974): 209.
29. Monchanin, *Swami*, 200.
30. Jules Monchanin, "The Quest of the Absolute," in *Indian Culture and the Fullness of Christ*, ed. Jules Monchanin and Swami Abhishiktananda (Madras: The Catholic Cen-tre of Madras, 1957), 50–51.

In so redefining the concept of divine personality, Monchanin believes that he can fulfill the deepest aspirations of Hinduism for a God who is absolutely simple and absolutely one, and who is not personal (if personal implies even the slender duality of an "I-thou" relationship of a conscious being with an object outside itself).[31] Monchanin's solution to the Hindu quest for a personal-impersonal God must be commended for its skillful blending of some elements of Western apophatic mysticism (the belief within some Christian mystical traditions that God can only be described by humans in terms of what cannot be said of him) with the *advaita* philosophy of Sankara. But it hardly does justice to the "full-blooded" personalism of the New Testament understanding of the Holy Spirit.

Swami Abhishiktananda (Henri Le Saux) develops the basic ideas of Monchanin in a somewhat more radical direction. Abhishiktananda also regards *advaita* as the highest form of Hinduism and is convinced that the deepest and best Hindu (*advaitic*) experience finds its true fulfillment in the Christian mystical experience. How does Abhishiktananda understand *advaita*? According to him, *advaita* simply means "neither God alone, nor the creature alone nor God plus the creature, but an indefinable non-duality which transcends at once all separation and all confusion."[32] All of his theology is thus conditioned by a commitment to this *advaitic* framework. As a result, he is much more deferential in his attitude toward *advaitic* Hinduism than either Upadhyaya or Monchanin.

The importance of the Spirit in Abhishiktananda's thought is determined by the fact that Christianity is primarily a spiritual reality, a living experience in the Spirit. The Christian life must, therefore, be lived at the level of the Spirit: "in the cave of the heart"—the secret and deep place where each individual meets God, the place of ultimate encounter, where the spirit of man becomes one with the Spirit of God.

Like Upadhyaya and Monchanin, Abhishiktananda follows the line of K. C. Sen in his understanding of the Trinity as *Saccidananda*. The Spirit is thus "the supreme revelation of Ananda, the Bliss of Being."[33]

31. Monchanin, *Swami*, 186.
32. Swami Abhishiktananda, *Hindu-Christian Meeting Point: Within the Cave of the Heart* (Delhi: ISPCK, 1976), 107.
33. Abhishiktananda, *Hindu-Christian Meeting Point*, 88.

It is difficult to see how Abhishiktananda can continue to speak of the Spirit in personal terms within his *advaitic* framework, although he does so on occasion: "the Unspoken and Unbegotten Person who . . . whispers in the sanctuary of the heart the eternal ABBA."[34]

A clue to the solution may lie in Abhishiktananda's reference to the Spirit as a personification of *ekatvam*, the mystery of *advaitic* unity. This may explain why he often speaks of the Spirit in abstract, impersonal terms. He likens the Spirit to the primal energy of *sakti*, "an immeasurable powerful energy," surging up from within man's own inner being, the innermost center of the soul.[35] This is far from the personal language of Christological trinitarianism, but Abhishiktananda leaves us in no doubt about his essential *advaitic* orientation in the following assertion: "In reality the *Advaita* lies at the root of the Christian experience. It is simply the mystery that God and the world are not two. It is this mystery of unity, *ekatvam*, that characterizes the Spirit in God, and in the whole work of God."[36]

Raimundo Panikkar, an influential proponent of the interreligious dialogue movement, devoted his theological endeavors to bringing the Hindu religious experience and Christian faith into a common form of expression.[37] In exploring the relationship between Christianity and Hinduism, Panikkar simultaneously attempts to harmonize two prominent schools of thought, *advaita* and *bhakti*, but his distinct preference for the former is evident in the basic orientation of his thought.[38] He thus finds it easy to blend the Christian and *advaitic* Hindu conceptions of the Supreme Being: "He [God] is the ultimate Subject, the Substance—the basis of everything—the *Brahman* identical to the *atman*, hence the primary Cause, the unmoved mover, the ultimate Creator, the infinite Goodness, the perfect Idea, the utmost Justice, the Supreme Being."[39] The influence of *advaita* philosophy on his concep-

---

34. Swami Abhishiktananda, *Prayer* (Delhi: ISPCK, 1967), 63.

35. Abhishiktananda, *Prayer*, 100.

36. Abhishiktananda, *Prayer*, 109; cf. Mattam, "Modern Catholic Attempts," 212.

37. J. B. Chettimattam, "R. Panikkar's Approach to Christology," *Indian Journal of Theology* 23 (1974): 219.

38. For a more detailed critique, see Vinoth Ramachandra, *The Recovery of Mission: Beyond the Pluralist Paradigm* (Delhi: ISPCK, 1999), 76–108; Ivan Satyavrata, "The Holy Spirit and Advaitic Spirituality," *Dharma Deepika* 1 (1995): 49–60.

39. Raimundo Panikkar, *Myth, Faith and Hermeneutics* (New York: Paulist, 1979), 356.

tion of God is evident in his distinct reticence to use personhood as a category for describing the essential nature of God. He thus warns against the "great temptation" of personalism, which he describes as anthropomorphism.[40]

Panikkar has his own distinctive understanding of personhood in relation to the Trinity. According to him the term "persons" cannot be used of the Trinity as a real analogy due to the absence of a viable point of reference for the analogy either within or without the Trinity itself. It is not true that God is three persons since "persons" in the Trinitarian context is an equivocal term, which has a different meaning in each case:

> There is no God except the Father who is his Son through his Spirit— but without three "who's" or "what's" of any sort. . . . There is not a *quaternitas*, a God-divine nature, outside, inside, above or beside the Father, the Son and the Holy Spirit. Only the Son is Person, if we use the word in its eminent sense and analogically to human persons: neither the Father nor the Spirit is a Person.[41]

God the Spirit is, in Panikkar's thought, the "immanent" God, whom he associates with the spirituality of intuitive inwardness, the *jnana* of *advaita* philosophy. Panikkar is deeply enamored of "the way par excellence of *advaita*," which with its emphasis on divine immanence offers the solution to some of the "enormous difficulties" posed by the classical personalist conception of God.[42]

Panikkar turns to the teaching of the *Upanishads* in quest of a solution to the question as to whether one can conceive of an authentic spirituality that is not based on interpersonal dialogue, in which God is not a "thou." The Spirit is thus clearly identified with the *atman* of the *Upanishads*, both signifying the same reality, divine immanence. Panikkar clearly does not conceive of this divine immanence in personal terms: "An immanent God cannot be a God-Person, 'someone' with whom I could have a 'personal' relationship, a God-Other. I cannot speak to an immanent God."[43] For him, the personal conception of

40. Raimundo Panikkar, *The Trinity and the Religious Experience of Man* (Maryknoll: Orbis, 1973), 24.
41. Panikkar, *The Trinity*, 52.
42. Panikkar, *The Trinity*, 27, 39.
43. Panikkar, *The Trinity*, 31.

God is clearly inadequate: "In short, is the mystery of God exhausted in his unveiling as Person?"[44] The God of the *Upanishads*—the immanent Spirit who is not other, not person, not one with whom we enter into relationship—seems to hold a deeper fascination for him.

The Spirit is, therefore, one whom we realize in the depths of our being—the Ground of Being beyond our outward self. We realize him inwardly through silence and through inwardness. Hence, the realm of the Spirit is the realm of mysticism and inward realization, not that of devotion or adoration of transcendent majesty: "One cannot have 'Personal relations' with the Spirit. One cannot reach the Transcendent, the Other, when one is directed towards the Spirit. One cannot pray to the Spirit. . . . One can only have a non-relational union with him."[45]

There are echoes here of a view of the Spirit's personhood, which we have earlier seen underlying the thought of Chakkarai, Monchanin, and Abhishiktananda, although in Panikkar the tendency is more explicit. His deference to *advaita* eventually leads him to empty the Trinity of any idea of selfhood and to an explicit denial of the Holy Spirit's personhood. For Panikkar, the spirit or the *atman* of *advaitic* Hinduism is merely an aspect of *Brahman*, the abstract, impersonal Absolute or Ground of Being. Panikkar's description of the Spirit's work amounts to little more than an attempt to clothe *advaitic* spirituality with the language of Christian theology.

Where the Holy Spirit Blows in India: A Summary Assessment and Prospects

There is a natural tendency in Indian Christian thought toward "pneumatomonism," in which it is easier to conceive of God as spirit (or Spirit), rather than the Holy Spirit as God. This is largely due to the fact that as a result of the influence of *advatic* Hindu non-dualism in India, it is easy for the Holy Spirit to be confused with the human spirit or to be viewed as an impersonal, immanent force. Consequently, the dominance of *advaita* in Hindu thought is reflected in the Christian discussion as well, with the impersonalist conception of the Absolute

44. Panikkar, *The Trinity*, 29.
45. Panikkar, *The Trinity*, 63.

by and large holding a greater attraction than the idea of a personal God for both Hindu and Christian thinkers alike.

With the clear exception of Nehemiah Goreh and A. J. Appasamy, the pneumatology of all the Indian thinkers surveyed bears the influence of *advaitic* non-dualism. Ram Mohan Roy's strict monotheism, focused on *Brahman*, the Supreme Being of Vedanta, had no place at all for a personal Holy Spirit. His successor Sen's conception of the Trinity as *Saccidananda* set the tone for a whole new approach in enculturation that sought to relate the Christian gospel to Hindu *advaita*. Sen accordingly identified the Christian view of God with the highest conception of God in Hinduism, the *nirguna Brahman* (undifferentiated Being) of *advaita*.

Following this line of thought, Brahmabandhab Upadhyaya attempted somewhat unsuccessfully to affirm divine tri-personhood within the framework of an *advaitic* interpretation of the Trinity. His theological successors, Jules Monchanin and Swami Abhishiktananda, move even further away from a personalist conception of the Spirit in their eagerness to demonstrate ontological continuity between Christian and *advaitic* mystical experience. Raimundo Panikkar's understanding of the Spirit as the "immanent God" of *advaita* represents the ultimate destination in this journey from Christian to *advaitic* spirituality since the idea of personhood in relation to the Spirit is emptied of any meaningful content.

The same tendency toward an impersonalist conception of the Spirit may also be observed in thinkers like Chenchiah and Chakkarai, who do not otherwise seem to display a conscious preference for *advaita* as a philosophical system. Even someone with strong personalist convictions like A. J. Appasamy feels the need to make room for an impersonal conception of God within his personalist *bhakti* framework. This mystical fascination with the *advaitic* impersonalist conception of Spirit/spirit among Indian Christian thinkers is not altogether inexplicable given the context in which they theologize. However, Claude Welch's insightful comment in the context of his discussion of the significance of the *filioque* clause helps highlight the crucial point at which Indian pneumatological reflection urgently needs to be more firmly grounded in the New Testament witness:

When the Christian speaks of the Holy Spirit, he does not refer to just any spirit or spirituality, certainly not to the spirit of man, or

merely to a general immanence of God, but to a Holy Spirit consequent upon the event of objective revelation and reconciliation in
Jesus Christ the Son. Where in Christian history the Spirit has not
been clearly recognized as the Spirit of the Son . . . there has arisen
what H.R. Niebuhr calls a "unitarianism of the Spirit."[46]

The neglect of this crucial perspective appears to be the main
weakness of Indian Christian pneumatology. The Holy Spirit is not just
any spirit and must not be confused with the human spirit, a general
divine immanence, or an impersonal monist conception of spirit such
as *Brahman-atman*. The Holy Spirit is preeminently the Spirit *of Christ*,
and the Christian concept of the Trinity is derived from the historical
fact of the incarnation.

There are profound implications of accommodating impersonalist conceptions of Spirit/spirit into Christian theology—a compromise
that has a far-reaching impact on the essential nature and perhaps even
the survival of the Christian faith. A major consequence of a notion of
spirit that is emptied of divine personhood is that it ultimately erodes
any basis for robust ethical engagement. The Christian ethic of loving
service is grounded in the biblical conception of God as tri-personal:
God as loving Father; the Son as divine love incarnate; and the Holy
Spirit as the one who pours out God's love into the hearts of Christ-
followers. Apart from the Holy Spirit's personhood, the foundation of
this ethic is considerably weakened, if not altogether eliminated.

A second, perhaps more serious, consequence relates to the emergence and growing popularity of the modern phenomenon called religious pluralism—the perspective that all religions, more or less, offer
equally valid ways of leading people to God. Religious pluralism celebrates diversity of religious experience and expression as good and
healthy and is skeptical of claims that any one religious tradition can
be normative for all. This perspective finds strong resonance in an influential strand of philosophical Hinduism that readily subsumes all
other religions within its doctrine of the essential unity of all religions
with direct realization of the Supreme Being as the ultimate goal of
a universal religion of the spirit. Religious pluralists in seeking to as-
cribe value to non-Christian religious experience thus often tend to

46. Claude Welch, "The Holy Spirit and the Trinity," *Theology Today* 8 (April 1951):
29.

stray away from biblical faith when they try to speak of the Spirit or the Trinity apart from the Christ-event in history.

John offers the following words of caution in his first epistle: "This is how you can recognize the Spirit of God: Every spirit that acknowledges that Jesus Christ has come in the flesh is from God, but every spirit that does not acknowledge Jesus is not from God" (4:2–3). The Holy Spirit is not the only spirit at work in the world—there are other "spirits" in the world. Spiritual discernment, the gift of "discerning of spirits" (1 Cor. 12:10), is thus a critical need if we are to have a biblically informed understanding of the Spirit's true identity in order to distinguish between genuine and counterfeit manifestations of the Holy Spirit's presence.

Jesus promised that the Spirit of truth would guide us into all truth and that he would testify about and bring glory to him (John 15:26; 16:13–14). This provides us with a helpful key for identifying where and how the Spirit is at work outside the church: we discern the authentic presence of the Spirit through his Christ-ward witness—the Spirit always points, attracts, and leads to Christ. A commitment to Christ-centeredness as normative in spiritual discernment thus enables us to follow the Spirit in freely pursuing truth, beauty, and goodness wherever they may be found. When we find such elements in the midst of non-Christian religions and cultures, we celebrate their presence, affirm them as pointers to Christ, and use them to deepen and enrich our understanding of the gospel of Christ.

Our survey of Indian Christian pneumatology has illustrated why the *advaitic* tradition within Hinduism, despite its influence, presents seemingly insurmountable obstacles to constructive dialogue. There is, however, a personalist *bhakti* strand within Hinduism that has held a great attraction for Indian Christians such as A. J. Appasamy, Narayan Vaman Tilak, and H. A. Krishna Pillai, among others.[47]

The term *bhakti*, rendered variously as "service," "worship," "loyalty," "homage," and "loving devotion to God," denotes in its widest sense adoration of and loving devotion to the deity.[48] It includes most of the principal aspects of Indian religion and has had widespread influence in India. While there are different schools of thought within

47. Boyd, *An Introduction*, 112–43.
48. G. M. Bailey and I. Kesarcodi-Watson, eds., *Bhakti Studies* (New Delhi: Sterling, 1992), 1–6.

the broader *bhakti* tradition, the essential core of *bhakti* includes the idea of a personal God who can be loved and worshiped, and remains distinct from the *bhakta* (devotee). The object of the *bhakta's* total emotional abandonment and singular devotion is her *ishtadevata*, the deity of her choice, who bestows his grace upon and fills her with his *anand*, indescribable peace and bliss.[49] The *bhakta* suffers the agony of separation until through single-minded devotion her soul finds ultimate realization in union with God.[50]

We find a positive Christian approach to *bhakti* spirituality best illustrated in a key Indian Christian figure of the previous century, Sadhu Sundar Singh.[51] A careful analysis of Sundar Singh's thought suggests that his Christian experience was subconsciously shaped by *bhakti* elements imbibed during his pre-Christian formative years, some of which were appropriated later in his Christian theological formation. The influence of *bhakti* on Sundar Singh's approach is pronounced, although his framework represents a synthesis of elements from different strands of the *bhakti* tradition.

The earliest extensive teaching on *bhakti* is to be found in the *Bhagavadgita*, a deeply devotional text, with *bhakti* as the central theme of its message, telling of the soul's immortality and of a caring God's saving and reassuring love for each individual.[52] Among the various Hindu scriptures Sundar Singh was exposed to in his early years, the *Bhagavadgita*, which he had memorized by the age of seven, was a key formative influence.[53] The *bhakti* framework thus seems to have served as a preparation for Sundar Singh's reception of the Christian faith.

Sundar Singh's pre-Christian *bhakti* framework prepared him for his experience of Christ at a number of significant points: the view of God as a loving, personal Creator, distinct from and yet immanent in

49. David Carlyle Scott, ed., *Kabir's Mythology* (Delhi: Bharatiya Vidya Prakashan, 1985), 23.

50. Scott, *Kabir's Mythology*, 22.

51. For a more detailed assessment of Sundar Singh's thought, see Ivan Satyavrata, *God Has Not Left Himself without Witness* (Oxford: Regnum, 2011), 139–96.

52. J. Miller, "Bhakti and the Rig Veda—Does it Appear There or Not?" in *Love Divine: Studies in Bhakti and Devotional Mysticism*, ed. Karel Werner (Richmond, Surrey: Curzon, 1993), 6, 21–24, 31; J. Lipner, *Hindus: Their Religious Beliefs and Practices* (London: Routledge, 1998), 134–35.

53. Friedrich Heiler, *The Gospel of Sadhu Sundar Singh*, trans. Olive Wyon (New Delhi: ISPCK, 1989), 37.

his creation; the acceptance of the possibility of the incarnation; the understanding of nature as a channel of divine revelation; the recognition of the divine authority of the written Word; the conception of sin as moral evil and salvation as the fulfillment of the soul's quest for union with God resulting in moral perfection of the soul; and the recognition that salvation comes at the gracious initiative of God. His understanding of salvation was strongly conditioned by the *bhakti* mystic quest for union with the divine. His view of the self in its relation to God resonates deeply with *bhakti* spirituality, in which mystical union with the divine is viewed as communion between two free personalities rather than absorption in the absolute: "God is our Creator and we are His creatures; He is our Father, and we are His children. . . . If we want to rejoice in God we must be different from Him; the tongue could taste no sweetness if there were no difference between it and that which it tastes. . . . To be redeemed does not mean to be lost or absorbed into God. We do not lose our personality in God; rather we find it."[54]

Sundar Singh observed the Spirit at work universally, as much in his mother's deep religious devotion as in his own dramatic conversion to faith in Christ. He believed that non-Christians, while needing "the fullest light" that Christ gives, already have some access to the Holy Spirit and to the light of Christ (the Sun of righteousness):

> Non-Christian thinkers also have received light from the Sun of righteousness. The Hindus have received of the Holy Spirit. There are many beautiful things in Hinduism, but the fullest light is from Christ. Every one is breathing air. So every one, Christian as well as non-Christian, is breathing the Holy Spirit, though they do not call it by that name. The Holy Spirit is not the private property of some special people.[55]

Within Singh's theological framework, people thus have direct intuitive and mystical access to the *Logos*-Christ and to the Holy Spirit: the essential *bhakti* aspiration for union with God is fulfilled in a mystical encounter with the "living inward Christ" of experience. How-

---

54. Quoted in Heiler, *The Gospel of Sadhu Sundar Singh*, 242.

55. Quoted in B. H. Streeter and A. J. Appasamy, *The Sadhu: A Study in Mysticism and Practical Religion* (Delhi: Mittal, 1987), 232.

ever, the historical facts concerning the life and ministry of Jesus as recorded in the New Testament are vital, ensuring continuity between the "inner Christ" of experience and the Christ of history. The *bhakti* mystical quest is thus fulfilled in an experience of mystical encounter with the "living inward Christ," in which the seeker's heart is transformed, is set free from sin, and finds true inner peace and bliss.

Sundar Singh's willingness to appropriate aspects of the Hindu tradition is also clearly evident in his adoption of the *sadhu* (holy person) lifestyle, an integral aspect of his expression of Christian discipleship.[56] He thus succeeded in embodying a form of Indian Christian discipleship that penetrated the heart of the gospel, and yet seemed "to have access to the innermost chambers of Indian spirituality."[57] The personalist *bhakti* devotional strand within Hinduism thus holds much more promise for Christian contextual engagement in India, and its influence can be observed in many grassroots Christian movements today. The popular Christian piety in mainline churches, many evangelical churches, and house church movements is commonly characterized by elements of *bhakti* devotional worship, and is especially evident in younger Pentecostal and charismatic church and mission movements.

Spirit-theology in India urgently needs to recapture a profound sense of the Holy Spirit's "holy-ness." The Holy Spirit is not merely an impersonal celestial force (*sakti*), or some abstract link between the Father and the Son (*ananda*). Nor must he be equated with any preexistent presence or influence already within humanity (*antaryamin*). He must not be confused with a general spiritual immanence, an impersonal divine influence, the human spirit, or some sort of supernatural spiritual being. He is the transcendent *Holy* Spirit, distinct and separate from his creation. He is the Spirit *of God* and *of Christ*, the personal presence of God himself: the dynamic personal, holy, *sakti* of Christ—the *Khrista-sakti*.

The Holy Spirit is the means by which God makes his personal presence felt among his people, the church, the community of the Spirit. The ultimate purpose of the Spirit's "floodlight"[58] ministry is to

56. Heiler, *The Gospel of Sadhu Sundar Singh*, 55–56.

57. Eric J. Sharpe, "The Legacy of Sadhu Sundar Singh," *International Bulletin of Missionary Research* 14 (1991): 161; cf. Heiler, *The Gospel of Sadhu Sundar Singh*, 231.

58. J. I. Packer's expression in *Keep in Step with the Spirit* (Grand Rapids: Baker, 2005), 57.

mediate the presence of the risen Christ, and to create and deepen an awareness of the reality of Jesus in human experience.[59]

> On the last and greatest day of the Feast, Jesus stood and said in a loud voice, "If anyone is thirsty, let him come to me and drink. Whoever believes in me, as the Scripture has said, streams of living water will flow from within him." By this he meant the Spirit, whom those who believed in him were later to receive. Up to that time the Spirit had not been given, since Jesus had not yet been glorified. (John 7:37–39)

Further Reading

Boyd, Robin. *An Introduction to Indian Christian Theology*. Delhi: ISPCK, 1991.

Christie Kumar, B. J. "An Indian Christian Appreciation of the Doctrine of the Holy Spirit: A Search into the Religious Heritage of the Indian Christian." *Indian Journal of Theology* 30, no. 1 (1981): 29–35.

Kim, Kirsteen. "The Holy Spirit in Mission in India: Indian Contribution to Contemporary Mission Pneumatology." *UBS Journal* 1 (2003): 57–66.

Lipner, Julius. *Hindus: Their Religious Beliefs and Practices*. London: Routledge, 1998.

Richard, H. L. "A Survey of Protestant Evangelistic Efforts among High Caste Hindus in the Twentieth Century." *Missiology: An International Review* 25 (1997): 419–45.

Stephen, M. *A Christian Theology in the Indian Context*. Delhi: ISPCK, 2001.

---

59. Satyavrata, *The Holy Spirit*, 80; cf. Packer, *Keep in Step*, 49–50, 56–58.

CHAPTER 3

Redefining Relationships: The Role of the Spirit in Romans and Its Significance in the Multiethnic Context of India

ZAKALI SHOHE

ABSTRACT

The relational aspect of the Spirit in the Pauline epistles is important to consider in understanding the place of the Spirit in Paul's thought. Furthermore, it is also significant in a multiethnic context. To this end the chapter investigates the role of the Spirit in Romans 8:14–17 and highlights its significance in the multiethnic context of India.

The context of India is one of diverse ethnic groups and races that are interdependent. This interdependence can be economic, political, or social. Yet despite this interdependence, there is also the tendency to protect one's own ethnic group and this can result in conflict and division. Hence, it is important to redefine boundaries, not abandoning distinct ethnic identities, religions, and denominations, while at the same time being open and accepting of differences in a multiethnic context. With this in mind, this chapter examines the role of the Spirit in Romans 8:14–17 from a relational perspective, and draws out its significance for Christians in India.

Studies on the Spirit and the ethical life have predominantly focused on the material *pneuma* (Spirit) as a means that provides an ontological transforming effect.[1] These studies regard Paul's notion of

---

1. Ernst Käsemann identifies Christ with *pneuma*, which transforms believers by their partaking in the sacrament of the Lord's Supper. *Pneuma* is seen as a sacramental gift through which the sacrament effects the transformation of people ("The

the Spirit as *Stoff* (matter). They focus on the transformation of believers that takes place through the *stofflich* (material) notion of the Spirit. Volker Rabens refers to this model as "static."[2] He proposes instead a relational model of the work of the Spirit based on the actual effects attributed to the Spirit in Judaism and Paul.[3] Rabens describes his model: "it is primarily through deeper knowledge of, and an intimate relationship with, God, Jesus Christ and with the community of faith that people are transformed and empowered by the Spirit for religious-ethical life."[4] The approach in this chapter is also relational, but it aims to investigate Romans 8:14–17 in particular within the context of Spirit-guided relationships.

A Brief Overview of Romans 8:14–17

In line with the view that Paul in Romans is addressing a mixed community of Jews and Gentiles,[5] this chapter looks at the Spirit language

---

Pauline Doctrine of the Lord's Supper," in *Essays on New Testament Themes*, Studies in Biblical Theology [London: SCM, 1964], 108–35, esp. 118–25). F. W. Horn also suggests an ontological transformation by the Spirit. According to him, Paul adopts the material concept of the Spirit, which is transferred sacramentally, especially through baptism (F. W. Horn, "Holy Spirit," in *The Anchor Bible Dictionary*, 6 vols., ed. David Noel Freedman [New York: Doubleday, 1992], 3:271–76). Volker Rabens in his monograph discusses this approach in detail. He especially analyzes the stand of Ernst Käsemann, Peter Stuhlmacher, and Friedrich Wilhelm Horn on the "infusion-transformation" approach (*The Holy Spirit and Ethics in Paul: Transformation and Empowering for Religious-Ethical Life* [Tübingen: Mohr Siebeck, 2010], 2–20).

2. For reasons, see Rabens, *The Holy Spirit*, 128.

3. Rabens, *The Holy Spirit*, 120.

4. Rabens, *The Holy Spirit*, 123.

5. See Karl Paul Donfried, *The Romans Debate*, rev. and expanded ed. (1977; reprint, Peabody: Hendrickson, 1991); Andrew Das, *Solving the Romans Debate* (Minneapolis: Fortress, 2007); John Murray, *The Epistle to the Romans*, New International Commentary on the New Testament, 2 vols. (Grand Rapids: Eerdmans, 1959, 1965), 2:172–74; Paul J. Achtemeier, *Romans: Interpretation* (Atlanta: John Knox, 1985), 215; W. S. Campbell, "Why Did Paul Write Romans?" *Expository Times* 85, no. 9 (1973–74): 268; C. E. B. Cranfield, *A Critical and Exegetical Commentary on the Epistle to the Romans*, International Critical Commentary, 2 vols. (Edinburgh: T&T Clark, 1975), 1:17–22; 1:694–96; Ernst Käsemann, *Commentary on Romans*, trans. and ed. G. W. Bromiley, 4th ed. (London: SCM, 1980), 366. Offering an alternate view that Paul is addressing a Gentile community are A. Andrew Das, "'Praise the Lord, All You Gentiles': The Encoded Audience of Romans 15:7–13," *Journal for the Study of the New Testament* 34, no. 1 (2011): 101–2;

in such a setting. In taking this stand, I do not intend to argue for
Jew-Gentile unification as Paul's sole purpose for writing Romans. In
recent years many studies have come up with a variety of reasons why
Paul wrote Romans.[6] The epistle itself gives evidence of the many purposes of Paul, but it is beyond the scope of this chapter to go into details. Hence, keeping in mind the Jew-Gentile context of Romans, this
chapter takes up the role of the Spirit in redefining relationships. In
looking at the pericope, I avoid a detailed discussion of every exegetical issue arising from the text. Instead, I concentrate on how Romans
8:14–17 contributes to the role of the Spirit in redefining relationships.
In relation to the Spirit language in Romans 8:14–17 this chapter highlights two aspects: the leading of the Spirit and the defining role of the
Spirit.

The Leading of the Spirit

For Paul the criterion for the status of children of God is the leading
of the Spirit (Rom. 8:14). It is generally accepted that *agontai* (being led)
with the dative *pneumati* (by Spirit) suggests the enthusiastic nature of
believers and is an active indication of being led by a spiritual force.[7]
The overtone of active and ecstatic behavior in the use of the dative
pneumati is also found in other Pauline epistles (e.g., 1 Cor. 12:2; Gal.
5:18). Furthermore, the notion of "being carried away" by a compelling
force or surrendering to a spiritual force was also dominant in the
Greco-Roman world, especially in magical texts, where *agein* (to lead)

Joshua D. Garroway, "The Circumcision of Christ: Romans 15:7–13," *Journal for the Study of the New Testament* 34, no. 4 (2012): 306.

6. See L. Ann Jervis, *The Purpose of Romans: A Comparative Letter Structure Investigation* (Sheffield: JSOT, 1991); A. J. M. Wedderburn, *The Reasons for Romans* (Edinburgh: T&T Clark, 1988); Lo Lung-Kwong, *Paul's Purpose in Writing Romans: The Upbuilding of a Jewish and Gentile Christian Community in Rome* (Hong Kong: Alliance Biblical Seminary, 1998); Robert Jewett, *Romans: A Commentary* (Minneapolis: Fortress, 2007), 80–91.

7. Ernst Käsemann defines this experience: "Paul was not so timid as his exposi-
tors. He could appropriate the terms of the enthusiast because he took 'Christ in us' seriously." *Commentary on Romans*, 226. James D. G. Dunn and Robert Jewett follow Käsemann in reading *agesthai* with the dative as indicating an enthusiastic and active force. Dunn embraces the NEB's rendering "moved by the Spirit." Dunn, *Romans 1–8*, 450; Jewett, *Romans*, 496.

was used in reference to gods, spirits, or ghosts of the dead. These agents were commanded to lead a person supernaturally.[8]

Romans 8:14 also reflects active indication, which need not necessarily be an audacious ecstatic experience.[9] Instead, it is possible to interpret "being led" by the Spirit in connection with "being led" by the cloud in the exodus narrative.[10] In the exodus narrative, the cloud is identified as the presence of God that leads the Israelites (Exodus 14). There is no direct reference to the Spirit in the text from Exodus, but Paul alludes to this event in 1 Corinthians 10:1–5 and links the Spirit with the exodus. In considering the Corinthians passage, it is possible to understand being led by the Spirit in Romans 8 as parallel to being led by the cloud. The cloud is the presence of God with the Israelites and the Spirit in Romans 8:14 can also be seen as the presence of God in the lives of believers.

Elabete (you received, 8:15) probably points to the initial experience of life in the Spirit, while *agontai* (being led, 8:14) refers to the ongoing leading of the Spirit. For the relationship does not stop with the initial experience, but the Spirit continues to guide believers by connecting them to God as well as to other believers. Paul's emphasis is on the ongoing Spirit-guided relationship in the experience of heirship, where all believers share Christ's heirship in the family of God (8:15–17). For the Spirit is active in guiding believers to a new status as children of God, and this status redefines their relationship within the family of God. It is the Spirit that defines the place of believers in the family of God.[11] This is further elaborated in verses 15–17 with the use of familial images.

The Defining Role of the Spirit

Having established the criteria for being called "children of God" (Rom. 8:14, 16), Paul goes on to highlight the defining role of the Spirit

8. For references to texts, see Jewett, *Romans*, 496 (esp. note 231).

9. Also, Jewett, *Romans*, 496. But not necessarily as in the Corinthian and the Thessalonian contexts (1 Cor. 12–14; 1 Thess. 5:19–22).

10. For this reading of *agō* I am indebted to Francis Watson, who introduced me to it in the course of our discussion at Trinity Theological College, Singapore, September 30, 2014.

11. See Dunn, *Romans 1–8*, 451.

with the use of familial images (8:15–17). He draws on powerful relationship language from the ancient Mediterranean world that binds its members together in kinship. The family was a basic social institution and references to it were used in people's everyday language in relation to one another.[12] The familial images in 8:14–17 also point to a relationship that, according to James D. G. Dunn, is a status by "divine choice."[13] Paul aims to redefine what it means to be adopted as children of God through receiving the Spirit of God.[14]

Four characteristics define the role of the Spirit of God. First, in 8:14–15 the Spirit is described as the "Spirit of adoption." In these verses the status of the children of God is defined in relation to the Spirit. This relationship is made possible through "adoption," which for Dunn is either through "the Spirit which effects adoption, or the Spirit which expresses adoption."[15]

The metaphor of adoption occurs throughout the Pauline epistles, especially in Romans (Rom. 8:15, 23; 9:4; Gal. 4:5; Eph. 1:1). It is possible that Paul uses the metaphor in his exhortation to the Roman believers because the notion of adoption was common in Greco-Roman law and custom.[16] This practice was not prevalent in its legal form among the Jews, but the notion of adoption, especially divine adoption, is also found in Jewish sources.[17] Ernst Käsemann rejects the original sense of adoption in the Greek term *huiothesia* (Rom. 8:15).[18] However, such rejection overlooks the overall intention of Paul, especially in terms of

12. Philip Esler, *Conflict and Identity in Romans: The Social Setting of Paul's Letter* (Minneapolis: Fortress, 2003), 247.

13. James D. G. Dunn, "Spirit Speech: Reflections on Romans 8:12–27," in *Romans and the People of God: Essays in Honor of Gordon D. Fee on the Occasion of His 65th Birthday*, ed. Sven K. Soderlund and N. T. Wright (Grand Rapids: Eerdmans, 1999), 83. See also Dunn, *Romans 1–8*, 526.

14. See Dunn, *Romans 1–8*, 451; Jewett, *Romans*, 497 (following Dunn's position).

15. Dunn, "Spirit Speech," 83.

16. It is beyond the scope of this chapter to discuss the Greco-Roman institution of adoption. See James M. Scott, *Adoption as Sons: An Exegetical Investigation into the Background of ΥΙΟΘΕΣΙΑ in the Pauline Corpus*, Wissenschaftliche Untersuchungen zum Neuen Testament 48 (Tübingen: Mohr Siebeck, 1992), 3–13.

17. God as the father and Israel as the son (Exod. 4:22; Isa. 43:6; Sir. 51:10; Tob. 13:5). Scott presents a detailed study in *Adoption as Sons*, 61–117. See also Cranfield, *Romans*, 1:397–98.

18. Käsemann, *Romans*, 227, following Theodor Zahn, *Der Brief des Paulus an die Römer* (Leipzig: Deichert, 1925).

the role of the Spirit as redefining boundaries. Dunn rightly comments that Käsemann's rejection "is both unfounded and misses the point." Dunn goes on to affirm that Paul draws *huiothesia* from the Greco-Roman world and his use of the term indicates that a believer is transformed not only from a slave to a freed man but also from a freed man to an adopted child of God.[19] It is thus possible to refer to the notion of adoption as redefining a person's relationship with God. This new status of believers is experienced through the guidance of the Spirit.

Second, the new status of believers gives them the privilege to cry "Abba Father" (8:15). *Krazomen* (we cry) is taken as referring to *pneuma* (Spirit), "in whom we cry." It can be either an intense and loud cry[20] or an "urgent and sincere crying to God," regardless of whether loud or soft, formal or informal, public or private.[21] However, we cannot conclude with certainty if *krazomen* stands for a loud, soft, spoken, or silent cry, but it is possible to regard it as an expression of connecting to God where believers can freely express themselves. Such connection with God is realized through the leading of the Spirit.

The filial address "Abba" in Paul's exhortation should not be interpreted merely on the basis of its semantics, but, more important, in the context of the divine-human relationship. Emphasizing the experiential side, M. M. Thompson hypothesizes that the "Abba"-cry (8:15) and the Spirit's bearing witness with our spirit (8:16) have been misinterpreted as an intimate relationship with God. Thompson states that *krazein* (to cry) cannot be an expression of an emotional state of believers, for it occurs in a prophetic context in Romans 9:27. It refers to the "Spirit-inspired nature of Isaiah's speech." She concludes that *krazein* in 8:15 emphasizes the "ultimate source," which points to the power of the Spirit at work.[22] The problem with Thompson's conclusion is her overemphasis on the experiential aspect of the Spirit over against the relational aspect. It is also a relationship since believers are adopted as children of God, pointing to a different level of relationship from slavery and fear. This relationship receives expression through the Spirit-inspired cry to God. In the words of Dunn, "it is a relationship he is describing, not just an experience. But Paul's language does not permit

19. Dunn, *Romans 1–8*, 452.
20. Dunn, *Romans 1–8*, 453.
21. Cranfield, *Romans*, 1:399.
22. Marianne Meye Thompson, *The Promise of the Father: Jesus and God in the New Testament* (Louisville: Westminster John Knox, 2000), 126.

us to forget that the relationship in view is one which for Paul was expressed in intensity of feeling as well as intimacy of expression."[23] Supporting the view that the "Abba"-cry is not just an experience but also connotes relationship, Rabens says: "The 'Abba'-cry does not designate isolated experiences but a continuous loving relationship which, like every active relationship, has an experiential side."[24]

Third, Paul is emphasizing joint witness. Romans 8:16 further affirms the role of the Spirit in redefining the place of believers: "The Spirit bears witness with our Spirit that we are children of God." The Greek *sun-* compounds (*sun*: with, together with) in relation to the Spirit appear often in Romans 8: the Spirit bears witness together with us (v. 16); the Spirit leads believers to a relationship with Christ, with whom they become "joint heirs," and also "suffers together with" in order that they might be "glorified together with" (v. 17); the Spirit comes along to offer aid in our weakness (v. 26); and the Spirit works all things together for good (v. 28). These *sun-* compounds emphasize a close "relationship between two people or matters."[25]

The prefix *sun-* (with) in the compound verb *summartureō* (bear witness together with) carries the meaning of accompaniment ("bear witness with"), but it can also refer to an intensive force ("bear witness to"; cf. Rom. 2:25; 9:1).[26] Some scholars prefer the latter meaning,[27] while others argue that the dual witness affirms the believer's new relationship to God.[28] The requirement of two or more witnesses is also found in Deuteronomy 17:6 and 19:5, in 2 Corinthians 13:1, and in the practice of adoption in the ancient Greco-Roman world.[29] In Romans 8:16, it probably refers to a joint witness in order to affirm the adoption by adding more than one witness. The Spirit confirms the

23. Dunn, "Spirit Speech," 85.

24. Rabens, *The Holy Spirit*, 226–27.

25. See Gordon D. Fee, *God's Empowering Presence: The Holy Spirit in the Letters of Paul* (Peabody: Hendrickson, 1994), 562.

26. See *BAGD*, 3rd ed., 617–19, on *martyreō* and its related roots.

27. Geoffrey W. Bromiley, ed., *Theological Dictionary of the New Testament*, 10 vols. (Grand Rapids: Eerdmans, 1967), 4:508–9; Cranfield, *Romans*, 1:402.

28. Rabens, *The Holy Spirit*, 216.

29. Rabens, *The Holy Spirit*, 216–17, follows James D. G. Dunn, *The Epistle to the Galatians* (Peabody: Hendrickson, 1993), 219; Trevor J. Burke, *Adopted into God's Family: Exploring a Pauline Metaphor*, New Studies in Biblical Theology 22 (Downers Grove: InterVarsity, 2006), 150–51. See also Douglas J. Moo, *Romans* (Grand Rapids: Zondervan, 2000), 504.

new status of believers in God's family. It is a change from slaves to children. Accordingly, Robert Jewett writes, "since the Spirit impels believers to utter their prayers directly to their 'Abba,' this is a powerful experiential confirmation of their status as children of God. Since the Spirit confirms that they belong to God, there is no longer any basis for anxiety about their status."[30]

Thompson offers a different view, noting that in Romans 8:16 Paul is explicitly referring to the work of the Spirit in enabling the Gentiles to acknowledge God as their source of life and not the believer's "sense of sonship."[31] I agree with Thompson that the Spirit enables the Gentiles, but focusing only on this aspect in verse 16 misses the filial relationship in verses 14–15, especially the work of the Spirit in witnessing with our spirit and in confirming the filial relationship that believers share with God.[32] For in their status as children of God, believers become heirs of God (8:17).

Fourth, believers share status with Christ as "co-heirs" (*sunklērono-moi*; Rom. 8:17; cf. Gal. 4:7). Christ is not directly addressed as the heir, but believers are called to share as co-heirs with Christ. In this regard Christ as heir suggests the concept of the "son of God" (Mark 12:7; Heb. 1:2). The Spirit leads believers to a new status as children of God through adoption and they share with Christ as co-heirs. This points to the relationship between God, Christ, and the Spirit. In the Pauline epistles (and the New Testament as a whole) there is no explicitly articulated doctrine of God as in the classical documents of the church like the Nicene Creed. However, as David S. Yeago argues, the New Testament contains implicit and explicit judgments concerning the crucified and resurrected Jesus of Nazareth.[33]

In Romans 8, the relationship of God and Jesus is that of Father and Son. Jesus is identified as an heir in God's family. As heir of God, Jesus has been identified with God, and as such shares God's unique privileges as the firstborn of all (Col. 1:15). The Spirit also acts on behalf of God as "the Spirit of God" (Rom. 8:14) by leading believers in relating to the Father in their identity as co-heirs with Christ. Romans 8 also reflects a community building and strengthening one another in the

30. Jewett, *Romans*, 500.

31. Thompson, *The Promise of the Father*, 128.

32. So also Rabens, *The Holy Spirit*, 227–28.

33. David S. Yeago, "The New Testament and the Nicene Dogma: A Contribution to the Recovery of Theological Exegesis," *Pro Ecclesia* 3, no. 2 (Spring 1994): 153.

Spirit. Furthermore, Jesus is identified as Christ in verse 17, signifying his exaltation, and in his exaltation Jesus has been identified with
God.[34] In looking at the text from the relational perspective it is possible to see the connection between God, Christ, and the Spirit. Christ
and the Spirit cannot be separated from God, for God is identified in
the person of Jesus as the "Son of God" and heir, and the Spirit in this
text is the presence of God, signifying the triune God.

Believers are co-heirs not through physical descent but through
divine call and appointment. As Jesus addresses God as "Abba Father"
so also believers address God as "Abba Father" and attest themselves
as children of God and co-heirs with Christ. The Spirit establishes this
relationship and links believers to Jesus. This then defines a person as
a believer.[35] Sonship and inheritance are grounded in a new creation.
The idea of inheritance is important in Paul, for the promise given to
Abraham is now mediated through Christ (cf. Gal. 3:16, 29; 4:1, 7) and
believers, both Jews and Gentiles, are co-heirs of the promise (Rom.
8:17; Eph. 3:18).[36]

Thus far, this chapter has analyzed the Spirit language in Romans
8:14–17 and highlighted two aspects. The first is the criterion for the
believer's status as a child of God, that is, the leading of the Spirit. The
second is the defining role of the Spirit with the use of familial images.
Having analyzed the role of the Spirit in the text, the next step is to
redefine relationship in the context of the Spirit.

Redefining Relationship in the Context of the Spirit

Spirit and Language of Intimacy

The word "relational" is not found in the Pauline epistles. In fact, Paul
does not even use the words "relationship" and "relational" in the context of the Spirit language. However, the concept of relationships plays

---

34. Yeago makes a similar argument in his discussion of the message of early
Christians on Jesus's exaltation, though not in relation to Romans ("The New Testament and the Nicene Dogma," 154).

35. See Dunn, "Spirit Speech," 84.

36. J. H. Friedrich, "*klēronomos, ou, ho*," in *Exegetical Dictionary of the New Testament*,
3 vols., ed. Horst Balz and Gerherd Schneider (Grand Rapids: Eerdmans, 1991), 2:298–99.

an important role in his ministry and theology.[37] This observation is also made by Dunn, who says, "Paul's theology is relational."[38] There are terms and phrases pointing to the idea of relationship, as is also found in Paul's approach to the Spirit. For example, the prepositions *sun* (with, together with) and *en* (in) point to relationship, particularly the notion of being in Christ or with Christ. Familial images like *huiou theou* (son of God), *huiothesias* (adoption), *abba ho patēr* (Abba Father), *tekna theou* (children of God), *klēronomoi* (heirs), and *sunklēronomoi* (co-heirs) highlight family relations (Rom. 8:14–17).

The relational approach is also discussed in detail by Rabens with exegetical evidence from the epistles of Paul.[39] Yet, unlike Rabens, the main question this chapter takes up is how the Spirit enables the redefinition of boundaries. My reading of Romans 8:14–17 indicates that the role of the Spirit in the redefinition of boundaries occurs in the Spirit-guided relationship. This relationship is made more significant with the use of familial language.

Spirit-Guided Relationship: A Redefined Boundary

Paul states that "in the Spirit" the Roman communities share a new identity, which is built on Israel's self-understanding of being people chosen by God. The new identity is emphasized with the use of diverse terms like *huiou* (son; Rom. 8:14, 19), *huiothesia* (adoption; 8:15, 23), and *tekna theou* (children of God; 8:16, 21).[40] In the context of the new relationship as children of God, K. K. Yeo makes an insightful remark from the perspective of honor and shame: "Believers made righteous by the act of God in Christ have been given the honor of being sons of God."[41]

---

37. This is also my hypothesis in "Paul's Use of 'Familial Images' and Their Significance for the Understanding of His Ministry" (MTh thesis, United Theological College, 2003). See Rabens for a list from the Pauline epistles (*The Holy Spirit*, 135–37).

38. James D. G. Dunn, *The Theology of Paul* (Grand Rapids: Eerdmans, 1998), 53.

39. Rabens, *The Holy Spirit*, 121–24.

40. See J. Ross Wagner, "'Not from the Jews Only, But Also from the Gentiles': Mercy to the Nations in Romans 9–11," in *Between Gospel and Election*, ed. Florian Wilk and J. Ross Wagner, Wissenschaftliche Untersuchungen zum Neuen Testament 257 (Tübingen: Mohr Siebeck, 2010), 418.

41. K. K. Yeo, "From Rome to Beijing: One World One Dream," in *From Rome to Beijing: Symposia on Robert Jewett's Commentary on Romans*, ed. K. K. Yeo (Lincoln: Kairos Stud-

In the light of the Spirit language in Romans 8, it is thus possible to look at the Spirit of God as the agent of honor. It guides believers to God through adoption and thus leads them to experience the honor of this new identity. It is the Spirit that guides believers and connects them to God through adoption. Their adoption into the family of God gives them the privilege of calling God "Abba Father."

The link between the Spirit and divine heirship broadens beyond people groups by defining believers at Rome as adopted into the family of God. Their status in the family of God is affirmed through a joint witness where "the Spirit" and "our spirit" witness together. This joint witness points to the importance of a community in relation building that redefines boundaries. Furthermore, the Spirit-guided relationship narrows the gap between Jewish and Gentile believers through their acceptance of one another. This relationship is given shape and made significant through the use of familial images. Thus, it is the Spirit that empowers and connects believers at the personal and the corporate levels of relationship.

Spirit-Guided Relationships: A Basis for Hope

The divine acceptance of believers as children of God allows them to enter into a new relationship. The entrance into a new relationship is not an end in itself, but the Spirit-guided status that believers share, as co-heirs with Christ and with one another as a faith community, provides an eschatological hope for the "unseen" (cf. Rom. 8:24–25; 15:13). Heirship is also grounded in future hope (8:23), for the inheritance of believers is also an object of hope.[42] Believers look forward to the promise of glorification (8:17).

Paul ends the section (8:14–17) on the believer's existence in the

---

ies, 2013), 16. The monograph *From Rome to Beijing* is important for its cross-cultural reading of Romans.

42. The word group *klēronomos* in its eschatological sense also occurs in the context of judgment (Matt. 25:34; 1 Cor. 6:10; Gal. 5:21). The phrase "inherit eternal life" also occurs within the eschatological frame (Matt. 19:29; Mark 10:17; Luke 18:18; 10:25; Col. 3:24). See W. Foerster, "The Word Group *klēronomos* in the LXX," in *Theological Dictionary of the New Testament*, 10 vols., ed. Gerhard Kittel, trans. Geoffrey W. Bromiley (1965; reprint, Grand Rapids: Eerdmans, 1984), 3:782–84; Friedrich, "*klēronomos, ou, ho*," 2:298–99.

Spirit with a condition (v. 17). He demands that as fellow heirs with Christ, believers "suffer with him so that we may also be glorified with him." The notion of present suffering and future glorification is further developed in 8:18–30. Believers look forward to the future glorification as fellow heirs with Christ, a hope that is unseen, but for which they patiently await (8:24–25). Believers remain part of the present world in which suffering and difficulties are inevitable (5:3–5). In their coming together as a worshiping community[43] believers strengthen one another and abound in hope as they look forward to final glorification (cf. 8:17; 15:7–13).

It is thus possible to say that the Spirit-guided relationship provides hope, for it involves a future relationship between individuals, communities, and groups. As Jürgen Moltmann puts it, "Every relationship to another life involves the future of that life, the future of the reciprocal relationship into which one life enters with another."[44] It is a "relational eschatology,"[45] for it concerns the ongoing relationship built on the truthfulness and the mercy of God (cf. chaps. 9–11; 15:8–9a). In accepting one another as fellow believers in the family of God, the members of the community continue to hope in nurturing their relationship in a meaningful direction. The hope of believers is a move toward building a sense of connectedness among Jews and Gentiles and their openness to accepting one another through the guidance of the Spirit. In 15:13, hope is connected with worship. Such a connection also appears in 5:2, where hope is connected with giving praise to God—a hope that is unseen (8:24–25) but kept alive through the common worship of Jews and Gentiles.

Summary

Thus far, this chapter has attempted to identify the role of the Spirit in redefining relationships. The concept of relationship is elaborated with the use of familial images. This relationship is redefined through the guidance of the Spirit at both the personal and the corporate lev-

43. While I understand that there are many home churches in Rome, in this chapter I use the singular, which also represents these home churches.

44. Jürgen Moltmann, *The Church in the Power of the Spirit: A Contribution to Messianic Ecclesiology*, 2nd ed. (London: SCM, 1992), 134.

45. The phrase "relational eschatology" is taken from Moltmann, *The Church*, 134.

els. From the above analysis of Romans 8:14–17 it can be said that the language used for the Spirit describes relationship, one expressed in openness to accept the "other," one not belonging to the same people group (15:7). The Spirit redefines or moves people in terms of boundaries; the Spirit guides believers not only in their present life as a faith community, but also gives them hope to look forward to final redemption. The Spirit guides individual believers in relating to God as children in the family of God as well as in their openness to accepting one another, both Jews and Gentiles. This Spirit-guided relationship also provides hope for believers in their coming together as a worshiping community. Having identified the relation-building nature of the Spirit, I now draw insights from my reading in the context of India.

A Pneumatological Relational Element in the Context of India

Context of India: A Brief Overview

India is a land of diverse cultures, faith traditions, and ethnic identities. The multiethnic context and rich cultural diversity provide an opportunity to be open to, learn from, and respect one another. Even people within the same region share rich cultural diversity, administration, and policies. This is true especially for the northeast region of India. Eight different states comprise northeast India: Assam, Arunachal Pradesh, Manipur, Meghalaya, Mizoram, Nagaland, Sikkim, and Tripura. The region is characterized by its rich ethnic, cultural, religious, and linguistic diversity.

However, the danger in the context of diversity lies in being overprotective of one's identity at the expense of the other people groups. When an ethnic identity or a faith tradition is rooted in pride, there is the danger that the dominant group's identity becomes a threat to others. In India, the Brahmanic, or Sanskritic, culture is meant to represent the Indian culture or what it means to be Indian.[46] The other people groups enter the mainstream by assimilating into the Hindu fold, whereby the tribes are identified in the Hindu polity.[47] This means

46. G. S. Gurye, *The Scheduled Tribes* (Bombay: Popular Prakashan, 1963), 211. See also G. N. Dash, *Hindus and Tribals* (New Delhi: Decent Books, 1998), 3.

47. Gouranga Chhattopadhyay, "The Problem of Tribal Integration to Urban In-

"entering the caste fold from the lowest level."[48] In such a context the minority communities are involved in conflict in order to preserve their ethnic or faith identity over against the dominant one; they may experience discrimination at the personal level in either workplaces or public places to varying degrees.

Today in India instead of celebrating diversity, there is a tendency among various groups to be suspicious. Mistrust stops people from being open and accepting of those who do not belong to their race, religion, or people group, and this is true even in an ecclesial setting. In such a context of conflict, differences, and atrocities, Christians as individuals and the church as an institution in India are called to redefine relationships in the ecclesial sphere as well as in the social sphere.

Spirit and Relationality

Paul's exhortation on the Spirit-guided relationship that moves beyond the traditional boundaries of people groups is relevant for Christians in India. In the pluralistic context of religions and multiethnicity, which continue to remain a challenging issue in the Indian context, S. J. Samartha refers to the Spirit that brings the unity of the Father and the Son and also brings believers in Christ together as the Spirit of oneness.[49] In Samartha's view the Holy Spirit "not only makes it necessary for us to enter into dialogue, but also to continue in it without fear, with full expectation and openness."[50] Chenchiah describes the Holy Spirit as a great creative power and energy that brings transformation in the political and social structures of the world.[51] Thus, the Spirit transcends the traditional understanding of the people of God and redefines relationships. It is the Spirit that redefines the people of God, for all who are led by the Spirit are children of God, heirs and

---

dustrial Society: A Theoretical Approach," in *The Tribal Situation in India*, ed. K. Suresh Singh (Simla: Indian Institute of Advanced Study, 1972), 491.

48. Hukato Shohe, "Developing a Christology from Sumi Naga Context" (PhD diss., Senate of Serampore College [University], 2014), 202.

49. Stanley J. Samartha, *One Christ—Many Religions: Toward a Revised Christology* (Maryknoll: Orbis, 1991), 83.

50. Stanley J. Samartha, *Two Cultures: Ecumenical Ministry in a Pluralist World* (Bangalore: Asian Trading Cooperation, 1997), 1–14.

51. P. V. Joseph, *Indian Interpretation of the Holy Spirit* (Delhi: ISPCK, 2007), 72.

co-heirs with Christ. In his chapter in this volume Wei Hua also high-lights the role of the Spirit in building new relationships in the life of believers. This notion of the Spirit is important especially in our under-standing of Pauline pneumatology because in Paul's writings we see that the Spirit redefines an individual believer's status before God, and that this is also the case in the incorporation of both Jews and Gentiles in the body of Christ. This creates space for openness to accept one another in a faith community.

The Spirit guides believers into community, where their acceptance of one another provides hope (Rom. 15:7–13), for it encompasses the future of the relationship that is established. In their acceptance and openness to one another believers abound in hope that strengthens and nurtures their relationship in a constructive and meaningful direction. The relationship does not end with its initial experience, but believers grow together as they look forward to the hope of final redemption.

This understanding of the Spirit as one who guides believers into community and openness by redefining boundaries is significant for Christians and the church in India. The relation building of the Spirit is obvious in the life of the church, in spite of the many limitations imposed on it by human-created structures in thought and attitude. In India, the church is seen as a remnant of the imperialist heritage. Christians are many times looked upon as agents of imperialism or traitors of nationalism or indigenous cultures and religions at worst or as passive or unconscious agents of Western culture at best. In this context, the reaching-out and relation-building nature of the Spirit continues to manifest itself in various ways in the ecclesial sphere. Both the church as an institution and individual believers continue to identify with and engage in diverse ways at the personal and the corpo-rate levels, in creating space for openness and acceptance, for building a community of faith, and for learning from one another through the guidance of the Spirit.

For instance, northeast India has a long history of insurgency. In fact, most of the states there in recent years have been affected by vi-olence and conflict. In Nagaland, the separatist violence started in the 1950s and the conflict has escalated, especially since the late 1970s.[52]

52. Ajai Sahni, "Survey of Conflicts and Resolution in India's Northeast," http://www.satp.org/satporgtp/publication/faultlines/volume12/Article3.htm#2, accessed Jan-uary 5, 2015.

The Nagas have had a long history of conflict with the government of India, and have also suffered at the hands of the Naga insurgency that is fragmented into various factions. The conflict between the government of India and the various people groups, particularly in the northeast region, has led to much hardship and animosity between the people of mainland India and those of the northeast region. There have also been various occasions when the churches or church-related nongovernmental organizations from mainland India and northeast India have come together to share their visions and missions and to create a platform where they can work together to address issues related to the conflict between mainland India and the various people groups.

The relational nature of the Spirit is visible in the witness of the church in Nagaland. Nagaland, a state in northeast India, is a land of ethnic diversities; yet 80 to 90 percent of the people there are Christians. The Naga society is multicultural and multilingual in nature. The different ethnic groups have been intolerant of one another since colonial times. This was mainly to protect their ethnic identity and their territory. In the past, different ethnic groups were seen as a threat to one another. However, the church as the body of believers in Christ has played its part at different levels. Today many Nagas have gone from being suspicious of the other ethnic communities to acceptance and acknowledgment of the contribution of others. The Nagaland Baptist Council of Churches (NBCC) creates platforms where the different ethnic groups can come together to share the visions and missions of their churches and work together to address issues related to conflict and social evils. The contributions of the members irrespective of ethnic group are appreciated and the members continue to learn from one another and grow together as a faith community.

The other platform where the relational nature of the Spirit is manifested at the ecclesial level is the effort of the Council of the Naga Baptist Churches (CNBC). This platform aims to bring the Nagas from different ethnic groups together at the ecclesial level, although administrative division within India and the international border between India and Myanmar divide them. While it is still at its nascent stage, it is one organization that brings all Nagas together under one umbrella. It may not sound like much to people unaware of the division and fragmentation of the Nagas living in different administrative states in India and Myanmar. For the people who have virtually no means of coming together, the CNBC is doing yeoman service in reaching out and creating a meeting point for building relationships, which has remained impossible since the schism of the national political parties fighting for independence.[53]

These are just a few instances where we find the relation-building nature of the Spirit manifested in the life of the church and its members. Nonetheless, in spite of the efforts that the church and individual Christians in some contexts are making, in general relationship building continues to remain a challenge in India.

Challenges for the Church in India

While the efforts of the church and its members provide glimmers of hope in building relationship between groups, other elements in this activity hinder the work of the Spirit. First, the long history of ethnocentrism of the various ethnic groups in India, as well as the different tribes in northeast India, has created stereotypes that hinder open and true relationships among the various people groups. Such stereotyped images are also visible in the life of the church among diverse ethnic Christian groups and denominations. Division and mistrust hinder the growth of Christians as a community of faith and a witnessing community. Second, the relation-building nature of the Spirit may be experienced beyond the ecclesiastical walls in a wider social sphere. For this, the church needs to create platforms for interracial-ethnic, interregional, inter-faith, and intra-faith efforts and participation to reflect on the social evils, injustices, and conflicts and to build a just community and restore positive rapport.

The Spirit guides the church to redefine relationships by creating space for openness to accept one another. However, on many occasions in a multiracial-multiethnic context, instead of seeing the beauty in diverse groups coming together people are building walls and forming divisions on the basis of race and ethnicity. There are also instances where the church has remained silent on the atrocities and violent acts committed in the name of freedom movements, nationalism, or integration. For example, India is a country of diversity, with many races, many ethnic people groups, and a plurality of religions, but aims

53. I am indebted to Hukato Shohe for the information about CNBC.

to promote unity in diversity. Yet, the problem of racism continues to exist in many parts of the country. The atrocities against the people from northeast India committed by the mainland Indians are a common experience for many residing or traveling outside their home states. These atrocities prevail at workplaces, in educational institutions, and in public places as well as in the private sphere. Christians at the personal level have shared their concern on different occasions, in their personal interactions as well as in social gatherings, but the church as an institution has remained silent on the atrocities against northeast India. People from mainland India also experience atrocities in northeast India. But the church in the region does not address this issue. Even when it comes to caste atrocities, the church as an institution has remained passive.

No one can fully blame the church in India for being silent on many issues since for some time it has been seen as an alien religion that entered the native land. However, the church in India as an institution needs to go beyond the ethnic, denominational, ritual, and doctrinal differences and address the atrocities against the minority groups. It needs to create awareness among its members on the importance of accepting and respecting people from all ethnic groups. One of the challenges for Christians in India is to acknowledge multiple identities and roles. Believers in Christ cannot be exclusively Christians in their personal relationship with God and ignore the community. Christianity does not draw away individual believers from the faith community of believers, the wider sphere of the society, or their own culture and traditions, but it demands that its members participate in a different way. Our multiple identities and roles continue to persist in life even after we become Christians, but they should be utilized for the service and the glory of God.

Thus, the church as an institution needs to be a model of openness by taking initiative in bridge building and creating platforms for meeting points. The church in India can draw insights from Paul's exhortation on the Spirit-guided relationship. The leading of the Spirit plays an important role in the life of believers. Thus, it is important to listen to the voice of the Spirit, for it is the Spirit that guides believers into community and openness. For at the heart of it is the notion of relationality. Such a relationship recognizes the "other" and is expressed in an openness to accept the "other" and strengthen one another as a witnessing community.

The Christian faith calls us to bring people together, transcending boundaries and building positive rapport. We need to go beyond our ethnic identities, denominational boundaries, and doctrinal boundaries, and redefine our boundaries as a witnessing community through the guidance of the Spirit. If the church in India can transcend the boundaries of ethnic groups and denominations and come on a common platform to discuss issues, this will be a witness that speaks louder than any proclamation.

The Spirit-guided relationship brings people together and promotes acceptance and harmony rather than divisions and conflict. It brings believers together as a faith community. As members belonging to the world, believers continue to strengthen one another in their trials and sufferings. In their openness to accepting one another, Christians in India through the guidance of the Spirit will be able to grow and build one another up despite their ethnic and denominational differences.

Christians can be witnesses in their coming together and looking forward to the eschaton. The hope for the future glorification in the Spirit-guided life provides strength and confidence for Christians in India as they persevere in their faith amid hardships and sufferings. C. René Padilla emphasizes the notion of the Spirit as one that provides hope in the context of suffering and hardship in his chapter in this volume. He looks at the work of the Holy Spirit as a power that provides hope in the context of poverty. Such a notion of the Spirit is important because the Christian hope provides a reason to press on and anticipate transformation and change in the face of hardship, poverty, injustice, and suffering. However, in this chapter I present the notion of the Spirit as one that provides hope within the context of the worshiping community. Being in a community of believers that is open and accepting of one another strengthens the members to abound in hope and gives them confidence to nurture and build their relationship in a meaningful direction as they look forward to the final glorification.

Conclusion

Virgilio Elizondo notes that it is not possible for borders to disappear and that differences cannot completely fade away. Nonetheless, differences need not necessarily divide people and keep them apart as me and you, we and they. Instead of becoming fences of separation, differences can serve as marking regional characteristics, which is definitely appealing and humanizing. Elizondo further stresses that each individual needs the other to be fully human; in encountering others, more about us is revealed as well as about others.[54] Elizondo's perspective enriches our redefining of boundaries, for every time a border is crossed and a bridge is built, Christians in India get another opportunity to critique the past and through the guidance of the Spirit move toward creating space for openness and being a witnessing community. Instead of seeing the diverse ethnic groups, denominations, and doctrines as the dividing line between individuals and groups, Christians can view them as a meeting point from which we build bridges and grow together in respect and solidarity. In this way the relation-building nature of the Spirit can be manifested in the life of the church, which itself will be a witness to the wider social sphere.

Further Reading

Dunn, James D. G. "Spirit Speech: Reflections on Romans 8:12–27." In *Romans and the People of God: Essays in Honor of Gordon D. Fee on the Occasion of His 65th Birthday*, edited by Sven K. Soderlund and N. T. Wright. Grand Rapids: Eerdmans, 1999.

Fee, Gordon D. *God's Empowering Presence: The Holy Spirit in the Letters of Paul*. Peabody: Hendrickson, 1994.

Jewett, Robert. *Romans: A Commentary*. Hermeneia. Minneapolis: Fortress, 2007.

Joseph, P. V. *Indian Interpretation of the Holy* Spirit. Delhi: ISPCK, 2007.

Rabens, Volker. *The Holy Spirit and Ethics in Paul: Transformation and Empowering for Religious-Ethical Life*. Tübingen: Mohr Siebeck, 2010.

Yeo, K. K., ed. *From Rome to Beijing: Symposia on Robert Jewett's Commentary on Romans*. Lincoln: Kairos Studies, 2013.

---

54. Virgilio Elizondo, "Transformation of Boundaries: Border Separation or a New Identity?" in *Negotiating Borders: Theological Exploration in the Global Era*, ed. P. Gnanapragasam and E. S. Fiorenza (Delhi: ISPCK, 2008), 28–29.

CHAPTER 4

Pauline Pneumatology and the Chinese Rites:
Spirit and Culture in the Holy See's Missionary Strategy

WEI HUA

ABSTRACT

After providing a brief survey of Chinese pneumatology in the field
of biblical studies, the chapter describes the evolution of the Chinese
rites controversy, which addressed the question of the traditional commemorating rites of ancestors and Confucius. It then draws insights
from Pauline pneumatology, focusing on the relationship between custom and law in Chinese culture and the Holy Spirit since it is only the
Holy Spirit who can initiate and maintain the identity of a Christian.
The commemorating rites of ancestors and Confucius are Chinese customs that should be acknowledged and absorbed into the Christian
faith through the fulfilling and transforming work of the Holy Spirit.
Historically, the rites controversy ended with the Roman Catholic Holy
See's concession and, in light of that issue, the chapter raises a theo-
logical question regarding the necessity and possibility of a *Chinese*
Christianity rather than Christianity *in China*.

As "an apostle to the Gentiles" (Rom. 11:13), Paul launched three missionary journeys, primarily to establish churches in Mediterranean
cities. Through his letter writing, he showed Jews and Gentiles the
path to Christian faith based on the cross of Christ and the work of
the Holy Spirit. With the help of a culturally sensitive and transformative missionary strategy and by means of countercultural accommodation, Gentile Christians soon became the majority of the church
in the first-century Jesus movement. Christianity spread rapidly in the

Roman Empire soon after and eventually "conquered" the empire as it became its state religion.

By comparison, in the third mission of Christianity to China, the Jesuit Matteo Ricci (1552–1610) advocated a missionary strategy of adaptation, which was well received by the Ming and Qing governments and Chinese intellectuals. He was attacked later by missionaries from other Catholic orders. In this so-called Chinese rites controversy, the Holy See banned Chinese Christians from practicing commemorating rites of ancestors and Confucius. Consequently, the Chinese emperor Kangxi (1654–1722) canceled the proclamation right of Christianity in China. This vigorous conflict led to a fatal failure of the Chinese mission over the next several hundred years.

It is widely believed that the Holy See should assume primary responsibility for this failure. However, significant questions remain: Why did the Holy See's judgment of the Chinese rites lead to a dead end? What mistakes did the Holy See make in its missionary strategy with regards to the dynamic of culture and the Spirit? Numerous studies have focused on the historical facts of the controversy, but this chapter deliberates on the theological causes behind it.

This chapter first presents a brief survey of Chinese pneumatology within biblical studies. It then traces the historical development of the Chinese rites controversy, detailing the two opposite views on this issue. Drawing insights from Pauline pneumatology, especially regarding the relationship between the Holy Spirit and Chinese custom and law, the chapter then argues that it is only the Holy Spirit who can initiate and maintain one's identity as a Christian, and that the Holy Spirit must be an agent of transformation in a culture receiving the gospel. In other words, the commemorating rites of ancestors and Confucius are Chinese customs that should be acknowledged and absorbed into the Christian faith through the fulfilling and transforming work of the Holy Spirit. We know that, historically, the rites controversy finally ended with the Roman Catholic Holy See's concession, and perhaps that in itself indicates a hindsight acknowledgment regarding the necessity and possibility of a Chinese Christianity.

Chinese Pneumatology

Many Chinese scholars have written commentaries on the book of Acts or a biblical theology of the Holy Spirit. Yet only a few take seriously the context of Chinese culture, and these scholars focus primarily on the relationship between biblical exegesis and dialogues with Chinese classics. In biblical exegesis, Watchman Nee (Nee Duo-sheng of Shanghai), a famous theologian and church leader, founded churches called "the Little Flock" or "the Local Church" in mainland China prior to 1949. He believed that in the Old Testament the Holy Spirit came "upon" (*epi*) people, which is an external endowment. But in the New Testament, besides coming "upon" people, the Spirit also comes to dwell "in" (*en*) people, which is internal empowerment. Nee saw two gifts of the Holy Spirit in the New Testament. After the resurrection, Jesus breathed on his disciples and they received the Easter gift of the Holy Spirit that would give them abundant life (John 20:22). Fifty days later, God himself filled the apostles with the Pentecost gift of the Holy Spirit (Acts 2:1–13), which would "grant them the power for Christian ministry."[1] Nee's exegesis of the Holy Spirit influenced deeply the house churches in mainland China and continues to do so today.

After the founding of the People's Republic of China in 1949, the center of Chinese biblical studies shifted to Hong Kong, Taiwan, and the Chinese diaspora. This new generation of biblical scholars, including Huiyuan Bao, Roland Y. K. Fung, and Zhibang Zhong, closely followed the exegetical methods and even the theological positions of their Western counterparts. Generally, these scholars agreed that the Hebrew term *ruah* corresponds to the Greek word *pneuma*, which can be translated into "wind," "breath," or "Spirit" in Chinese. *Pneuma* can refer to the human spirit or to the Holy Spirit, "the mediator and way of salvation for all human beings."[2] Receiving the Holy Spirit is a necessary step in the process of repentance, baptism, and rebirth.

Not contradicting the biblical exegesis on pneumatology of other Chinese scholars, K. K. Yeo has devoted much of his work to going beyond exegesis to promoting a dialogue between the Bible and Chi-

---

1. See Watchman Nee, *The Communion of the Holy Spirit* (New York: Christian Fellowship, 1994), 37–43, 49–67, 79–83. See also Archie Hui, "The Pneumatology of Watchman Nee: A New Testament Perspective," *Evangelical Quarterly* 75, no. 4 (2003): 3–29.

2. See Zhibang Zhong, *Commentary on the Gospel of John*, 2 vols. (Shanghai: Shanghai Sanlian, 2008), 1:190–91.

nese classics in an attempt to address contextual issues faced by his Chinese readers. In his earlier work, he investigated the problem of eating idol-meat in 1 Corinthians 8 and 10 and proposed a rhetorical and cross-cultural hermeneutics that addresses Chinese ancestor "worship" or reverence.[3] His recently published monograph, *Musing with Confucius and Paul: Toward a Chinese Christian Theology*, critically synthesizes Confucius's ethical teachings in the *Analects* and Paul's theology in Galatians. He sees the work of the Holy Spirit as more effective than Confucius's benevolence (*ren*), thus fulfilling *ren* and overcoming human or cultural differences because "love your neighbors" and "love your enemies" (Matt. 5:43-48; Luke 6:27-36) can truly consolidate the five Confucian basic relationships (*wulun*).[4]

The Chinese Rites Controversy

During the final years of the Ming dynasty, the Jesuits introduced Christianity to China.[5] Matteo Ricci arrived in Macau in 1582, and then preached the Christian faith in south China. In the next several years, he dressed first as a Buddhist monk and later as a Confucian mandarin. He made friends with Chinese intellectuals and officials, and even wrote books in Chinese. Regarding the "term question" (which name should be used for God), he translated "God" into *Shang-ti* (Heaven), a word that appeared frequently in ancient Chinese classics. He did not regard the rites commemorating ancestors and Confucius as idolatry, but permitted Chinese Christians to participate in them. This missionary strategy of adaptation, called "the Rules of Ricci," was followed by other Jesuits.

3. See K. K. Yeo, *Rhetorical Interaction in 1 Corinthians 8 and 10: A Formal Analysis with Preliminary Suggestions for a Chinese, Cross-Cultural Hermeneutic* (Leiden: Brill, 1995), 180–211.

4. See K. K. Yeo, *Musing with Confucius and Paul: Toward a Chinese Christian Theology* (Eugene: Cascade, 2008), 253–66; K. K. Yeo, "Paul's Way of *Renren* in Romans 13:1–10," in *From Rome to Beijing: Symposia on Robert Jewett's Hermeneia Commentary on Romans*, ed. K. K. Yeo (Lincoln: Kairos Studies, 2013), 469–79.

5. For the historical details of the Chinese rites controversy, see George Minamiki, *Chinese Rites Controversy: From Its Beginning to Modern Times* (Chicago: Loyola University Press, 1985); Tiangang Li, *Chinese Rites Controversy: Its History, Literature and Significance* (Shanghai: Shanghai Classics, 1998); and Liwei Wu, *The Chinese Rites Controversy: The Encounter of Civilizations and Powers* (Shanghai: Shanghai Classics, 2007).

The Jesuits and other missionaries fiercely debated two questions: whether the "God" of Christianity could be translated as *Shang-ti* (Heaven or Lord of Heaven), or could only be transliterated into Chinese; and whether Chinese rites were idolatrous and consequently prohibited among Chinese Christians. In Chinese missionary history, this debate is called the Chinese rites controversy. However, in the earlier period, the term question gave way to the rites question.[6] The Jesuits and other missionaries, the Holy See, and the Chinese emperor Kangxi were all involved in the debate on these Chinese rites.

In 1643, arising out of his opposition to the Jesuits' missionary strategy of adaptation, the Dominican Juan Bautista de Morals submitted his seventeen opposing opinions to the Holy See. In 1645, Pope Innocent X issued an encyclical that disapproved of the adaptive Jesuit strategy and banned Chinese rites among Chinese Christians. Martino Martini, a Jesuit working in China, was called back to Rome by the Society of Jesus to make a counterargument, claiming that Chinese rites were essentially secular and political rites that simply honored ancestors or Confucius. In 1656, Pope Alexander VII issued another encyclical permitting the Chinese rites.

Nevertheless, in 1693, as a vicar apostolic managing church affairs in Fujian province, Charles Maigrot imposed a ban in his diocese. He insisted that the encyclical issued in 1656 was based on Martini's misleading report and, as a result, Chinese Christians were not permitted to participate in the rites commemorating ancestors or Confucius. The rites controversy agitated the Chinese emperor Kangxi. In 1704, Pope Clement XI issued an encyclical in favor of Maigrot's decision, and sent Carlo Tommaso Maillard de Tournon to publish it in China. Without notifying the Qing government beforehand, the ambassador published this encyclical in Nanjing the following year, and ordered the Jesuits to be obedient to the Holy See or face excommunication. Emperor Kangxi was outraged. He ordered the detention of the ambassador and Maigrot and expelled them from China. As for the other missionaries, he reassured them that, as long as they abided by "the Rules of Ricci" and received a permission paper, they would be granted free missionary privileges in China. In addition, on three occasions Emperor Kangxi

---

6. For more details, see Zi Wang, "How to Understand a Biblical God in Chinese: Toward a Cross-Cultural Biblical Hermeneutics," in *The Trinity among the Nations: The Doctrine of God in the Majority World* (Grand Rapids: Eerdmans, 2015), 140–60.

sent messengers carrying his letters to the Holy See, in hopes of continuing the diplomatic negotiations.

In 1715, Pope Clement XI issued a new encyclical, *Ex illa die*, which reiterated the previous ban against the traditional rites. In the following year, again without notifying the Qing government in advance, the encyclical was published in Beijing. Emperor Kangxi gave the order to arrest the publisher and send all copies back to Rome. Dispatched by the Holy See, Charles Ambrose Mezzabarba arrived in Beijing in 1720. Emperor Kangxi read the Chinese translation of the ban and, in 1721, gave the order to revoke the legal status of the Chinese mission. In 1742, Pope Benedict XIV issued an encyclical, *Ex quo singulari*, which reaffirmed the ban of 1715 and even prohibited missionaries from debating these issues further.

Paul on the Holy Spirit, Law, and Custom

The Chinese rites controversy involves numerous significant historical details. However, "the difficulty is not how to restate this controversy, but how to explain it."[7] The challenge is to explain it theologically. The controversy seems to center on the debate about whether the commemorating rites of ancestors and Confucius constitute idolatry. A deeper analysis will show that the controversy erupted because the Holy See did not correctly understand the relationship between the Holy Spirit and Chinese custom and law.

In first-century missionary circumstances, Paul demonstrated the role of the Holy Spirit in initiating, sustaining, and consummating the Christian faith. He dealt with the relationship of the Holy Spirit, the Jewish law, and Gentile custom by focusing on the agency of God's Spirit among cultures.

"Having Started in the Spirit" (Gal. 3:3)

In contrast to John the Baptist's water baptism for repentance, Jesus baptized with the Holy Spirit for rebirth (Matt. 3:11; Mark 1:8; Luke 3:22; John 1:33; 3:5). Jesus also promised that, after his ascension, the

---

7. Sun Shangyang, *Chinese Christianity before 1984* (Beijing: Xueyuan, 2004), 369.

Holy Spirit, the Advocate, would be sent upon believers, teaching his disciples everything so that they could preach his gospel to the ends of the earth (Mark 13:11; John 7:39; 14:26; 15:26; 16:13; Acts 1:5). The disciples received the Holy Spirit at Pentecost, and "began to speak in other languages" (Acts 2:4). Paul asked the Ephesian disciples, "Did you receive the Holy Spirit when you became believers?" (19:2). After receiving a negative response, he baptized them in the name of Jesus, and laid his hands upon them as the Spirit baptized them. John 3:8 reads, "The wind blows where it wishes, and you hear its sound, but you do not know where it comes from or where it goes. So it is with everyone who is born of the Spirit." Indeed, rebirth in the Holy Spirit should be the starting point of Christian faith for everyone.

New Testament pneumatology suggests that following Jesus before his death or just hearing the gospel does not constitute a fully Christian process. Believers in Christ need to be baptized by the Holy Spirit so that their discipleship and religious identity become completely confirmed.[8] Paul understood that the reception of the Holy Spirit was an identity marker that confirmed the faith of any Christian, whether Jewish or Gentile. James D. G. Dunn argues that although "in Christian tradition it has become customary to think of the gift of the Spirit as a deduction to be drawn from a correct confession or properly administered sacrament," in Pauline pneumatology, the "definition of a Christian" originated in receiving the Holy Spirit, not in a confession or a sacrament. Paul illuminates this principle when he writes, "for all who are led by the Spirit of God are children of God" (Rom. 8:14), and "anyone who does not have the Spirit of Christ does not belong to him" (8:9).[9] Paul tells the Galatians explicitly that, "having started with the Spirit" (Gal. 3:3), they must "also be guided by the Spirit" (5:25), in order that they may bear good fruits for God and build a close relationship with God.

Having received the Holy Spirit, Jews and Gentiles are called "Christians" (Acts 11:26) because they share the same religious identity and become children of God. This spiritual relationship makes them all heirs of the inheritance of Abraham promised by God. Having the

8. David Coffey, *"Did You Receive the Holy Spirit When You Believed?": Some Basic Questions for Pneumatology* (Marquette: Marquette University Press, 2005).

9. James D. G. Dunn, *The Theology of Paul the Apostle* (Grand Rapids: Eerdmans, 1998), 430–31.

same religious identity does not cancel national, racial, cultural, or gender differences among Christians, nor does it erase economic, legal, or social inequalities. These differences and inequalities are now transformed into a Christian *koinonia*, which is a new marker of how the Spirit of God is working in a diverse community. What is most significant about this marker is that human differences have been released from the power of sin and, consequently, are accepted by God in the hope of eternal life. As Paul writes, "There is no longer Jew or Greek, there is no longer slave or free, there is no longer male and female; for all of you are one in Christ Jesus" (Gal. 3:28).[10] Differences among human beings are not erased, but domination arising from these differences is eliminated. The work of the Holy Spirit is therefore to foster the uniqueness of individuals and cultures, but also to rid them of the discrimination these differences might bring to any community.

While the role of the Holy Spirit is universally recognized, the early church also faced a difficult and urgent question, that is, whether and how the Jewish law was still abiding for Jewish and Gentile Christians. This is not simply a question of "right theology," but a theological question embedded in a dynamic cultural context. In the first century, some Jewish Christians thought that, besides receiving the Holy Spirit, Gentile Christians also had to abide by the Jewish law, especially circumcision and the law of purification, in order that they might join in the holy covenant between God and Israel. They believed this was "right theology." However, Paul thought of both theology and culture, so he admonished the Galatians that becoming a Christian was not about subscribing to the Jewish works of the law (becoming a Jew), but about God's grace enabling one to receive the Holy Spirit in order to be fully who one is (as created by God, i.e., "a Gentile").

Paul's assertion, "If you are led by the Spirit, you are not subject to the law" (Gal. 5:18), may appear to be an exegetical issue. In fact, without the cultural context, this verse does not make a lot of sense. For circumcision and the law of purification are cultural symbols to Jews that may still have religious meaning. To Gentile Christians, however, cir-

---

10. As J. Louis Martyn comments, "Religious, social, and sexual pairs of opposites are not replaced by equality, but rather by a newly created unity." J. Louis Martyn, *Galatians: A New Translation with Introduction and Commentary* (New Haven: Yale University Press, 1997), 377.

cumcision of the flesh would mean ceasing to be a Gentile (in the most robust sense and therefore without the tainting of sin) and instead becoming a Jew, although the concern about becoming a believer is there too. To address both ethnic (Gentile) and salvation (Christian) issues, Paul teaches that circumcision of the flesh has been replaced by circumcision of the heart (Rom. 2:29) and a water baptism that does not have racial, gender, or social distinctions. Paul explains that the inheritance was promised to Abraham long before the promulgation of the Mosaic law, and now "in Christ Jesus the blessing of Abraham might come to the Gentiles" (Gal. 3:14), making the point that inclusion of Gentiles among God's people is more highly prioritized (in Abraham) than Jewish distinctiveness (in Moses).[11] Therefore, after receiving the Holy Spirit, Gentile Christians by faith become "born according to the Spirit" (4:29) and are fully qualified to inherit the Abrahamic blessings originally announced to the First Testament people of God.

The Jewish Law

For Jews, the law given by God through Moses is holy and irrevocable; circumcision of the flesh even becomes a sign of their cultural and religious identity as the "people of God." In the Gospel narratives, we read that Jesus frequently "violated" the written laws, as he understood the Jewish law self-critically, out of his deep conviction that "until heaven and earth pass away, not one letter, not one stroke of a letter, will pass from the law until all is accomplished" (Matt. 5:18). In other words, a self-critical practice of the Jewish law will bring about its fulfillment and greater effectiveness and benefits to more people, but "blind" obedience from others may actually reduce the power of the law for good. When asked the basic tenets of the Jewish law, Jesus explained that all the law could be summarized by two commandments: love God (Deut. 6:4–6) and love your neighbor (Lev. 19:18). This is the mega principle of the law and also of the work of the Holy Spirit. For Jesus, the law is sacred. It is a means to allow God's love to touch more people, not to yoke them to the fine print of the law and restrict their behavior.[12] No

11. See Yeo, *Musing with Confucius and Paul*, passim.

12. See Yeo, *Musing with Confucius and Paul*, 258–59, for a discussion of the ritualizing process of the law in accordance with the Confucian understanding of *li* (ritual).

wonder Jesus proclaims, "The Sabbath was made for humankind, and not humankind for the Sabbath" (Mark 2:27). Paul's teaching in the book of Romans confirms this view of the law.

In his gospel mission to the Gentiles, Paul accurately grasps the two sides of the law. On the one hand, the law promulgated to the Jewish people "is holy, and the commandment is holy and just and good" (7:12). On the other hand, the purpose of the law is to reveal to the human race the power of sin that entraps them, first with the Jewish people: "through the law comes the knowledge of sin" (3:20). But the law does not make them stop sinning or become righteous. In other words, in theological terms, the purpose of the law is Jesus Christ because "Christ is the end of the law" (10:4).[13] After the advent of Christ, Paul thinks that the Jews are released from the law and justified by God, not by obeying the law but by believing in Christ. That is to say, the law has been fulfilled or accomplished by Christ's faithfulness. However, this faithfulness does not abolish the law. For example, as a Jewish Christian, Paul not only followed his Jewish vow and had his hair cut off in Cenchrea (Acts 18:18), but he also circumcised Timothy and made a sacrifice in the temple (16:3; 21:23–26). Indeed, Jews are not compelled to be Gentiles upon conversion any more than Gentiles are compelled to be Jews.

Jewish Christians still may observe the law, but as a marker of their religious identity only. The law by itself is insufficient to be a sign of salvation and must be affiliated with the work of Christ.[14] As a Jewish tradition and custom, the Jewish law cannot justify or save Jews, for the Jewish custom and tradition have been fulfilled by the gospel and love of Jesus Christ (Rom. 13:10). K. K. Yeo argues that, facing the agitators in Galatia, Paul criticized the cultural and religious imperialism of his Jewish opponents. Paul uses the crucifixion of Christ to deconstruct Jewish ethnocentrism and reconstruct the Jewish law via the Spirit of the law in love. What Christ had accomplished on the cross has been illustrated by the coming of the Holy Spirit because "the Spirit is the one who fulfills the promise of God." In other words,

13. See Robert Jewett, *Romans: A Commentary* (Minneapolis: Fortress, 2007), 634.

14. Just as Augustine argued later, the Jewish law never was intended to have a divine function in salvation, but because of its long history, it now becomes "an ancient tradition" (*paternarum traditionum*) and "an enduring custom" (*diuturnam consuetudinem*) for the Jewish people. See Augustine, *De mendacio* 5.8; *Contra Faustum Manicheum* 19.17.

it is the Holy Spirit who has transformed or extended the salvation of God from a Jewish law-centeredness in the old age to the Spirit-led grounding in the new age.[15]

Circumcision and the law of purification can distinguish Jews from Gentiles, but they cannot be used to differentiate Christians from non-Christians because national and ethnic identities will constantly need to be challenged and fulfilled by religious identity. In other words, the Spirit of God constantly engages cultures to overcome ethnocentrism and to transform them into cultures that will reflect God's glory and kingdom values. Gentile Christians joined the holy covenant, not by obeying the law, but through faith in Jesus Christ and in the power of the Holy Spirit. Jewish agitators and opponents in Galatia stubbornly insisted that, for Gentiles, obeying the law was a prerequisite for becoming a Christian. Thus they committed the error of "nationalistic presumption and ethnic restrictiveness."[16]

The Gentile Custom

As a part of daily life in the Mediterranean world, people usually sacrificed wine and meat to pagan gods during local festivals, which included many non-Christian religious elements. Being invited to join in a banquet in a pagan temple also was a token of friendship. Jewish Christians in the diaspora were sometimes bothered by these activities, and Gentile Christians in Corinth were confused by this invitation. Christian theology viewed sacrifice to pagan gods as idolatrous, and joining in such a banquet as idol worship (1 Cor. 8:7-10; 10:19-21). If this was so, could Gentile Christians enter pagan temples, and then drink wine and eat meat with their pagan families, relatives, or friends? If they did these things, were they participating in idol worship? Like the Chinese rites controversy, these questions created a fierce conflict in the early church and still do so in the church today in China.

In the Corinthian church, believers were divided into two groups: "the weak conscience ones," who regarded consuming food offered to

15. Yeo, *Musing with Confucius and Paul*, 83–84, 310.
16. John M. G. Barclay, "'Neither Jew nor Greek': Multiculturalism and the New Perspective on Paul," in *Ethnicity and the Bible*, ed. Mark G. Brett (Leiden: Brill, 2002), 202.

idols as idolatry, and "those who possess knowledge," who believed this kind of eating and drinking was not idolatrous. As we can see, the use of such labels highlights the mutual misunderstanding among Corinthian Christians. To ease tensions, Paul postulates two main principles. First, no idols really exist because we know that "an idol is nothing at all in the world and that there is no God but one" (8:4). For "those who possess knowledge," participating in such a banquet does not necessarily lead to idolatry. Yet, Paul seriously limits their participation in banquets held within the confines of pagan temples (such as the Asklepion) because a temple banquet is no doubt honoring a pagan god.[17] In essence, as Paul argues, this pagan sacrifice is a sacrifice to devils, for one may not participate in the table of the Lord and the table of devils (10:21). Second, for "the weak" eating meat in temple banquets should be prohibited since the practice cannot heal their weak conscience. Instead, it defiles them. Due to community concerns, knowledge is less important than love of brothers and sisters, for "knowledge puffs up, but love builds up" (8:1). Taking Paul himself as an example, personal freedom or right has to give way to the edification and salvation of others (9:19–22).[18]

Although not all traditional customs are prohibited, there are limits to the practices. These are defined by concerns for the well-being of others in the community. In the new community life in which Christ is the head, brothers and sisters are "all made to drink of one Spirit" (12:13). In the same faith of Christ, the Holy Spirit has granted them the same religious identity; no longer is anyone able to boast of her glory based on her national, cultural, or social status. Every Christian becomes a child of God and equal in faith.[19] In Pauline pneumatology, this same identity will not cancel their differences, but the Holy Spirit opens the way for believers to view their cultural differences anew, that is, not in the old way of cultural discrimination but now from a new perspective of appreciating other cultures (especially cultural ideals) in order to overcome cultural blind spots. Being a Christian does not require Jewish Christians to abandon the law or Gentile Christians to obey the letter of the law (to be proselytized into Judaism), but

---

17. Joseph A. Fitzmyer, *First Corinthians: A New Translation with Introduction and Commentary* (New Haven: Yale University Press), 331.

18. Yeo, *Rhetorical Interactions*, passim.

19. Jewett, *Romans*, 137.

it does require both Jewish and Gentile Christians to observe the spirit of the law (2 Cor. 3:6).

As to the role of the Holy Spirit, Paul states the following.

First, the theological function of the holy law has been fulfilled by faith in Christ and in the power of the Holy Spirit. Jewish Christians may still obey the law but with a new sense of spiritual renewal whereby the Spirit of God in the end-times is baptizing Gentiles to his kingdom. Jewish Christians cannot impose the Jewish law on Gentile Christians.

Second, the cultural function of pagan customs has been revised and renewed also by faith in Christ and in the power of the Holy Spirit. After a person receives the Holy Spirit, the Jewish law and pagan customs are not obstacles to the Christian faith, but can be accomplished and updated in the love of God and neighbors. Any controversial actions should be delimited and guided by this love.

The Commemorating Rites of Ancestors and Confucius: Chinese Custom or Law?

In the Chinese rites controversy, the Jesuits aligned with the Chinese emperor and Chinese intellectuals, and they submitted their statements of defense to the Holy See to argue for the secular, political nature of the commemorating rites of ancestors and Confucius. There are six kinds of sacrificial rites involved in the controversy: sacrifice in funeral mourning; sacrifice to a town-god by local officials; sacrifice to Heaven by the emperor; commemorating rites of ancestors; commemorating rites of Confucius; and rites to living people.

The commemorating rites of ancestors and Confucius are the most controversial ones. In the first rite, participants are descendants of a family or patriarchal clan, and other people are not allowed to enter the family temple. Participants display meat and fruits in front of the ancestors' memorial tablets, and they burn incense and candles, kowtow, and then share food in a family banquet. In the second rite, participants usually are Chinese intellectuals who have a good reputation for knowledge and some social status. Many of them are imperial officials. On the first and fifteenth days of the month, they enter a Confucian temple, kowtow, and burn incense in front of Confucius's memorial tablet. Every spring and autumn, the central and local governments must hold a grand commemorating rite in the Confucian temples. As in the first rite, participants display meat and fruits, and then share them in a friendly banquet.

As we can see, Chinese rites have social, political, cultural, ethical, and religious dimensions, and these dimensions are clearly intertwined. By participating in these rites, Chinese people can consolidate their close relationships among families, clans, and social strata—being filial to parents, loyal to superiors, trustworthy to friends, and reverent to the cosmic Logos. Furthermore, they can show their respect to Confucius and thus loyalty to emperors, for an empire is also regarded as a family, with the emperor as its father.

The challenge comes when we seek to distinguish between culture and religion, secular and sacred. This is not possible. Every religious belief is developed in a certain culture, and every culture also contains a kind of religious belief. For example, in its external form, the commemorating rites of ancestors are similar to worship rites in Chinese folk religions. Even the common people who do not possess knowledge pray to their ancestors for protection. Unsurprisingly, these two rites may be suspect as being idol worship by foreigners, such as Western missionaries in the time of the Qing dynasty.

The task of a theologian is to attempt to delineate culture from religion, or better still, as Yeo advocates, to read ethics theologically and to read cultures Christologically, thus finding creative ways to fulfill cultural aspirations.[20] As Yeo explains, we cannot "speak of Confucianism as a religion, because for me and many Chinese it is more a way of life in pursuit of virtue and in the formation of community."[21] Indeed, the essence of the Chinese rites differs from that of Roman pagan rites, first, in that the objects of Chinese commemorating rites are not powerful gods, but deceased relatives and loved ones, including fathers, grandfathers, and Confucius, who was regarded as a sage on morality and knowledge. Second, unlike religion or idolatry, the purpose of the Chinese commemorating rites is not to pursue any supernatural power, but to express thanksgiving to ancestors and to pay secular respect to Confucius. We can see that neither of these is an idol in the Christian sense. Also, the word "worship" is too strong. Thus, "reverence" may be a better word. Our biblical hermeneutic needs to

20. Yeo, *Musing with Confucius and Paul*, 80–83, 385–86.
21. Yeo, *Musing with Confucius and Paul*, 80.

take on the power of the Spirit in order to access our cultures not in their outward forms only, but more important, contextually through their inward spiritual dynamics.

It is noteworthy that another author in this volume, Zakali Shohe, analyzes the role of the Spirit in Romans 8:14–17 from a relational perspective precisely to bring about a similar pneumatological effect in Asian contexts. Shohe convincingly demonstrates that the Spirit redefines the broader identities of people, including ethnic, cultural, economic, political, and religious ones. These identities will guide Christians to a new status as children of God and then bear witness to a new religious identity in Christ.

The commemorating rites of ancestors and Confucius have two functions. For ordinary people, they are Chinese folk customs and become part of their daily lives, like the customs of Gentiles in Paul's day. But for intellectuals, these rites have been practiced for more than two thousand years and have constituted the core of Chinese traditional ritual and law (*lifa*), which constructed a social order and a moral system for China. Similar to Jewish law, Chinese ritual and law shape national and cultural identities for Chinese people.

By using a hermeneutics of pneumatology to respond to the rites controversy, I do not mean to suggest Chinese rites are perfect, but that the Spirit of God will continue to renew such rites, leading the Chinese people to their intended purpose. In his early work, Yeo has suggested how Chinese ancestor "worship" can be renewed by Chinese Christian theology today. If practitioners have any fear or bondage at all, the gospel can proclaim a message of hope and freedom to them.[22]

As the founder of Confucianism, Confucius criticized sharply the sacrificial rites of the Shang and Zhou dynasties, as he attempted to remove any superstitious elements and retain only their edifying (moral) function. Therefore, Confucius's allowable sacrifices were not part of religion or idol worship. If distortions have crept into sacrificial practice, then of course it is proper to address the issue of distortion and engage it with the gospel of Christ.

Confucius did not believe in the existence of gods or ghosts: "The

---

22. Yeo, *Rhetorical Interactions*, 217–20. See also his "The Rhetorical Hermeneutic of 1 Corinthians 8 and Chinese Ancestor Worship," *Biblical Interpretation* 2, no. 3 (1994): 298–311, and his *Ancestor Worship: Rhetorical and Cross-Cultural Hermeneutical Response* (Hong Kong: Chinese Christian Literature Council, 1996) (in Chinese).

topic the Master did not speak of was prodigies, force, disorder, and gods" (*Analects* 7.21).[23] He denied the ancient practice of divination. Nevertheless, he supported practice of sacrifice and the commemorating rites of ancestors. He even paid much attention to the rightfulness of sacrificial objects and rites: "Unless I enter into the spirit of a sacrifice, it is as if I did not sacrifice" (*Analects* 3.12). In other words, if Chinese rites are done merely for show, then they lose the power to shape identities of people; the Spirit of God can empower Chinese to practice these rites out of their intended purpose of living a moral life, thus exhibiting the fruits of the Spirit (Galatians 5).

Regarding filial behaviors, Confucius insisted that "when your parents are alive, comply with the rites in serving them; when they die, comply with the rites in burying them and in offering sacrifices to them" (*Analects* 2.5). The reason for this seeming paradox is that Confucius highly valued the moral edifying function of these rites. Offering sacrifices to gods can enlighten a person about his natural position in the entire universe and encourage him to imitate the Dao (the Way) of the cosmos. In this ritual of imitation, he will constantly improve his intelligence and moral conscience. Meanwhile, offering sacrifices to ancestors can enlighten him about his position in society, and make him call to mind his parents' and ancestors' virtue and merits. In this reminiscence, "the virtue of the common people will incline toward fullness" (*Analects* 1.9). This Confucian language of morality is compatible with Paul's language of sanctification, but Paul believes that it is the Holy Spirit that enables believers to live a life of holiness, rather than an individual's effort.

As Confucius demanded, each person must be filial to his parents and offer sacrifices to them when they die. After that, his parents also become the object of commemorating rites. In this edifying process, he will retain love and a good moral conscience from his childhood; recognize the social relations between husband and wife, father and son, emperor and subjects; abide by established social regulations and moral principles; and gradually become a virtuous and peace-loving citizen. "It is rare for a man whose character is such that he is good as a son and obedient as a young man to have the inclination to transgress against his superiors; it is unheard of for one who has no such

23. For the *Analects*, this essay uses D. C. Lau, trans., *The Analects* (Beijing: Zhonghua, 2008).

inclination to be inclined to start a rebellion" (*Analects* 1.2). Thus, after these stages of life, he will accomplish good merits like his parents and ancestors. The Holy Spirit can baptize all these teachings to allow Chinese Christians to live out the spirit of the biblical law in Chinese contexts.

From the Han dynasty to the Qing dynasty, Confucius and his teachings were highly praised. He became a brilliant model of knowledge and morality. In such a long history, he was enshrined as "The Holiest Master and Teacher." The Confucian classics were assigned as sole references for imperial examinations, and the commemorating rites of Confucius also became significant political affairs from the court to local places. According to Confucius, these commemorating rites were intended to express respect to him. Yeo points out that often in Chinese history, however, royal cults would distort and use Confucius's ethic for their own concentration of power. It is this abusive power of the government that needs critical engagement with the democratic and salvific work of the Holy Spirit.[24]

Historically, the commemorating rites of ancestors and Confucius constitute a long custom or even a holy law for the Chinese people, although this holiness was not stated explicitly as coming from God. Chinese Christians can nevertheless, based on their biblical understanding, know that much of Confucius's teaching is in line with biblical teaching. This is a significant point regarding how the Spirit of God has revealed, created, worked, moved, and shaped cultures that are not explicitly traced to the Bible. Amos Yong's chapter in this volume is particularly reflective as we discern this issue. As he advocates, a Spirit-oriented approach is "anchored in the revelation of God in Christ and . . . being open to wherever and however the wind of God blows." The Spirit of God has always blown and moved in Chinese cultures, from ancient times until today.

Unlike the Gentiles in Paul's time, participants in Chinese rites do not worship any pagan gods. But as we saw in the case of the Jewish law, participants in Chinese rites are performing the spirit of the biblical commandments. For example, showing filial piety to parents is one of the core teachings of the Ten Commandments (Exod. 20:12) and forgoing rebellion is similar to fulfilling Jesus's and Paul's social principle of serving God and Caesar (Mark 12:17; Rom. 13:1–7). Moreover, this edi-

24. See Yeo, "Paul's Way of *Renren*," 469–79.

fying process is similar to the sanctifying work of the Holy Spirit in the Christian language. Filialness, loyalty, trustworthiness, and reverence all are encompassed in the commandment to love one's neighbors. In Paul's theology, "love (*agape*) is made virtuous by overcoming human differences in the power of the Spirit."[25]

The Missionary Failure and Its Theological Causes

Liwei Wu notes that in ancient Chinese society "a rite is not merely a cultural symbol, but plays an indispensable role in the social administration. As a part of social regulations, Chinese rites also represent a kind of imperial power."[26] If a Chinese person does not participate in the commemorating rites of ancestors and Confucius, his choice signifies a betrayal of his family and rebellion against the Chinese government. If the Chinese people are banned from these rites, then they are asked not to be Chinese. As a result, they would rather simply reject Christianity. In this context, Matteo Ricci advocated a missionary strategy of adaptation, which gave Chinese Christians freedom of choice, but a freedom in line with how the Spirit of God is creating and blowing in the Chinese land and culture. Ricci even argued for the secular nature of these rites through his industrious study of Chinese classics, which may be seen as cultural fulfillment in the process of the meeting of the Bible and Chinese classics.

Dressed as Western Confucians, the Jesuits maintained a close association with Chinese intellectuals and officials. Because of their contributions to the empire, they quickly gained the favor of the emperor. Emperor Kangxi even legitimized their mission in China. As we know, the early church experienced numerous persecutions, which finally ended with the Edict of Milan issued by Constantine, the emperor of the Roman Empire. Compared to their predecessors, the Jesuits' conversion of the Chinese people to Christianity went well. However, the missionaries of other orders did not understand Chinese language, culture, and customs, looking only at the outward forms rather than at the spirit of the rites. Thus, they concluded that the commemorating rites of ancestors and Confucius were idolatry and banned Chinese

25. Yeo, *Musing with Confucius and Paul*, 261.
26. Wu, *The Chinese Rites Controversy*, 102.

Christians from observing them—not knowing that the ban killed the spirit of a culture and almost eliminated the soul of a group of people.

In this controversy, Chinese Christians became the biggest victims. Contrary to the situation in the Corinthian church, almost all Chinese Christians believed that Chinese rites had nothing to do with idolatry but were endowed with a deep spirituality in line with teachings of the Bible. Participation in Chinese rites never disturbed their faithful conscience, but allowed them to make peace with the empire and Confucian society in which they lived, while allowing the Spirit of God to work out salvation in changing cultures. Not surprisingly, the ban from the Holy See met with fierce opposition from the Jesuits, the Chinese emperor, and Chinese Christians.

The ban lasted until the 1930s, when the Holy See eventually lifted the ban on the Chinese rites while dealing with the "Sophia University event" in Japan and the official commemorating rites of Confucius in the pseudo-Manchukuo. In 1939, the Propaganda Fide published the encyclical *Plan compertum est* issued by Pope Pius XII, in which Chinese Christians were allowed to participate in Chinese commemorating rites. Although never acknowledging the former encyclicals' error, the Holy See actually reverted to its 1656 position, which recognized that the Jesuits' judgment on the nature of the Chinese rites was correct, namely, that these rites in essence were not idolatry but a long-term Chinese custom and tradition. In 1941, the Propaganda Fide issued an additional order that reflected the spirit of Pauline pneumatology: "You should absolutely avoid drafting a list of what is prohibited or permitted, in order that these old disagreements would not stir up again a fierce controversy in its new form," but "should let those priests and good laity to make their decision in individual circumstances according to their own conscience."[27] That is to say, with the love of God and brothers and sisters, Chinese Christians have the freedom to participate in Chinese commemorating rites because they have received the Holy Spirit.

In the Chinese rites controversy, there were at least three critical issues, from which we can learn important lessons regarding culture and the Holy Spirit.

---

27. Ray Noll, trans., *100 Roman Documents concerning the Chinese Rites Controversy (1645–1941)* (San Francisco: Ricci Institute for Chinese-Western Cultural History, 1992), chap. 100.

First, the Holy See debated with the Jesuits on the relationship between the catholicity of the Christian faith and its contextualization in China. The focus was whether this universalized faith could be localized and indigenous in various contexts. The Pentecost event in Acts, with multiple tongues in gospel proclamation, confirms that contextual theologies of the gospel are the will of God and involve the movement of God's Spirit. It will take faith in the Spirit to allow the Spirit to work in new lands, cultures, languages, and contexts.

Second, the Holy See debated with the Chinese emperor on the relationship between church and state. The focus was whether the Holy See should respect the political authority of the Chinese Empire and offer criticism only when church and state assumed an uncritical alliance that concentrated power and downplayed kingdom values. The Jesuits asked the Holy See to follow their admonition: "Do not violate the principles of Confucianism, and never try to intrude into the imperial power."[28] Here, Paul's discussion of the responsibility of Christians and government leaders to serve the Roman Empire in Romans 13 suggests a dual citizenship of Christians.[29]

Third, the Holy See debated with Chinese Christians on the relationship among the Holy Spirit, custom, and law, and the focus was whether it was necessary to abandon national customs once the Chinese received the Holy Spirit. This was the core of the controversy. In the seventeenth and eighteenth centuries, the Holy See neither followed the teachings of biblical pneumatology nor kept a more open attitude for an equal and patient dialogue with their Chinese counterparts. The simple and crude ban issued in 1742 did nothing positive for the Chinese mission, but only intensified the Holy See's conflict with the Jesuits, the Chinese government, and Chinese Christians—resulting in a fatal end to its oriental missionary project.

Conclusion

Just as the Jewish law had been fulfilled in the power of the Spirit by Gentile Christians, and the Roman customs had been renewed in Paul's time, so also the Chinese commemorating rites can be renewed

---

28. Wu, *The Chinese Rites Controversy*, 81.
29. See Yeo, "Paul's Way of *Renren*," 469–79.

and obeyed by Chinese Christians as "humanizing" etiquette (*li*) in the power of the Holy Spirit, who moves and works through all believers.

As a historical event, the Chinese rites controversy has passed. But for China, the problem of a Chinese Christianity is still a heated topic for the church and the government. After the revolution of 1911, China was no longer a dynastic empire, but became the People's Republic of China. By that time, the Chinese government recognized and respected freedom of belief and religion, and the question of understanding and living that freedom often hinged on the letter or the spirit of the law. As the Chinese rites controversy demonstrates, the Holy Spirit plays a critical role in initiating and maintaining Christian identity in a changing culture or context. If we wish to find the right way for the Christian faith to spread in China, we must trust the power of the Spirit at work in diverse cultures and acknowledge the spirit of Chinese traditional customs and absorb the ideals of Chinese civilization into the Christian faith. In this mutual inspiration, promotion, critique, and fulfillment, Christianity will accomplish its localization and indigenization, while also growing and learning from the global church's multiple cultures. May the Spirit of God help the global church in China not to be Christianity *in China*, but to be *Chinese* Christianity.

Further Reading

Jewett, Robert. *Romans: A Commentary*. Minneapolis: Fortress, 2007.

Minamiki, George. *Chinese Rites Controversy: From Its Beginning to Modern Times*. Chicago: Loyola University Press, 1985.

Noll, Ray, trans. *100 Roman Documents concerning the Chinese Rites Controversy (1645–1941)*. San Francisco: Ricci Institute for Chinese-Western Cultural History, 1992.

Wu, Liwei. *The Chinese Rites Controversy: The Encounter of Civilizations and Powers*. Shanghai: Shanghai Classics, 2007.

Yeo, K. K. *Musing with Confucius and Paul: Toward a Chinese Christian Theology*. Eugene: Cascade, 2008.

Yeo, K. K. *Rhetorical Interaction in 1 Corinthians 8 and 10: A Formal Analysis with Preliminary Suggestions for a Chinese, Cross-Cultural Hermeneutic*. Leiden: Brill, 1995.

CHAPTER 5

Pneumatology: Its Implications for the African Context

SAMUEL M. NGEWA

ABSTRACT

The visible aspect in relation to the role of the Holy Spirit, in the African context, has been more divisive than unifying. Many of those who have claimed to have been blessed with the gifts of the Holy Spirit, especially the gifts of healing and speaking in tongues, have always assumed spiritual superiority over those who do not have such gifts. Sermons promoting such an understanding have often been drawn from the book of Acts, particularly Acts 2, where we have an account of what happened on the Day of Pentecost. The main objective of this chapter is to underline that the Holy Spirit of the book of Acts, and for that matter the New Testament as a whole, is a unifying Spirit and not a divisive one. He brings together not only individuals but also races to think together and serve God as one united family of God. When this unifying role of the Holy Spirit is placed in the forefront, all his gifts, as shown in other parts of the New Testament, fall neatly into place.

"Pneumatology" comes from two Greek words, *pneuma* and *logos*. *Logos* literally means "word," but when it is put together with another word it means "study of."[1] *Pneuma* means "spirit," whether spirit of

---

1. We add *logos* to *theos* (God) to derive "theology" (study of matters related to God), to *kosmos* (world) to derive "cosmology" (study of the universe), and to *astēr* (star) to derive "astrology" (study of stars), for example.

man[2] or Spirit of God.[3] It is also translated "wind."[4] In this chapter *pneuma* refers to the Spirit of God (Holy Spirit) and so pneumatology means "study of the Holy Spirit."

Most works on the Holy Spirit have two main sections, one dealing with the person of the Holy Spirit and the other dealing with the work of the Holy Spirit. The section on his person deals with such matters as his deity and whether he is actually a person or a thing, while the section on his work deals with what he has done (e.g., in the Old Testament, in the life of Jesus, and in the New Testament church) and does (e.g., his ministries of indwelling a believer and giving gifts for ministry to church and society). By its very nature, an examination of his person tends to be philosophical, while a study of his works is usually more descriptive. The descriptive rather than the philosophical is characteristic of the African context.

Jesus in John 3:8 compares the work of the Holy Spirit with wind and says, "You hear its sound, but you cannot tell where it comes from or where it is going." One implication of this is that the Holy Spirit's work can be evident even without a philosophical analysis of who he is in his essence. There may be little systematic analysis of who the Holy Spirit is in the African context, but there are millions of people in whose lives he has left a tremendous impact. We can learn about him by examining what he has done.

Being one of the three persons of the Trinity,[5] the Spirit is eternal and therefore his work is eternal. For the purpose of this chapter, however, I limit the discussion to his work in the African context, particularly in the eastern part of Africa, in the twentieth century and into the twenty-first century.

One major and documented story on the Holy Spirit at work in Africa is the East Africa Revival, referred to by Timothy C. Morgan as "Africa's Azusa Street."[6] Notable at its beginning was a team of a mis-

2. Examples include Acts 7:59 (spirit of Stephen) and Acts 18:25 (spirit of Apollos).
3. Some examples are Acts 2:17 (my Spirit) and Acts 16:7 (the Spirit of Jesus).
4. John 3:8 is a good example.
5. The three persons of the Trinity are God the Father, God the Son, and God the Holy Spirit (Matt. 28:19; 2 Cor. 13:14).
6. Timothy C. Morgan, "Africa's Azusa Street," March 28, 2006, www.christianitytoday.com/ct2006 marchweb-only/113–23.0.html. The Azusa Street Revival in Los Angeles under William J. Seymour, April 9, 1906–15, was marked by unrelenting preaching against sin and some miraculous signs like speaking in tongues (en.wikipedia.org/wiki/Azusa_Street_Revival, accessed January 29, 2015).

sionary (Joe Church) and an African (a Ugandan, Simeon Nsibambi). All differences set aside, these two saw the need for the African church to live out its theology. It is one thing to say that we believers are the "salt" and "light" of the world (Matt. 5:13–16) and it is another for our lives to reflect that truth. Morgan says these two men were moved by "the lifelessness of African churches, the ruthlessness of colonialism, society's pervasive corruption, and the moral failure of Christian leaders."[7]

Church (a graduate of Cambridge University working as a missionary in Gahini in Rwanda) had gone to Uganda in 1929 to catch up on some rest. There he providentially met Nsibambi and as the two studied the Bible and prayed together, their spirits were united in advancing a life of holiness for the church of Christ.[8] As Church worked from his mission station in Rwanda in the following years and Nsibambi devoted himself to the ministry of preaching in Uganda, the fire of revival caught momentum. Its effect was felt not only in Rwanda and Uganda, where it originated, but also in Burundi, Kenya, Tanzania, and Congo. Its effect, to some degree, has lasted to this day. Festo Kivengere (d. 1988), who has been labeled as the Billy Graham of Africa,[9] was the product of this movement. Its chief characteristic was confession of sin and commitment to live a life of holiness. In some extreme cases, some of its members saw themselves as "holier" than those who were not in the movement. There were also situations where the confession of sin was taken as the central mark of spirituality, making some members confess sins that they actually had not committed. In such cases, the desire to appear spiritual led to the sin of pretence. Such weaknesses did not help in keeping the movement as steady as it should have been, and so what we have today is more of the effect of the revival than continuity with it. Overall, however, it was evident that the Holy Spirit was at work in Africa.

Another story testifying to the work of the Holy Spirit in Africa centers on the ministry of Joe Kayo (b. 1936), who in 1970 founded the Pen-

---

7. Morgan, "Africa's Azusa Street."

8. For a detailed history of this relationship, see Richard Gehman, "The East African Revival," *East Africa Journal of Evangelical Theology* 5, no. 1 (1986): 36–56, and Kevin Ward, "Tukutendereza Yesu: The Balakole Revival in Uganda," www.dacb.org/history/Uganda.balakole.html, accessed January 28, 2015.

9. "Festo Kivengere, 1919–1988," www.dacb.org/stories/Uganda/Kivengere_festo.html, accessed January 28, 2015.

tecostal Deliverance Church of Kenya[10] but also ministered in Uganda and Zambia.[11] It is from Kayo that in 1971 I heard the most convincing message about the need for speaking in tongues. His sermon was taken from Acts 2, and on reflection (I was one of those who did not speak in tongues during the meeting) I wondered whether he was right to use a narrative to promise all of us the gift of speaking in tongues if we were truly saved. There are many today who carry Kayo's message, citing Acts passages as proof texts. This is an issue that is at the center of this chapter and is discussed extensively below. In summary, however, many like Kayo and their disciples have given the impression that the power of the Holy Spirit is "a private possession of those who have been baptized in the Spirit."[12] This feeling, just as was the case among some members of the East Africa Revival, resulted in a holier than thou attitude. Many looked at believers in the mainline denominations as unsaved just because they did not speak in tongues. Instead of unifying the church, it brought division and factions in some quarters.

While the East Africa Revival as promoted by Church and Nsibambi and the Pentecostal Deliverance Church under Kayo stand out, they do not exhaust the story. Many African independent (at times called instituted or indigenous) churches also "place emphasis on the Holy Spirit, with accompanying manifestations of joy, tongues and power, on healing and exorcism, on personal testimony."[13] This is not to mention the ministries of Assemblies of God fellowships[14] and the many mainline denominations that recite the Apostles' Creed every Sunday. In this creed is the statement, "I believe in the Holy Spirit."

Experience must be founded on knowledge, just as knowledge without experience is not adequate. The personal experiences among the members of revival and charismatic movements cannot be downplayed. However, they would be richer if founded on good exegesis of the Scriptures. The impatience "with the idea of using the Bible for sustained teach-

10. www.pewforum.org/2010/08/05-historical-overview-of-pentecostalism-in-Kenya, accessed January 28, 2015.

11. www.dacb.org/stories/kenya/kayo-Joseph.html.

12. Albert Nolan, *God in South Africa: The Challenge of the Gospel* (Grand Rapids: Eerdmans, 1988), 115.

13. Diane Stinton, "Africa, East and West," in *Introduction to Third World Theologies*, ed. John Parratt (Cambridge: Cambridge University Press, 2004), 119.

14. The Assemblies of God has fellowships in many parts of the continent, and emphasizes the work of the Holy Spirit, particularly the gift of speaking in tongues.

ing on theological issues"[15] must be replaced with a careful examination of the passages on which we build our experiences. Since the book of Acts has been used extensively in promoting the claims of these experiences, this chapter sets out to examine some of those key passages exegetically and from them draw some lessons for the church of Christ in Africa today.

Theological and Exegetical Examination

Almost all mainline denominations recite the Apostles' Creed every Sunday. What it contains, however, is just an assertion that belief in the Holy Spirit is one of the pillars of the faith. The Nicene Creed (325) says a little more, for it states that the Holy Spirit is "the Lord and Giver of Life; who proceedeth from the Father and the Son; who with the Father and the Son together is worshipped and glorified; who spake by the Prophets."[16] The creed states something about his deity (he is worshiped and glorified with the Father and the Son), his being sent by the Father and the Son as taught in John 14:16 and 16:17, his role in inspiration (he spoke by the prophets), and his ministry in the life of a believer (he is the Lord and Giver of Life). Thus, though this creed was meant to answer some wrong teachings of the time, it touches on the most essential teachings of the Scriptures concerning the Holy Spirit. He is a person[17] and not a thing (e.g., power or influence of God),[18] he is equal with the Father and the Son, and he has a ministry to do. These facts need to be kept in mind even as we examine his work in the passages from Acts below.

As we do so, it is important to keep in mind that the book of Acts is a narrative, and narrative's primary function is to tell us what happened and not what should happen. This does not take away the fact

---

15. Ward, "Tukutendereza Yesu."

16. This is cited from Wayne Grudem, *Bible Doctrine: Essential Teachings of the Christian Faith* (Leicester: Inter-Varsity, 1999), 474.

17. In spite of the Greek noun *pneuma* (Spirit) being neuter, the New Testament uses a personal pronoun (*ekeinos*) whenever referring to the Holy Spirit.

18. In his determination to safeguard the unity of God, Arius (d. 336) identified only the Father as God, labeling the Son as God's first creation while reducing the Spirit to God's power or influence. This wrong teaching is today propagated by the Jehovah's Witnesses, who are zealous in door-to-door visitation. While their Kingdom Halls may not be fully packed, their enthusiasm in evangelism is felt in many parts of Africa.

that the God who did something in the past is the same God today and so can do the same thing again. However, it serves as a caution not to impose demands on a sovereign God for what he chooses to do, when to do it, and how it will be done.

Four key passages to be considered in this chapter are Acts 2, 8, 10, and 19. These four passages are about the outpouring of the Holy Spirit in Jerusalem on the Day of Pentecost, in Samaria, in the house of Cornelius, and in Ephesus, respectively.

Acts 2

The focus of Acts 2 is Jews. Jewish believers are the first to receive the Holy Spirit. The story, however, begins earlier than chapter 2, for in 1:8 Jesus had told the apostles (*apostoloi*)[19] that they would be his witnesses (*martyres*)[20] in all of Judea (beginning in Jerusalem), in Samaria, and to the ends of the earth. The timeframe for this was given as after the Holy Spirit had come upon them (1:8).[21] Even more significantly, Jesus said that their new status would be one in which they had "power" (*dynamis*).[22] Once the Holy Spirit had come upon them, they would be equal to the task.

19. "Apostles" in Acts 1:2 is taken to refer to the eleven (the twelve less Judas Iscariot). This is made clearer by the addition of "whom he [Jesus] had chosen."

20. The significance of a witness is that the person qualified to be one is someone who has gone through an experience needed to achieve that status. The eleven were to be witnesses concerning Jesus because they had been with him—seeing what he was doing and hearing what he was teaching.

21. This is not to be understood as if the Holy Spirit was inactive in the lives of God's people before the Day of Pentecost. The Old Testament uses such terms as "coming upon," "filling," and "putting on" to describe his activity in the lives of judges like Othniel (Judg. 3:10), Gideon (6:34), Jephthah (11:29), and Samson (14:6); civil administrators like Moses (Num. 11:17), Saul (1 Sam. 10:10), and David (16:13); craftsmen like Bezalel (Exod. 31:4); and prophets like Ezekiel (Ezek. 11:15) and Micah (Mic. 3:8). All these, however, were task-oriented fillings. On the Day of Pentecost the Holy Spirit came to dwell (Rom. 8:11; 1 Cor. 2:12; 6:19–20), seal (2 Cor. 1:21–22; Eph. 1:13; 4:30), and empower (1 Cor. 12–14). God the Father was the most involved in the affairs of his people in the Old Testament, God the Son in the Gospels, and God the Holy Spirit after the Day of Pentecost. It would be wrong, however, to assume that the other two persons of the Trinity were inactive when in a given period the focus was on one of them.

22. The idea behind *dynamis* is the needed energy to perform the task. When a car or machine is said to have lost power, it means that something that makes it keep moving has gone wrong. When that is fixed, the power is restored. The apostles

Jesus's promise that the apostles would receive power upon their reception of the Holy Spirit was fulfilled on the Day of Pentecost[23] and when they were "all" (*pantes*) in one place (2:1).[24] Whether only the 12 or the 120 (the more popular view), these were persons who had experiences to share and a message to pass on. Views are divided on whether the "one place" was a private house or a hall within the temple, and there is no good reason for anyone to be dogmatic in support of one against the other.[25] In any case, its location was such that

---

needed the person of the Holy Spirit to move the good news they had witnessed Jesus teach and do, in both near and far locations. Their activities were accomplished with *dynamis* and their gospel was a gospel of *dynamis*, even as Paul said in Romans 1:16.

23. Pentecost, also referred to as the Feast of Weeks, was one of the three major feasts for Jews (the other two being the Passover and the Feast of Tabernacles). It was celebrated in June when the weather was generally good, and so many people were normally in attendance. It was a fitting time for many to witness the fulfillment of the promise that the Holy Spirit would fill Jesus's followers at Jerusalem.

24. The group meant by "all" here could be the 12 (at this point Matthias has been chosen to replace Judas Iscariot; 1:26) or the 120 mentioned in 1:15. Luke uses the term "apostles" (*apostoloi*) for the 12 (1:2) and "brothers" (*adelphoi*) for the 120. The term "brothers" here is used of all who identified with the apostles on the issue of the message from and about Jesus. Acts 1:14 mentions some women as part of this group also. While I take the position that the "all" is the 12 apostles, the reasons are not strong enough to totally dismiss the view that it can be the 120 brothers. The "all," however, needs to refer to a group the crowd can single out (2:7). The 12 had some identity as Jesus's apostles. See C. S. C. Williams, *A Commentary on the Acts of the Apostles* (New York: Harper & Brothers, 1957), 62, and F. W. Beare, "Speaking with Tongues: A Critical Survey of the New Testament Evidence," *Journal of Biblical Literature* 83 (1964): 236. For the view that 120 were meant, see W. G. MacDonald, "Glossolalia in the New Testament," *Bulletin of the Evangelical Theological Society* 7 (Spring 1964): 60; William Neil, *The Acts of the Apostles*, New Century Bible (Greenwood: Attic, 1973), 72; F. F. Bruce, *The Book of Acts: The English Text with Introduction, Exposition and Notes*, The New International Commentary on the New Testament (Grand Rapids: Eerdmans, 1981), 68; John Williams, *The Holy Spirit: Lord and Life-Giver* (Neptune: Loizeaux Brothers, 1980), 190; I. Howard Marshall, *Acts,* Tyndale New Testament Commentaries (Leicester: Inter-Varsity, 1980), 68; John B. Polhill, *Acts: An Exegetical and Theological Exposition of Holy Scripture*, The New American Commentary (Nashville: Broadman, 1992), 97; Joseph A. Fitzmyer, SJ, *The Acts of the Apostles*, The Anchor Bible (New York: Doubleday, 1998), 238; Craig S. Keener, *Acts: Exegetical Commentary*, vol. 1, *Introduction and 1:1–2:49* (Grand Rapids: Baker Academic, 2012), 795.

25. See Keener, *Acts*, 1:796–99. For the private house view, see Heinrich A. W. Meyer, *A Critical and Exegetical Handbook to the Acts of the Apostles* (Winona Lake: Alpha, 1883), 83; R. C. H. Lenski, *The Interpretation of the Acts of the Apostles* (Minneapolis: Augs-

a crowd could gather to hear the message being proclaimed. What is most significant is what happened that day.

The manner in which the Holy Spirit came upon this group of Jews was "as a sound like the blowing of a violent wind" and "what seemed to be tongues of fire" (2:2–3). The wind symbolism here may be taken to signify real power in action though invisible, while the tongues of fire may signify the presence of the Lord (cf. Exod. 3:2). The incident left no doubt that the promised Holy Spirit had come.

The result of this incident is fourfold: all were filled with the Holy Spirit (2:4), all began to speak in other tongues (2:4), Peter preached the main message for the day (2:14–40), and about three thousand believers were added that day (2:41).

The act of filling with the Holy Spirit may have as its focus either character or service. When the focus is character, it may be viewed as a permanent endowment. It is a status that controls the manner in which a person responds to life in general.[26] Paul summarizes this in what he refers to as the fruit of the Spirit in Galatians 5:22–23. When the focus is service, however, the act is accompanied by a task performed.[27] It is service that is the focus of Acts 2:4. Filling in this sense is an enabling that may go with a short-lived assignment or a long-term task. It can be repeated as many times as there are tasks to be performed. We see it repeated in the cases of Peter[28] and Paul[29] and this was also the sense in which believers of Acts 4:31 were filled with the Holy Spirit. These two foci of the filling of the Holy Spirit must always be kept in mind when we express our theological positions on a given passage. While character-related filling of the Holy Spirit is expected of all believers (Eph. 5:18), task-related filling may be limited to those assigned a specific task. Also, while character-related filling is meant to be a permanent status, service-related filling may be seasonal. God may fill us with the Holy Spirit in a special way for a task in the twenty-first century that was

---

burg, 1934), 58; and Polhill, *Acts*, 97; for the hall within the temple view, see Neil, *Acts of the Apostles*, 72; Bruce, *The Book of Acts*, 67.

26. Examples of this include Acts 6:3, 11:24, and 13:52.

27. Examples of this include Luke 1:41 and 1:67.

28. Peter must have been a participant in the filling of Acts 2:4 since he turned out to be the preacher of the day, and Luke reports the same experience for him in 4:8.

29. In 9:17–20, Saul (Paul) was filled with the Holy Spirit and spoke in the synagogue; in 13:9–11, he was filled with the Holy Spirit and announced punishment on Elymas.

not a necessary task in the twentieth century. In such a case, what makes the difference between us in the twenty-first century and those in the twentieth century is not the level of spirituality but the nature of tasks. The task of establishing the church in Jerusalem called for a filling that was special. We see it in the further results.

The first outcome of the filling of the Holy Spirit was that "all" began to speak in tongues (Acts 2:4). If we limit the "all" to the team of twelve (see discussion above) referred to as apostles, we can say that the apostles spoke in tongues. It is clear that *glōssa*, translated as "tongue" here, has several meanings.[30] What interpreters are divided on is when it needs to be viewed as a language and when it needs to be viewed as some kind of ecstatic utterance. We also need to be careful not to read into Acts what we have in 1 Corinthians, and vice versa, for this may result in misinterpretation of one or the other.[31] Each passage must be read within its own context and literary type.

We observe in Acts 2 two phrases: "in other tongues" (*heterais glōssais*) in verse 4 and "in our tongues" (*hēmeterais glōssais*) in verse 11. Luke's choice of words makes it clear that the *glōssai* here do not point to speech out of this world but speech within the context of the languages spoken by those listening.[32] Luke says about the speech in Acts 2 that some of those who heard it described it as "declaring the wonders (*ta megaleia*) of God" (v. 11). A list of those who heard is given in 2:9–11. These not only took home the miracle of Galileans (v. 7) speaking in languages of many

30. It can mean the physical tongue (Luke 1:64; 16:24), nation or people (Rev. 5:19; 7:9; 10:11; 14:6), or a language or ecstatic utterance. No references are given for the last two, but they are at the center of the discussion above.

31. Even if there may be other passages (e.g., Eph. 5:18–20; Col. 3:16; 1 Thess. 5:19–20) that some interpreters regard as relevant to the issue of tongues (see I. J. Martin, "Glossolalia in the Apostolic Church," *Journal of Biblical Literature* 63 [1944]: 126), it is the book of Acts and 1 Corinthians 12–14 that deal with the matter directly. Mark 16:17, of course, mentions it specifically, but the ending of Mark has its own textual difficulties.

32. The attempts to present what happened in Acts 2 as a miracle of hearing (see George B. Gutten, *Speaking with Tongues: Historically and Psychologically Considered* [New Haven, CT: Yale University Press, 1927]) rather than a miracle of speaking goes against Luke's choice of words. Menzies's position that the incident combined a miracle of speaking unintelligible tongues and a miracle of understanding those tongues (Robert P. Menzies, "The Role of Glossolalia in Luke-Acts," *Asia Journal of Pentecostal Studies* 15, no. 1 [January 2012]: 52) is based more on assumption (to support "tongues" in Acts 2 as glossolalia) than the more plain reading of the narrative.

parts of the world but also a message of what God had done. Though not stated specifically, part of the message of the twelve here must have been that Jesus had risen from the dead. God had raised Jesus up, sealing the fact that Jesus was his Son and not even death could hold him in the grave. This is a message so close to God's heart that we should not be surprised if he gives the same gift to a missionary of the twenty-first century, enabling her to declare the wonders of God in Christ.

The other outcome of the filling in this incident of Acts 2 centers on Peter. In verse 14, Luke says that Peter addressed the crowd.[33] His sermon on the Day of Pentecost and as reported by Luke in verses 14–39 begins by showing that what was happening was fulfillment of Scripture,[34] followed by a summary of the Christian message[35] and concluding with the invitation to repent and be baptized. Peter tells his hearers that their obedience to his invitation to repent will be followed by their reception of the Holy Spirit. The literal translation of the Greek, in verse 38, as to what they will receive is "the gift of the Holy Spirit" (NIV), which can be understood as the gift that comes from (taking "of the Holy Spirit" as genitive of source) or is connected with (qualitative genitive) the Holy Spirit.[36] It is better, however, to read this in view of Acts 1:8. The Holy Spirit who had come upon those gathered together on the Day of Pentecost is a blessing to be enjoyed by all those who repent and believe in the Lord Jesus Christ. The Holy Spirit himself (epexegetical genitive) is that gift.[37] What accompanies

33. We are not told what language (*glōssa*) Peter spoke in addressing the mixed crowd, but he probably spoke a language everyone present would be assumed to understand, even if it would be a second language. His primary audience was the Judeans (Jews) who may also have been the ones making the comment of Acts 2:13, for they did not know some of the dialects (2:6, 8). In any case, Greek, Aramaic, and Hebrew were languages possibly spoken among the disciples and proselytes (R. H. Gundry, "The Language Milieu of First Century Palestine: Its Bearing on the Authenticity of the Gospel Tradition," *Journal of Biblical Literature* 83 [1964]: 404–8) and Aramaic was the lingua franca of commerce for countries listed in 2:9–11 (F. J. Foakes-Jackson, *Acts of the Apostles* [London: Hodder and Stoughton, 1931], 12).

34. Acts 2:16–21. Joel had prophesied what was taking place.

35. Acts 2:22–36. Jesus of Nazareth's death was in the plan of God. He was raised and lives forevermore as Lord. He is God's provided object of faith.

36. It is this particular understanding of this passage that has led to some reading the gift of tongues into it, of course, raising the question why one gift from the Spirit, out of many as listed in 1 Corinthians 12 and 14, would be singled out.

37. See also Wayne Jackson, "What Is the 'Gift of the Holy Spirit' in Acts

the reception of him is secondary. For the Jews on the Day of Pentecost, it was accompanied by the gift of speaking in other languages. They were enabled to proclaim the good news to all who had come together for the Feast of Pentecost. Luke reports that three thousand people were saved that day (2:41). The church was born in response to a message whose central character was Jesus. It was born in response to faith in this risen Jesus, and everyone who believed received the Holy Spirit. This, however, was a congregation of Jews and proselytes (2:5). Witnessing in Jerusalem and Judea (Acts 1:8) had taken place.

Acts 8

In New Testament times, the three broad categories of communities were Jews, Samaritans, and Gentiles. Acts 2 focuses on how Jews received the Holy Spirit. The focus of Acts 8 is Samaritans. Jews regarded Samaritans as one degree nearer than Gentiles, but still not full-fledged members of the house of Israel.[38] Different happenings in history[39] had brought the Jewish general attitude toward Samaritans to a level where a Jewish rabbi would instruct his fellow Jews, "Let no man eat bread of Cuthites (the Samaritans) for he who eats their bread is as he who eats swine's flesh" and would also teach Jews to pray "and Lord, do not remember the Samaritans in the resurrection."[40] In Acts 8:17, however, Samaritans received the Holy Spirit—the same person that Jews had received in Acts 2. The significance of this was that God, the owner of the church, welcomes to his family Samaritans just as he welcomes Jews. There are some key details in the narrative that should be noted:

1. The Samaritans who received the Holy Spirit were persons[41] who

---

2:38?" https://www.christiancourier.com/articles/175-what-is-the-gift-of-the-holy-spirit-in-acts–2–38, accessed January 29, 2015.

38. T. H. Gaster, "Samaritans," in *Interpreter's Dictionary of the Bible*, vol. 4, ed. G. A. Buttrick (Nashville: Abingdon, 1962), 191.

39. See a summary of these happenings in Samuel M. Ngewa, *The Gospel of John for Pastors and Teachers* (Nairobi: Evangel, 2003), 473–74.

40. R. Kent Hughes, *Acts: The Church Afire* (Wheaton: Crossway, 1996), 111.

41. Luke in Acts 8:5 says that these were the dwellers of "the city of Samaria" ([*tēn*] *polin tēs Samareias*). Since "Samaria" was used for the region in New Testament times, identification of the exact city has included Sebaste, which was the capital city

had been preached to by Philip but had not received the Holy Spirit at the point of their believing (8:5, 16). Some have argued that the delay needs to be seen within the context of Philip's limitations in clarity of message or authority.[42] Others have maintained that the delay needs to be explained within the context of the Samaritans' faith being deficient.[43] These, however, seem to be conclusions that do not have full support from the narrative.[44] The reason seems to lie elsewhere, as I will mention below.

2. The Samaritans' reception of the Holy Spirit was in the presence of, and under the ministry of, Peter and John. The apostles in Jerusalem had sent Peter and John (8:14) after they heard that Samaria had received the word of God. We are not told how they had heard, but it is possible that Philip himself was party to the message sent to the apostles. The message could have been that the Samaritans had received the word of God but there was no external evidence that they had received the Holy Spirit. The standard of measuring or for knowing whether the Holy Spirit had come would have been the experience of the Jews in Acts 2. This had not happened to the Samaritans though they had believed and had been baptized (8:12) and it would have concerned Philip.

3. The ministry of Peter and John to these Samaritans included "laying hands on them" (8:17) and the result was that the Samaritans received the Holy Spirit. By implication, there was some external indicator that this had happened. Whether this was speaking in

---

of the region (Barclay M. Newman and Eugene Nida, *A Translator's Handbook on the Acts of the Apostles* [London: United Bible Societies, 1972], 173; Fitzmyer, *Acts*, 402); Neapolis, which was the religious headquarters (Lenski, *Interpretation of the Acts of the Apostles*, 316); or even Gitta, the birthplace of Simon the Magician, if the Greek article is left out of the text, reading "a city" (Bruce, *The Book of Acts*, 183).

42. Johannes Munck, *The Acts of the Apostles: Introduction, Translation and Notes*, The Anchor Bible, rev. William F. Albright and C. S. Mann (Garden City: Doubleday, 1967), 75; G. H. C. Macgregor, "The Acts of the Apostles," in *The Interpreter's Bible*, vol. 9, ed. G. A. Buttrick (Nashville: Abingdon, 1954), 110.

43. J. D. G. Dunn, *The Baptism of the Holy Spirit* (Naperville: Alec R. Allenson, 1970), 65; A. Hoekema, *Holy Spirit Baptism* (Grand Rapids: Eerdmans, 1972), 32.

44. For example, the narrative does not tell us that Peter and John preached a clearer message than Philip had preached but simply that they prayed for them (8:15) and laid hands on them (8:17). Also the comment of Luke in 8:16 (the Holy Spirit had not fallen on any of them) implies that there was some abnormality to what would be expected under normal circumstances.

tongues, as we see later in Acts 10:46, or another sign we cannot say for sure. It is, however, reasonable to assume that God did provide an indicator that was visible to all. The laying on of hands was also an external demonstration of fellowship.

The situation, therefore, seems to be one in which the Samaritans believed but did not receive the Holy Spirit as would have been expected. Philip is not sure why this is the case and so sends a message to the apostles in Jerusalem on the matter. The apostles send Peter and John to evaluate the situation. They pray for and lay hands on the Samaritans and the Samaritans receive the Holy Spirit. The delay in receiving the Holy Spirit is caused by neither the weakness of Philip's preaching nor the deficiency of the Samaritans' believing. The delay is God's providence that the apostles, and for that matter the representatives of the Jerusalem church, would be part of and witnesses to the Samaritans also receiving the Holy Spirit. This in itself would be God's own stamp on the oneness of the church of Christ, whether Jews or Samaritans. Barriers are broken in Christ and that is confirmed by the Samaritans being partakers of the same Spirit as the Jews in Acts 2.[45] At a secondary level, there is also the vivid picture of one of the seven deacons (6:3–5) and two of the twelve apostles (Peter and John) cooperating in the mission of God.[46] They show a unity as the leaders and that unity is to be lived by all—whether Jews or Samaritans (and later, in chap. 10, Gentiles also).

Acts 10

The third key passage is Acts 10, with the narrative extending from 10:1 to 11:18. While Acts 2 centered on Jews and Acts 8 centered on Samaritans, this passage centers on Gentiles (11:1, 3). From the perspective of Jerusalem, while Jews belonged to the inner circle and Samaritans to the middle circle, Gentiles belonged to the outer circle. The Gentile

---

45. I. Howard Marshall describes this overcoming of hostility between Jews and Samaritans as "a step towards the greater of bringing Jews and Gentiles together." He then adds, "If this is correct, it may provide the clue to the undoubted problem presented by the fact that the Samaritan believers did not receive the Spirit until the apostles laid hands on them" (*Acts*, 153).

46. C. K. Barrett, *Acts*, vol. 1, International Critical Commentary (Edinburgh: T&T Clark, 1994), 412.

representative in the narrative is Cornelius, who was a centurion (man of authority) as well as a God-fearer (10:1–2). The narrative presents to us some notable details, including the following:

1. Divine preparation of Peter for the ministry to and on behalf of Cornelius, his household, and his friends (10:9–21). Peter had his views about Gentiles and those views had to be refuted by the Lord's own intervention through a vision.
2. Divine guidance of Cornelius and his messengers (10:1–8, 21–23). The Lord gave specific instructions to Cornelius as to whom he would send for and where that person would be found.
3. Peter's obedience and the results (10:24–29, 44). The message to Peter was clear. He was left with the options of obeying and doing what in his view had seemed as impossible or disobeying and knowing that he was acting against the Lord's clear instructions.
4. Shock of those in Jerusalem (11:1–3) and Peter's explanation of what exactly happened (11:4–17) followed by those in Jerusalem having no choice but to accept what had happened (11:18). It all pointed to the providence of God.

Some of the key phrases (or statements) related to the narrative and pointing us to the providence of God in uniting all believers into one body include the following:

1. God is no respecter of persons (*ouk estin*[47] *prosōpolēmptēs ho theos*; 10:34b). Peter says that this is a fact that he has been taught (*katalambanomai*;[48] 10:34a) through the vision God used to prepare him. If it had been left up to him, Gentiles were meant to stay outside

---

47. The verb "is" (*estin*) is here to be taken as a gnomic present, that is, God's nature once we come to know who he is for sure. Peter was aware of this truth before but only on theoretical terms. Now he knows it practically. In God there is no discrimination or class. He accepts all on the basis of faith in his Son Jesus Christ even as Peter preached in this narrative (10:36–43).

48. Literal translation of this verb is "I realize, understand, perceive" and in this context can be translated, "I have come to understand" (perfective present), for it is a status that God's preparation of him has helped him to achieve. God has caused him to look beyond the limitations of his earlier perceptions. In other words, God has prepared him to see people the way God sees them and not the way the ordinary Jew would.

the kingdom of God or come into it by way of passing through the path of Judaism. God, however, says that they also need to have direct access and Peter has now learned this. The vision was not for Peter's glorification but for his education in the school of God. He learned that "it is God's will that Gentiles become part of God's people without the obligation of obeying prescriptions of the Mosaic law."[49]

2. Every person, from any nation, is accepted by God (*dektos autō estin*; 10:35)[50] so long as there is fear of God in him. This is another statement of Peter's newest education in this narrative. He now knows this.

3. Those of the circumcision (Jews) who were believers were astonished (*exestēsan*)[51] because the gift of the Holy Spirit[52] was poured on Gentiles also (10:45). The fact that Jews and Gentiles stood on equal footing before God was clear, and, as Hughes puts it, "There was no denying that fact now. Seven[53] witnesses had seen it, including an apostle!"[54]

The "pouring" (*enkchutai*;[55] 10:45) of the Holy Spirit captures the same thing as the "falling" (*epepesen*;[56] 10:44) of the Holy Spirit upon all those who heard the word, and the speaking in tongues (10:46) is not what is described here as the gift of the Holy Spirit (see note 52) but the external demonstration that the Holy Spirit (who himself is the gift) had been received by Cornelius and his relatives and close friends also.

49. Fitzmyer, *Acts*, 448.

50. This is also a gnomic present. It is what God does on the basis of his nature.

51. The literal meaning of *existēmi* is "to stand outside oneself, to be out of one's mind," and in this context it has the idea of being surprised, for what was happening was out of the expected. For a Gentile to have equal spiritual experience with a Jew was not normal.

52. The gift of the Holy Spirit (*hē dōrea tou hagiou pneumatos*) here may be taken as the Holy Spirit himself, taking the genitive *tou hagiou pneumatos* as epexegetical.

53. In Acts 11:12, Peter mentions brothers who had gone with him.

54. Hughes, *Acts*, 152.

55. The verb *encheō* (I pour out) focuses on the source. In this case, it is God who pours out.

56. The verb *epipipto* (I fall on) focuses on the recipients. Taking it in relation to *encheō* (see above), the experience of the Gentiles was that they experienced the Holy Spirit falling on them while at the same time the Jews were surprised at the act of God pouring the Holy Spirit on the Gentiles.

The center of this phenomenon is, therefore, not that Gentiles spoke in tongues but that they received the Holy Spirit,[57] the reception of which was confirmed by the external demonstration of speaking in tongues. They received the same Holy Spirit the Samaritans had received in chapter 8 and the Jews had received in chapter 2. In other words, Jews, Samaritans, and Gentiles were equal guests in God's house, to dine on the same food and enjoy the same blessings. By the same Holy Spirit, God had sealed the unity of all the communities of the first century. Jews, Samaritans, and Gentiles were brought together into one body, and all of them on equal footing. The issues that had led to the separation of and discrimination between Jews and Samaritans, and the fact that Gentiles could only be accepted by partaking of "Jewishness" were all broken down. In Christ all are one family, the family of God.

Acts 19

Acts 19 does not focus on ethnic distance from what would have been expected in view of God's earlier dealing with the Jews as his chosen nation but on distance in terms of location. It represents "a remote part of the earth" (1:8) when Jerusalem is seen as the beginning point. The narrative tells us about the following:

1. Paul going to Ephesus, on his third missionary journey, and finding twelve disciples who were baptized only in the baptism of John (19:1, 6)
2. Paul asking them whether they had received the Holy Spirit when they believed and their answering, "No, we have not even heard there is a Holy Spirit" (19:2)
3. Paul, on realizing that they had received only John's baptism, explaining to them the meaning of John's baptism and its relationship to Jesus (19:3–4)
4. Paul baptizing them, placing his hands on them, and their reception of the Holy Spirit and speaking in tongues (19:5–7)

---

57. It is the reception of the Holy Spirit that Peter also emphasizes (Acts 11:15) when he states his case to the effect that God had received Gentiles just as he had received Jews and when that happened, Peter had no choice but to accept it (11:17) and allow it to change his perception.

The identity and spiritual state of these twelve have been matters of discussion in scholarship. There are some who have advanced the view that the twelve had been disciples of Apollos who himself knew only about the baptism of John (18:25) until Priscilla and Aquila "explained to him the way of God more accurately" (18:26).[58] Others have suggested that they were disciples of John the Baptist.[59] These two positions are not incompatible. They could have been disciples of John the Baptist who also looked up to Apollos as their teacher.

As to their spiritual state, there are some who view them as not saved, [60] while there are others who view them as believers.[61] While it may be difficult to be 100 percent certain, there are some details in the text whose weight cannot be ignored:

1. Luke's use of "disciples"[62] (*mathētai*) without qualifying them to be John the Baptist's, Apollo's, or someone else's. It is not unreasonable to see Luke's use of the term here to be equivalent to "believers," that is, disciples of Jesus Christ. The argument that these twelve men only had the appearance of being disciples but they were not[63] seems to take away from Luke the more obvious meaning when he simply says, "he (Paul) found some disciples."[64]

58. Examples include Merrill F. Unger, *New Testament Teaching on Tongues* (Grand Rapids: Kregel, 1971), 64, and Bruce, *The Book of Acts*, 385.

59. Examples include Marshall, *Acts*, 306, and Bastiaan van Elderen, "Glossolalia in the New Testament," *Bulletin of the Evangelical Theological Society* 7, no. 2 (1964): 55.

60. Hoekema (*Holy Spirit Baptism*, 42), William J. Larkin Jr. (*Acts*, The IVP New Testament Commentary Series [Downers Grove: InterVarsity, 1995], 272), Marshall (*Acts*, 305), Fitzmyer (*Acts*, 643), and Ajith Fernando (*Acts*, The NIV Application Commentary [Grand Rapids: Zondervan, 1998], 506) are examples of those who take the view that these twelve were not saved.

61. Examples include Ned B. Stonehouse ("Repentance, Baptism and Gift of the Holy Spirit," *Westminster Journal of Theology* 13 [1950–51]: 12), Lenski (*Interpretation of Acts*, 780), and Bruce (*The Book of Acts*, 385).

62. Other places where Luke uses the title "disciples" in Acts are 6:1, 9:10, and 11:26, and in these passages the title is interchangeable with the term "Christians."

63. Larkin (*Acts*, 272) says that Luke uses "disciples" for the twelve because "at first their outward identification with believers led Paul to take them as such." Marshall (*Acts*, 306) also says, "they appeared to be disciples but they are not . . . Luke describes them as they appeared to Paul." But then, why would Luke promote the same misunderstanding years later?

64. The Greek is *kai eurein tinas mathetas* with the aorist verb *eurein* simply reporting what happened. It is a fact of history.

2. The use of the aorist participle *pisteusantes*[65] (believed) gives some support to the view that these twelve were believers (no matter how deficient their understanding was) whose reception of the Holy Spirit had not taken place yet.

The key issue for our argument here is that they had not received the Holy Spirit though they had believed. However, after Paul baptized them in the name of Jesus (19:5) and laid his hands on them, "the Holy Spirit came on them and they spoke in tongues prophesying" (19:6). Fitzmyer's statement that Paul laid his hands on these twelve as a representative of the twelve apostles[66] is in agreement with what God seems to be doing in the book of Acts, namely, bringing people of all races and nations under the same umbrella.

What happened in these four incidents can be summarized as follows:

The Group	Spiritual Status	Historical Timing	Significance
12 or 120 Jews	Disciples of Christ	Day of Pentecost	The Counselor (John 14:26) has come, and a movement of Spirit-indwelt and -empowered believers has begun.
Samaritans	Believers	After Philip preached to them and Peter and John laid hands on them	Samaritans are in also.
Gentiles	Believers	As Peter was speaking	Gentiles are in also.
12 disciples at Ephesus	Believers (disciples)	After Paul laid hands on them	Believers from the uttermost part of the earth are in also.

Looking at Acts 8, 10, and 19, one wonders why persons who have believed do not receive the Holy Spirit, as would be expected in view of

65. The aorist participle is usually used for an action antecedent to the action of the main verb though it can also be simultaneous with the action of the main verb if the main verb is also in the aorist tense. Paul presumes here that the twelve had believed, and it is on that basis that he is asking them whether they had also received the Holy Spirit.
66. Fitzmyer, *Acts*, 644.

such passages as Romans 8:9 and Ephesians 1:13.[67] The mystery lies in what God wants to establish in the context of these four outpourings of the Holy Spirit recorded in Acts. Acts 2 marked the fulfillment of the promise of 1:8 and the other three outpourings marked the uniting of other people groups into that body of believers established on the Day of Pentecost. Samaritans (chap. 8), Gentiles (chap. 10), and those living at the uttermost parts of the world (chap. 19) were fully welcomed into the same body established in chapter 2. There would no more be classification of persons who have joined this movement on the basis of race, whether Jews, Samaritans, or Gentiles, whether near Jerusalem as the beginning point or as far away from there as Ephesus.

Implications for the Twenty-First-Century Church

When we put together Acts 2, 8, 10, and 19, we see a God who is involved in mission to make his own people from Jewish, Samaritan, and Gentile communities. He not only controls the timing of events, but he also provides visible demonstration of the oneness he is creating so that everyone who is genuine cannot question the evidence. This has implications for us today:

1. There is only one God[68] for all the races of the world. It is not every race or tribe with their God or a Supreme Being who should not be disturbed,[69] but one God on a mission for all. He does not need "a whole army of inferior gods and a long line of ancestral spirits"[70]

---

67. In these passages and others, a believer receives the Holy Spirit immediately after exercising faith in Christ. In fact, Romans 8:9 asserts that anyone without the Holy Spirit is not a believer.

68. The God of Isaac (Yahweh) was also the God of Ishmael (Gen. 17:19–27). There is no reason why Muslims and Christians (in Africa) or Jews and Palestinians (in the Middle East) cannot find a basis for unity as they relate to each other. Calling the Creator of heaven and earth by different names should be seen as a matter of the tongue (languages) and not a necessary basis for irreconcilable differences.

69. Samuel Ngewa, "The Biblical Idea of Substitution versus the Idea in African Traditional Sacrifices" (PhD diss., Westminster Theological Seminary, 1987), 59.

70. Charles Salala, "The World of the Spirits: Basukuma Traditional Religion and Biblical Christianity," in *Issues in African Christian Theology*, ed. Samuel Ngewa, Mark Shaw, and Tite Tienou (Nairobi: East African Educational, 1998), 136.

to connect with his people. He himself is at work among his people.

2. There is only one Savior[71] for all races of the world. It is no longer each people group with their set sacrifices, but God's Son has been given as a sacrifice for the salvation of all.

3. There is the same Spirit for all races of the world. It is no longer the ancestral spirits serving as intermediaries,[72] but God's gift (third person of the Trinity) baptizing believers into one body, one family.

4. There is one family of God, no matter the people group.[73] All the tribes are given a common identity, membership in God's family that is found in the church of Christ.

5. All divisions on the basis of race, tribe, or the like have no place in the church of Christ. We do not deny that different races and tribes exist but in terms of how we relate they should not make any difference.

6. God's true servants allow God to change their perceptions about people even when the inherited perceptions had drawn lines of demarcation on the basis of race or tribe. History cannot be erased. There were colonizers and the colonized, the "them" and the "we," but all these become things of the past as we are united in Christ.

As believers, unity defines our mission and goal in life. God laid the foundation and we must build on it if we desire to be judged by him as "faithful servants." Oneness also increases our level of effectiveness.[74] The principle of "united we stand, divided we fall" has been

71. The fact that God has declared One as Savior of the world is a fact that one who believes the Bible to be God's word cannot run away from. It is not a creation out of a sense of superiority but acceptance of God's own declaration (Matt. 3:17; Luke 9:35; John 3:16). This, therefore, should also not be seen as a basis for animosity against each other. It should be viewed as a point of difference of opinion (some accepting God's declaration and others not) but should not be a basis for wars.

72. Kenneth Little, "The Mende in Sierra Leone," in *African Worlds: Studies in the Cosmological Ideas and Social Values of African People*, ed. Daryll Forde (Oxford: Oxford University Press, 1954), 115.

73. Paul captures this well in Ephesians 4:4–6.

74. There has been, in our times, the unfortunate withdrawal of ministry funds from a kingdom of God-related ministry, not because the needs of the ministry had ceased but simply because the person who had sourced the funds (whether Jew, Samaritan, or Gentile—using these figuratively) had moved. That contradicts the fun-

proven over and over again. It is not only true in political and social arenas, but also in our spiritual ministry. Shuler's statement, "it is hard to change what has been ingrained,"[75] is totally accurate, but we must choose to act like our God, who purposely provided a church that is unified, no matter what boundaries had existed before.

Once the unity established on the basis of Acts is guarded, the exercise of the gifts of the Spirit as taught in the epistles becomes a blessing rather than a curse. We use the gifts for the good of the one family of God. Exercise of gifts should by no means be a source for division. God started a united church and it is our mission to maintain that unity, even as we use our different gifts among ourselves.

With this as our understanding of the will of God in doing his mission, we may ask, How are we doing in the African context, and beyond, in following his footsteps? How are we doing in accepting all people groups as God accepts them? As a way of challenge, not condemnation, it is ironic that in the very country (Rwanda) where the East Africa Revival started, one of the worst genocides was witnessed in 1994, with division on ethnic lines being in the background.[76] It is also equally surprising that in the very country (Kenya) where Joe Kayo's ministries started, there were clashes in 2007 causing the loss of many lives, with division along tribal lines being evident.[77] The unfortunate thing is that even persons who claimed to be Christians were involved in such killings. These serve as examples of many such conflicts all over the continent of Africa and beyond. Even within the church itself, there have been deep conflicts, with some of them centering on such

---

damental principle God established as he united the church in the first century. We need to keep dear to us God's deep desire that the church lives and acts as one—no matter the location.

75. Clarence Shuler, *Winning the Race to Unity: Is Racial Reconciliation Really Working?* (Chicago: Moody, 1998), 59.

76. It is estimated that between 500,000 and 1,000,000 persons were killed in 100 days (April 7 to July 15, 1994) with some sources putting the figure at 800,000 (en.wikipedia.org/wiki/Rwandan-Genocide and www.history.com/topics/rwandan .genocide). If one works with the 800,000 figure, this comes to 8,000 persons per day.

77. It is estimated that between 800 and 1,200 lives were lost ("Deadly Clashes in Kenya Fuel Fears of Election Violence," www.theguardian.com/world/2012/sep/13/ kenyan-tribal-clashes–116-dead, and "Death Toll Nears 800 as Post-Election Violence Spirals out of Control in Kenya," www.theguardian.com/world/2008/jan/28/kenya .international); the killers were apparently targeting people on the basis of their ethnic background.

matters as speaking in tongues and other such dramatic gifts of the Holy Spirit. No wonder George H. Williams laments, "It is regrettable that in the course of Christian history the great scene constructed by Luke has repeatedly led to divisions and factions among Christians."[78] Who has failed? Is it the Holy Spirit, or is it us? Certainly not the Holy Spirit! His uniting work is with us just as it was in the accounts discussed here from Acts. What then is it that we need to relearn again and again about the Holy Spirit as we see his work in the book of Acts?

1. The Holy Spirit removes all barriers—whether racial, tribal, status, or any other. He removed the wall between Jews, Samaritans, and Gentiles and formed one body, his church. When we see divisions in the church, then there is lack of obedience to the will of God. The church must model what it means to live as members of one family, and society will follow suit.

2. The Holy Spirit breaks down all prejudices. Peter was taken through a dramatic experience before he could imagine himself ministering to Cornelius for direct access to the kingdom of God. Prejudices stood in his way and those had to be broken. We are all familiar with the stereotyping that goes on—most of it along racial or tribal lines. No matter how historically correct some of the observations behind the stereotyping are, they must all be broken down once we are in Christ. We are called to view others the way God does. He treats Jews, Samaritans, and Gentiles the same, on the basis of faith in Christ.

3. The Holy Spirit uses us at the level of our gifts or assignments, calling all of us into a ministry of cooperation. God used the deacon Philip and the apostles Peter and John together to bring the Samaritans in, as full-fledged members of God's household. What matters is not who or what we are (bishop, pastor, professor, lecturer, etc.), but what God wants to use us for. Such an attitude removes all unhealthy competition and envy. We thank God for the gifts he gives us (1 Corinthians 12–14; Eph. 4:11–12) and pray that we will manifest his fruit (Gal. 5:22–23) as we serve him in the twenty-first century, each of us in our corner.

78. George H. Williams and Edith Waldvogel, "A History of Speaking in Tongues and Related Gifts," in *The Charismatic Movement*, ed. Michael P. Hamilton (Grand Rapids: Eerdmans, 1975), 104–5.

As a continent of fifty-four countries and hundreds of people groups, Africa provides a fertile ground for differences and conflict. The story, however, does not have to be as gloomy as it appears at times. Most African countries have a high percentage of Christians, and Bible preaching is on almost every corner. God on his part has given to every believer, no matter the race, tribe, or status, the gift of the Holy Spirit, the Spirit of unity. The church in Africa is called on to practically demonstrate what unity is all about. It is not loss of personal identity but a breaking down of all the barriers that hinder us from relating to others as members of one family. After the church has lived this truth out, then it has the authority to preach it to others. Acts 2, 8, 10, and 19 provide the basis on which to build as we strive to this end. A continent of conflict and strife can be turned into a continent of harmony and love by obeying what God shows us to be his will from the Acts accounts. Such harmony is a blessing not only within the context of the church but also in society at large for it addresses the "us" and "them" mentality that is the core cause of tribalism, nepotism, tribal clashes, civil wars, and other such social evils the African continent often suffers from.

Further Reading

Bruner, Frederick Dale. *A Theology of the Holy Spirit: The Pentecostal Experience and the New Testament Witness.* Grand Rapids: Eerdmans, 1970.

Gaffin, Richard B., Jr. *Perspectives on Pentecost: New Testament Teaching on the Gifts of the Holy Spirit.* Phillipsburg: P&R, 1979.

Gehman, Richard. "The East African Revival." *East Africa Journal of Evangelical Theology* 5, no. 1 (1986): 36–56.

Hamilton, Michael P., ed. *The Charismatic Movement.* Grand Rapids: Eerdmans, 1975.

Parratt, John. *Introduction to Third World Theologies.* Cambridge: Cambridge University Press, 2004.

CHAPTER 6

Who Is the Holy Spirit in Contemporary African Christianity?

David Tonghou Ngong

ABSTRACT

This chapter briefly tells the story of how the contemporary African theology of the Spirit came to emphasize the function of the Holy Spirit rather than the place of the Spirit in the Trinity, and proposes that the functional understanding of the Holy Spirit ought to be recalibrated. Moreover, the place of the Spirit in trinitarian life needs to be addressed.

In order to better understand who the Holy Spirit is in contemporary African Christianity, one needs to undertake a panoramic survey of the phases of Christianity in Africa.

Phases of the Christian Theology of the Spirit in Africa

African Christianity can roughly be divided into three phases: (1) early Christianity in Roman North Africa, Egypt, Nubia, and Ethiopia; (2) precolonial African Christianity that saw the continuation of Christianity in Egypt and Ethiopia, was dominated by Roman Catholicism in sub-Saharan Africa, and was found especially in regions such as present-day Nigeria (Benin and Warri) and Angola and Democratic Republic of Congo (the Kongo); and (3) colonial and postcolonial Christianity. The first phase is traditionally thought to have begun in first-century Egypt and what is left of it today is Coptic Christianity in

Egypt and Ethiopian Christianity. The second phase mostly began in the late fifteenth century and had almost completely disappeared by the middle of the eighteenth century. The third phase was heralded by the rise of the modern missions movement in the late eighteenth century but gained significant traction from the nineteenth century. The Christianity brought to Africa during this third phase is currently the most vibrant form of Christianity in the continent and is the focus of this chapter.[1]

First Phase

There were significant reflections on the person and work of the Holy Spirit during the first phase of Christian presence in Africa, especially as demonstrated in the works of early African theologians such as Tertullian of Carthage, Cyprian of Carthage, Augustine of Hippo, Origen of Alexandria, and Athanasius of Alexandria.[2] When debates about the nature of the Christian God were just beginning, it was Tertullian of Carthage (ca. 160–ca. 220), partly influenced by his membership in the Holy Spirit movement known as Montanism, who argued that God should be understood as three distinct and related *persona* (persons), Father, Son, and Holy Spirit.[3] Even before contemporary African Pentecostals began speaking of the Holy Spirit as transformer of persons, Cyprian of Carthage (ca. 200–ca. 258), who is mostly known for his doctrine of the centrality of the church in the Christian life, had noted that transformation of human beings is an important function of the Holy Spirit. Cyprian maintained that

1. For a good introductory work on the history of Christianity in Africa, see Elizabeth Isichei, *A History of Christianity in Africa: From Antiquity to the Present* (Grand Rapids: Eerdmans, 1995).

2. Carthage is in present-day Tunisia, Alexandria in present-day Egypt, and Hippo in present-day Algeria. Roman North Africa includes present-day Libya, Algeria, and Morocco.

3. *Against Praxeas* 1–2. Even though the extent to which Montanism influenced Tertullian's theology is debated, Tertullian seems to suggest in *Against Praxeas* 2 that his understanding of trinitarian theology is based on instruction from the Paraclete, or the Holy Spirit. For this debate, see Jaroslav Pelikan, "Montanism and Its Trinitarian Significance," *Church History* (June 1956): 99–109, and Andrew McGowan, "Tertullian and the 'Heretical' Origins of the 'Orthodox' Trinity," *Journal of Early Christian Study* 14, no. 4 (2007): 437–57.

the Holy Spirit played this transformative role in his own conversion to the Christian faith.[4]

Origen of Alexandria (ca. 185–254), who began the systematic process of reflecting on the Trinity that significantly influenced how the Trinity would be understood in Christian theology, argued that, as a member of the Godhead, it is the Spirit who probes the things of God and makes the knowledge of God available to human beings. In other words, Christian spirituality is dependent on a proper understanding of the place of the Spirit in trinitarian life.[5]

When in the fourth century some Christians questioned whether the Holy Spirit was God, it was Athanasius of Alexandria (ca. 296–373) who argued that the Spirit should be understood as fully God, thus contributing to the theology of the Spirit that was to influence the Nicene-Constantinopolitan Creed, or Nicene Creed, of 381.

Augustine of Hippo (354–430) is in a league of his own in the pneumatological reflections of this phase because his statement of who the Holy Spirit is came to form the official position of the Western church and contributed to the split between the Western and Eastern churches. Augustine argued that the Holy Spirit proceeds from the Father and the Son (*filioque*), contradicting the Nicene position that the Holy Spirit proceeds from the Father alone. Augustine's idea that the Holy Spirit is a gift from the Father and the Son and the communion, or love, that unites them, has also been influential in reflections on the Holy Spirit in the Western church.[6]

The above are brief examples of the significant reflections on the person and work of the Holy Spirit in the first phase of the church in Africa. Even though the focus of this chapter is not on the pneumatological reflections of this first phase, contemporary African pneumatology can benefit from appropriating some elements of the pneumatology of this phase.

---

4. Michael A. G. Haykin, "The Holy Spirit in Cyprian's *To Donatus*," *Evangelical Quarterly* 83, no. 4 (2011): 321–29.

5. Gregory K. Hillis, "The Holy Spirit and Prayer in Origen's *On Prayer*," *Cistercian Studies Quarterly* 49, no. 1 (2014): 3–26.

6. Adam Kotsko, "Gift and *Communio*: The Holy Spirit in Augustine's *De Trinitate*," *Scottish Journal of Theology* 64, no. 1 (2011): 1–12.

Second Phase

During this phase there was little, if any, pneumatological reflection in Africa. Christianity in North Africa and Nubia had been eliminated, Coptic Christianity in Egypt had declined due to the expansion of Islam, and Ethiopian Christianity continued. Explorers, traders, and missionaries from Europe, especially from Portugal, Spain, and Italy, began to engage sub-Saharan Africa. Beginning in the fifteenth century, Roman Catholic missionaries began to evangelize the people on the coasts of west, central, and southeast Africa.[7] While Christianity was fleeting in west and southeast Africa, it took root to some extent in central Africa, especially in the Kongo. Even though this second phase would not last, partly because Christian missionaries became entangled in the slave trade, it contained one of the most important manifestations of popular pneumatology in African Christianity.

This popular pneumatology appeared toward the end of the seventeenth century in the Kongo through the work of a charismatic young woman, Dona Beatrice Kimpa Vita (d. 1706), whose pneumatology could be seen as perhaps the earliest example of enculturation of the Christian faith in sub-Saharan Africa. As we will see below, versions of her pneumatology are still found in Africa today. She was trained as a *nganga*, or spirit medium/healer, but she later became a Christian when she experienced miraculous healing through the spirit of Anthony of Padua (1196–1231), a Portuguese Franciscan saint who was popular in Kongolese Christianity through Portuguese evangelization of the Kongo.[8] Borrowing from the language of spirit possession common in African indigenous religions, Kimpa Vita claimed that she had been possessed by the spirit of Anthony and she went about healing and preaching what would today be called an Afrocentric gospel. She said that Mary, Jesus, and the apostles of Jesus were all Africans and that Jerusalem was in the Kongo. She was declared a heretic and, like Joan of Arc, burned at the stake in 1706.[9]

---

7. There was no Protestantism at the time.

8. This Anthony is not to be confused with the Egyptian hermit, Antony the Great.

9. See Sigbert Axelson, "Arguments about 'Fetishes' in Europe and Kongo during the Great Awakening of Kimpa Vita (1684–2 July 1706)," *Swedish Missiological Journal* 96, no. 2 (2008): 127–38; John K. Thornton, *The Kongolese St. Anthony: Dona Beatriz Kimpa Vita and the Antonian Movement, 1684–1706* (Cambridge: Cambridge University Press, 1998);

Third Phase

The focus of this chapter is on the pneumatological reflections of the third phase of African Christianity that began with the missionization and colonization of Africa in the nineteenth century. Contemporary African pneumatology should be understood as partly a reaction against the Western Christianity that was brought to Africa by Christian missionaries and partly the desire of Africans to make their belief in the Holy Spirit meaningful in their various contexts. Generally speaking, the reaction has been rooted in the call for Christianity in Africa to be led by Africans and expressed in African idioms and life-worlds. This call is made against the background of Western demonization and denigration of things African in favor of things Western, so that becoming Christian in Africa came to be synonymous with becoming Western. The demonization of African life-worlds meant that Africans had to become Western if they were to be "good" Christians. It is this perception of the gospel and Western culture as equivalent that much of contemporary African theology and pneumatology is contesting.

Roughly four reactions against Western, or colonial, Christianity may be outlined in this phase. The first is the emergence, in the nineteenth century, of what is called Ethiopian Christianity, a form of African Christianity that emphasizes African, rather than Western, leadership in African churches. Here Africans broke away from some of the churches that were planted by missionaries and started African-led churches that were similar in most respects except leadership to the churches from which they had broken away. A second reaction, which may be connected to the first, is the moratorium movement in the mid-twentieth century, where African church leaders demanded that there should be an end to Western missionary leadership in African mainline churches. This vision has been realized because most African churches today are led by Africans.

A third reaction, which began in the early twentieth century, is the development of what has been called African independent churches or African initiated churches (AICs). These are prophetic movements that were led by charismatic leaders and they include the Harrist, Kimbanguist, Aladura, Roho, and Zionist churches that began with an empha-

---

Alexander Ives Bortolot, "Donna Beatriz: Kongo Prophet," *The Metropolitan Museum of Art*, http://www.metmuseum.org/toah/hd/pwmn_4/hd_pwmn_4.htm.

sis on the presence of the Spirit of Jesus Christ in the life of Christians. With the arrival of Western Pentecostalism in Africa in the early twentieth century, there would later emerge a fourth reaction, which is now described as Neo-Pentecostal/Charismatic.[10] The third and fourth reactions to Western Christianity have been described as Pentecostal-type churches, and contemporary African pneumatology, both popular and academic, has largely been centered on the beliefs and practices of these churches.[11] This chapter also focuses on these churches.

With the Pentecostalization of African Christianity, a phrase that describes the tendency to stress the presence of the Spirit in most African churches today, one may say that a dominant theological theme in contemporary African Christianity is pneumatology.[12] However, most of the popular and academic reflections on the Holy Spirit coming from Africa have been focused on what the Holy Spirit does rather than on the place of the Spirit in the Trinity. At one level, this is understandable given that the person and work of the Spirit, like the person and work of Christ, can hardly be separated. This notwithstanding, Christian theology, as expressed in the Nicene Creed, speaks of the Holy Spirit as the third member of the Trinity and it is necessary to reflect on what this means.

The remainder of this chapter first discusses some of the current themes of African pneumatology, arguing that this pneumatology has focused on the functions, rather than the person, of the Spirit. It

---

10. See Ogbu Kalu, ed., *African Christianity: An African Story* (Trenton: Africa World, 2007); Ogbu Kalu, *African Pentecostalism: An Introduction* (New York: Oxford University Press, 2008); and J. Kwabena Asamoah-Gyadu, *Contemporary Pentecostal Christianity: Interpretations from an African Context* (Eugene: Wipf and Stock, 2013).

11. For other classifications of this phase of African Christianity, see Birgit Meyer, "Christianity in Africa: From African Independent to Pentecostal-Charismatic Churches," *Annual Review of Anthropology* 33 (October 2004): 444–74; Ogbu U. Kalu, "The Third Response: Pentecostalism and the Reconstruction of Christian Experience in Africa, 1970–1995," *Journal of African Christian Thought* 1, no. 2 (December 1998): 1–21; Allan H. Anderson, *African Reformation: African Initiated Christianity in the 20th Century* (Trenton: Africa World, 2001).

12. For examples of pneumatological reflection in non-Pentecostal contexts, see Elochukwu Eugene Uzukwu, *God, Spirit, and Human Wholeness* (Eugene: Pickwick, 2012); Ferdinand Nwaigbo, "*Instrumentum Laboris*: The Holy Spirit and the Signs of the Times for the Second Synod for Africa," *AFER* (December 2010): 598–624; George Bebawi, "With the Desert Fathers of Egypt: Coptic Christianity Today," *Road to Emmaus* 10, no. 3 (Summer 2009): 3–37.

then makes three proposals for future reflections on the Holy Spirit in Africa. The first is that the reactive nature of African Christian discourse in general, and African pneumatology in particular, needs to be questioned in light of the contribution of such discourse in defining African identity in the modern world in which the continent is marginalized. Second, African pneumatology needs to engage the question of religious pluralism in the continent. Third, African pneumatology needs to address the question of the Spirit as the third member of the Trinity.

Themes in Contemporary African Pneumatology

Rejecting Western Enlightenment rationalism has been crucial to current reflections on the Holy Spirit in Africa. Western missionaries and the churches they planted in Africa were influenced by Enlightenment rationalism that denuded the world of the spiritual, making the human mind the arbiter of all truth. Rationalism undermined the spiritual imagination by declaring it to be superstitious, primitive, and a stage in human life that would eventually be overcome by advances in science and technology. This view of things led Western missionaries and the churches they planted not to take seriously the African cosmology that sees the universe as spiritually charged. In this cosmology, causation is not only material but also spiritual, and human beings make sure to carefully negotiate both the physical sphere and the spiritual sphere in order to ensure their well-being. Because missionaries and the churches they planted did not take this life-world seriously, they failed to appeal to the African masses because most people saw these churches as saying and doing things that did not directly address their concerns. According to this narrative, the critical concerns of most Africans can only be adequately addressed if African cosmology is taken seriously.

The above point may be connected to the African understanding of religion: religion in African cosmology is not concerned with the otherworldly but rather with how life is lived in the here and now. In fact, religion in Africa is focused on ensuring that humans live long and fruitful lives, characterized by having offspring (preferably many) and enjoying overall material well-being. Thus, religions that do not engage the spirit world with the aim of helping people experience this fullness of life will hardly travel far in Africa. By neglecting to address the connection between the spiritual world and the material world in the quest for human flourishing, Western missionaries and the churches they planted are accused of missing a significant opportunity to speak to the concerns of Africans. It is argued that the AICs and other pneumatic churches take this life-world seriously and thus appeal to the people, hence resulting in the significant growth of the church in Africa today.

This life-world is taken seriously through acknowledging that belief in the existence of spirits is not irrational, primitive, or superstitious. Rather, it is a legitimate way to perceive the world. Thus, the solution to the concerns that this life-world raises is to be found not in denying its basic assumptions, as Enlightenment rationalism did, but in positing the Spirit of Jesus Christ as the power that can address the concerns of the African universe and ensure human flourishing.[13] However, this pneumatology does not focus on discussing how the Holy Spirit is the Spirit of Jesus Christ but rather on the function of the Spirit in helping Christians deal with the concerns of their life-world. It is understood that one can only experience the power of the Spirit through Jesus Christ. When people accept Jesus Christ as their Lord and Savior, they begin to experience the power of the Spirit through various manifestations of the Spirit, including speaking in tongues, personal transformation, empowerment, protection, prophecy, and healing, among others.[14] We are going to look at each of these manifestations in turn.

Speaking in tongues (glossolalia) does not carry equal weight for all Christians who emphasize the presence of the Spirit in Christian life. Sometimes, those who speak in tongues tend to see such pneumatic expression as something that all genuine Christians must experience, so that speaking in tongues seems to be what distinguishes genuine from non-genuine Christians.[15] However, there are other Christians who emphasize the presence of the Spirit but do not see glossolalia as

13. It is important to note here that the Holy Spirit is understood to be the Spirit of Jesus Christ. In fact, the Holy Spirit is often conflated with Jesus Christ as the power in the name of Jesus is also the power of the Spirit.

14. For more on this, see J. Kwabena Asamoah-Gyadu, *African Charismatics: Current Developments within Independent Indigenous Pentecostalism in Ghana* (Leiden: Brill, 2005).

15. Francis Muchingura, "The Significance of Glossolalia in the Apostolic Faith Mission, Zimbabwe," *Studies in World Christianity* (April 2011): 12–29.

a central marker of the presence of the Spirit. In spite of these differences, the debate about the doctrine of subsequence, the idea that, after conversion, a Christian has to experience an additional "in-filling" of the Holy Spirit, has not been dominant in African popular and academic pneumatology, as has been the case in the West.[16]

Another important manifestation of the Spirit is personal and communal transformation. We saw above that Cyprian of Carthage was one of the earliest to speak of the transforming function of the Holy Spirit, holding up his own conversion as an example. Such personal transformation could be seen as the process of sanctification because it is expected that once a person accepts Christ as his Lord and Savior, his character has to change. This change in character means that one has become a new creation who lives by the ways of God rather than the ways of the world. This transformation is often described as a "born again" experience. This born again experience is especially manifested in how one relates to elements of African traditional cultures. One who is being transformed by the Spirit is expected to refrain from participating in elements of African traditional cultures that are thought to be inimical to both the Christian life and one's personal well-being. Thus, one of the evidences of spiritual transformation is to "make a complete break with the past."[17] Refraining from participating in activities such as those that venerate the ancestors and in certain funeral rites are among the means of making this break with the past. The goal of making this break seems to be that the life of a Christian should be different from that of a non-Christian.[18]

The transformative function of the Spirit is, however, not limited to individual lives; it extends to the rest of society. Kimpa Vita of the Kongo was perhaps the first to link the presence of the Spirit with the

16. See James D. G. Dunn, *Baptism in the Holy Spirit* (Philadelphia: Westminster, 1977), 2; Roger Stronstad, "Forty Years On: An Appreciation and Assessment of *Baptism in the Holy Spirit* by James D. G. Dunn," *Journal of Pentecostal Theology* 19 (April 2010): 3–11.

17. It has been suggested that this call for a complete break with the past has actually not been successful since much of African Christianity is still conducted against the background of African traditional religious cultures. See Birgit Meyer, "'Make a Complete Break with the Past': Memory and Post-Colonial Modernity in Ghanaian Pentecostal Discourse," *Journal of Religion in Africa* 28, no. 3 (1998): 316–49; Matthew Engelke, "Past Pentecostalism: Notes on Rupture, Realignment, and Everyday Life in Pentecostal and African Independent Churches," *Africa* 80, no. 2 (2010): 177–99.

18. Benson Ohihon Igboin, "Bias and Conversion: An Evaluation of Spiritual Transformation," *Evangelical Review of Theology* 37, no. 2 (April 2013): 166–82.

transformation of society as a whole when, indwelt by the spirit of Anthony of Padua, she preached the vision of a transformed Kongolese society. Some may find the fact that Kimpa Vita was indwelt by the spirit of Anthony to be troubling, given that the spirit of Anthony is not the Holy Spirit. Reading her narrative in this way would, however, not do justice to the context in which she lived and preached. Hers was a context in which the Spirit was spoken of in the idiom of spirit possession, which is still the case in much of Africa today.

In much of Africa, it is believed that people can be possessed by certain spirits.[19] Even though these spirits may be said to be different from the Holy Spirit, some scholars have seen the idea of spirit possession as significant to the development of Pentecostalism in America. The fact that the Azusa Street Revival, which is seen as the genesis of Pentecostalism in America, was led by a black person, William J. Seymour, has led some to posit this African spirituality of spirit possession as standing at the roots of Pentecostalism in America. The experience of spirit possession, which often led to trance experiences, was carried over by African slaves who were brought to the Americas and this informed their practice of the Christian faith in America. The Azusa Street experience of the Spirit is seen as a manifestation of spirit possession, interpreted in light of the Holy Spirit.[20]

Thus, the fact that Kimpa Vita was indwelt by the spirit of Anthony should be placed within a context in which spirit possession and pneumatology go together. The spirit of Anthony could therefore be seen as shorthand for the Holy Spirit who sometimes works through holy people. Because Anthony was a holy person, his spirit was holy and thus a manifestation of the Holy Spirit. Even though some evangelical thinkers would find this view controversial, speaking of the spirit of a saint should not be unmoored from the broader theological and pneumatological context in which a saint's life is understood because the spirit of a saint is not just a personal spirit, but also a spirit that participates in the divine Spirit. In essence, it is a spirit that has been divinized.

When this spirit inhabited Kimpa Vita, she preached not only a

19. See Susan J. Rasmussen, "Spirit Possession in Africa," in *The Blackwell Companion to African Religions*, ed. Elias Kifon Bongmba (Oxford: Wiley-Blackwell, 2012), 184–97.

20. For more on the African influence on the beginnings of Pentecostalism in America, see Walter J. Hollenweger, *Pentecostalism: Origins and Developments Worldwide* (Peabody: Hendrickson, 1997), 18–24; see also Estrelda Y. Alexander, *Black Fire: One Hundred Years of African American Pentecostalism* (Downers Grove: InterVarsity, 2011), 28–60.

gospel of personal transformation but also one of societal transformation. In fact, she preached a gospel that called for the burning of all fetishes, making no distinction between crosses and rosaries that Europeans carried and the talisman that the Kongolese carried. All were to be burned because carrying them did not demonstrate reliance on the power of God for protection. Growing up in a war-torn society, Kimpa Vita also preached a gospel that called for peace and restoration of society as a whole. This vision of the Spirit as transformer of society continues in the preaching of many African churches and Christians today.[21]

The theme of transformation is often connected to that of empowerment. It is the Holy Spirit who empowers people for personal transformation. It is the Holy Spirit who empowers societies so that they can be transformed. In fact, without such empowerment there can be no transformation. The empowerment of the Holy Spirit enables people to do and be what they would otherwise not be able to do and be. Thus, people develop moral excellence and spiritual insight only through the empowerment of the Holy Spirit. People succeed in business and jobs only through the empowerment of the Holy Spirit. Many Christian worship services are interspersed with testimonies of specific ways in which the Spirit has empowered people for personal transformation.

Further, Christian missions would not be possible without the empowerment of the Holy Spirit. In a recent reflection on the place of the Spirit in the missions of AICs, Ghanaian scholar Thomas Oduro has argued that AICs do not so much rely on money for missions as they do on the Holy Spirit.[22] He tells the story of how a leader of an AIC in Nigeria, Agnes Okoh, told her congregants in 1963 that the Spirit had informed her that the first foreign land where the church would do missions would be Ghana. It took thirty-four years for this prophecy to be fulfilled as the church waited on the movement of the Spirit! The

21. See Philomena Njeri Mwaura, "Integrity of Mission in the Light of the Gospel: Bearing Witness of the Spirit among Africa's Gospel Bearers," *Mission Studies* 24 (October 2007): 189–212; Clifton R. Clarke, "Pan-Africanism and Pentecostalism in Africa: Strange Bedfellows or Perfect Partners? A Pentecostal Assist towards a Pan-African Political Theology," *Black Theology* 11, no. 2 (July 2013): 152–84.

22. Thomas A. Oduro, "'Arise, Walk Through the Breadth and Length of the Land': Missionary Concepts and Strategies of African Independent Churches," *International Bulletin of Missionary Research* 38, no. 2 (April 2014): 86–89.

prophecy was fulfilled when someone in Ghana invited the church to do mission work there.

All in the church are empowered for Christian missions through charismatic gifts. As recorded in 1 Corinthians 12, different spiritual gifts are given to members of the church so that they can together work for the building up of the church. With the prominence of Pentecostalism in African Christianity, some have argued that there has been a democratization of charisma, that is, an emphasis is now placed on the fact that all members of the church are (to be) endowed with spiritual gifts. In this case, members of the clergy are not the only ones who are especially endowed with charismatic gifts; every member of the church has an important role to play in the ministry of the church because everyone is given a spiritual gift to be used in the church. Ghanaian scholar of Pentecostalism Asamoah-Gyadu has used the expression "12/70 paradigm shift" to make this point.[23] In this equation, 12 is related to the 12 apostles of Jesus Christ and 70 is related to the 70 disciples Jesus sent out for mission in Luke 10. The 12 apostles, in this scheme, represent the members of the clergy and a situation where the ministry of the church is left to the members of the clergy. However, the 70 disciples Jesus sent out represent the whole congregation rather than only members of the clergy. Thus, through the Spirit's dispensing of charismatic gifts, all members of the church have a role to play in the church's ministry.

This democratization of charisma notwithstanding, not all gifts of the Spirit are created equal. One of the spiritual gifts that is playing a significant role in contemporary African Christianity is the gift of prophecy.[24] Prophecy in this case does not so much have to do with the speaking of truth to power, as many prophets in the Hebrew Bible did, but rather with the ability to peer into spiritual things, to see spiritually what is past and what may happen in the future, the ability to unveil future hidden things, as found in the book of Revelation. Prophecy here is not so much directed toward society as a whole, as many Old Testament prophecies were, but rather toward particular individuals or a particular congregation. These prophets

---

23. J. Kwabena Asamoah-Gyadu, *Contemporary Pentecostal Christianity: Interpretations from an African Context*, Regnum Studies in Global Christianity (Eugene: Wipf and Stock, 2013), 59–78.

24. Cephas N. Omenyo and Wonderful Adjei Athur, "The Bible Says! Neo-Prophetic Hermeneutics in Africa," *Studies in World Christianity* (April 2013): 50–70.

are akin to African traditional seers or medicine men and women who perform diagnostic and healing roles, discerning the causes of particular maladies and then prescribing solutions. For example, if someone fails in a venture, she may visit a seer to find out why she did not succeed.

Through divination, the seer may say, for example, that the failure is due to the fact that one has not paid due recognition of a particular ancestor and it is the anger of this ancestor that is orchestrating the failure. The seer will then prescribe what needs to be done in order to appease the wronged ancestor and so earn his benevolence. Sometimes, Christian prophets may stipulate that in order for one to succeed, one would need to sever all ties to traditional religions, which may include family ties. Traditional religions, in this context, are often seen as avenues for demonic blockages and they need to be set aside for blockages to be unclogged. This is part of the context in which Christians are urged to make a complete break with the past. The past (connection to elements of African indigenous religions, such as ancestor veneration) may still be affecting the present in a negative way and in order for this negative influence to be arrested, ties with the past need to be severed. The prophet, like the seer in indigenous religions, helps Christians to navigate the various intricacies of the spiritual realm in order to sever such ties and so enhance their well-being. The prophet, like the seer, is also seen as a healer because she not only diagnoses but also makes prescriptions for a cure. Some have argued that the charismatic gift of prophecy sometimes overshadows the Holy Spirit because the prophet, rather than the Spirit, is seen as the source of the healing power.

The healing ministry of the prophet brings us to the theme of the Holy Spirit as healer.[25] This is another important pneumatological theme in African Christianity. Here the Spirit is seen as healer of all kinds of illnesses, from cancer to HIV and AIDS to barrenness. The power of prayer for miraculous healing is important, but healing is also mediated through holy people (like prophets), holy places, and holy things. While prayer can be conducted anywhere, some places have

25. See Cephas N. Omenyo, "New Wine in an Old Wine Bottle? Charismatic Healing in the Mainline Churches in Ghana," in *Global Pentecostal and Charismatic Healing*, ed. Candy Gunther Brown (New York: Oxford University Press, 2011), 231–50; Paul Gifford, "Healing in African Pentecostalism: The 'Victorious Living' of David Odeyopo," in *Global Pentecostal and Charismatic Healing*, ed. Brown, 251–66.

been especially established as places of spiritual power, such as Moria for the Zion Christian Church in South Africa.[26] Holy objects that may be used for healing are holy water and anointed oil. Again, the connection between these holy people, holy places, and holy things and the Holy Spirit still needs to be given clearer theological articulation in African Pentecostal pneumatology. That is, theological arguments for why the Spirit works through these things rather than other objects or why the Spirit works through these objects rather than no object at all needs clearer articulation if Christians are to be spared from being tethered to these things rather than the immaterial Spirit.[27] One way of thinking about this is that acknowledging that some objects have special healing power is to acknowledge the distinction between the sacred and the profane. Thinking in terms of sacred and profane may be helpful, but it may fall afoul of the much-needed element of African spirituality that stresses that everything is sacred.[28] Serious work needs to be done in this area.

Finally, the Spirit is seen as protector against all malevolent spirits. Special focus is directed at malevolent spirits because these are spirits that affect human life in negative ways, thus diminishing human flourishing. Of particular concern to most African Christians is the belief in witchcraft. Witchcraft, roughly stated, is the belief that some human beings possess the ability to appropriate spiritual powers in selfish ways that benefit them but harm others. As it was in the Middle Ages in Europe, many African Christians hold witchcraft responsible for various human misfortunes such as certain illnesses, poor harvest, deaths, and accidents. Because life has become increasingly harder for many Africans in a world that is modernizing, elements of this hardship are often interpreted in terms of witchcraft.[29] In pre-Christian Africa, people often shielded themselves from the effects of witchcraft through the help of medicine men or women who provided medicines

26. Anderson, *African Reformation*, 100–101; Asamoah-Gyadu, *Contemporary Pentecostal Christianity*, 51–52.

27. Recently some Christians in Ghana died in a stampede when they went to obtain holy water from a holy man from Nigeria. See "Ghana Stampede Kills Four at TB Joshua's Church," *BBC News*, http://www.bbc.com/news/world-africa–22595573, May 20, 2013.

28. Laurenti Magesa, *What Is Not Sacred? African Spirituality* (Maryknoll: Orbis, 2013).

29. See Jean Comaroff and John Comaroff, eds., *Modernity and Its Malcontents: Ritual and Power in Postcolonial Africa* (Chicago: University of Chicago Press, 1993).

that acted as vaccines against witchcraft activities. For many Christians, however, protection against witchcraft is the work of the Spirit of Jesus Christ. Thus, it is widely believed that those who are Christians, especially Christians who belong to Pentecostal churches, become immune to the activities of witches because they are protected by the Spirit. However, in cases where one is already affected by witchcraft or other negative spiritual powers, deliverance or exorcism is often performed.[30]

From the pneumatological themes discussed above, it can be seen that the focus is on how the Holy Spirit functions in the Christian life to enable human flourishing. This emphasis on human flourishing is understandable given that most Africans face daunting threats to their survival. The recent spread of the Ebola virus in some West African countries highlighted the urgency of some of these threats. These are threats that need to be overcome through the power of the Spirit. The emphasis on human flourishing has, however, led to the dominance of what is called the gospel of health and wealth, or the prosperity gospel, especially in popular pneumatology. This prosperity gospel has received significant critique by those who see it as an inadequate understanding of the gospel.[31] While there is some truth to these critiques, there are three directions that pneumatological reflections in African Christianity may fruitfully pursue.

First, African pneumatology should reconsider the relationship between the supposedly Western rationalistic worldview and the supposedly African spiritualistic worldview. Second, African pneumatology has to engage the question of religious pluralism, especially in an Africa that seems to be increasingly experiencing conflicts that have religious dimensions. Third, African pneumatology must place more focus on the place of the Spirit in the Trinity, reading the third person of the Trinity as divine gift and love who unites divine life, on the one hand, and who unites human and divine life toward eschatological consummation, on the other.

---

30. See Opoku Onyinah, "Deliverance as a Way of Confronting Witchcraft in Modern Africa: Ghana as a Case History," *Asian Journal of Pentecostal Studies* 5, no. 1 (January 2002): 107–34.

31. Paul Gifford, "The Prosperity Gospel in Africa: Expecting Miracles," *The Christian Century*, July 10, 2007, 20–24; Lovemore Togarasei, "The Pentecostal Gospel of Prosperity in African Contexts of Poverty: An Appraisal," *Exchange* 40 (October 2011): 336–50.

Concluding Proposals

With the rise of the discipline of world Christianity, it has become important to demonstrate how Christians around the world practice the faith differently.[32] Situated in the context of postcolonialism, voices that were stymied by colonial discourses are now being raised in the postcolonial era. Also, the tendency toward homogenization that seems to be engendered by globalization is being resisted through appropriation of the local. In these contexts, it makes sense for African Christian theologians to stress the African difference in pneumatological reflections by pitting the African against the Western. However, pitting a supposedly African spiritualistic worldview against a supposedly Western rationalistic worldview does not sufficiently take into account the complex nature of African and Western worldviews, thus leading to a slanted pneumatology. What is taken to be the African spiritualized life-world is only a part of the African life-world. While it should be admitted that the life-world of most Africans is highly spiritual in nature, it should not be forgotten that it is also highly rationalistic and even instrumental. One African theologian has even suggested that the African life-world is so highly pragmatic that it may discourage belief in God.[33] This is so because many Africans often seek what works in life so that their reliance on God is based on their understanding that God will improve their lives. Gods that are seen as indifferent to human well-being are sooner abandoned.[34]

It is also the case that what is depicted as a Western rationalistic worldview is only part of the Western imagination. In the West, we find highly spiritualistic worldviews, which explains why Pentecostalism is flourishing not only in Africa and among adherents of indigenous religions but also in Western countries such as the United States. Even more, what is depicted as the African life-world today has historically been a significant element of the Western imagination.[35] Life-worlds everywhere historically have both spiritualistic and rationalistic ele-

32. Lamin Sanneh, *Whose Religion Is Christianity? The Gospel beyond the West* (Grand Rapids: Eerdmans, 2003).

33. See Eloi Messi Metogo, *Dieu peut-il mourir en Afrique? Essai sur l'indifférence religieuse et l'incroyance en Afrique noire* (Paris: Karthala, 1997).

34. Toyin Falola, *Culture and Customs of Nigeria* (Westport: Greenwood, 2001), 35.

35. See Richard Fletcher, *The Barbarian Conversion: From Paganism to Christianity* (New York: Holt, 1997).

ments so that the separation of the two is only a recent phenomenon. Separating the two has often led to an emphasis on rationality, as was the case during the Enlightenment, or on ecstatic spirituality, as is the case in contemporary African pneumatological reflections. An adequate pneumatology is one that sees the Spirit as active in both the ecstatic and the rationalistic, the imaginative and the technical, the spiritual and the scientific.[36] Seeing the Spirit as manifested in both the ecstatic and the rationalistic is especially important because many of the problems Africa faces today are to be addressed not only miraculously but also technically or scientifically.

Take the Ebola outbreak in 2014 as an example. The spread of the virus was made worse not only by the fact that Ebola is an inherently deadly virus but also by the fact that the medical infrastructure was shamefully lacking. A recent study has demonstrated how measures by the International Monetary Fund (IMF) contributed to the weakening of medical infrastructures in the West African countries that have been significantly affected by the virus.[37] The imagination that seeks scientific causes of human failure and success should not be seen as bereft of the Spirit, but rather as part of the movement of the Spirit to enable human flourishing. In fact, during the Ebola outbreak, one of the leading Pentecostal healers in Africa, the Nigerian T. B. Joshua, cautioned those infected to stay in their countries rather than come to him for healing. While he is believed to be able to heal some illnesses miraculously, he demonstrated his limits during this outbreak.[38]

Another important area that needs to be investigated in African Christian pneumatology is the multireligious context of the continent. As the Nigerian scholar of religion Jacob Olupona has recently observed, "interreligious relations in Africa today have achieved a nearly

36. For more on the importance of bringing together the ecstatic and the scientific in contemporary African pneumatology, see David T. Ngong, "Stifling the Imagination: A Critique of Anthropological and Religious Normalization of Witchcraft in Africa," *African and Asian Studies* 11 (2012): 144–81. For more on the Spirit as entailing both the ecstatic and the rational, see John R. (Jack) Levison, "Recommendations for the Future of Pneumatology," *Pneuma* 33 (2011): 79–93.

37. Alexander Kentikelenis et al., "The International Monetary Fund and the Ebola Outbreak," *The Lancet* (December 21, 2014), http://www.thelancet.com/journals/langlo/article/PIIS2214-109X%2814%2970377-8/fulltext.

38. Ben Ezeamalu, "Nigeria: T. B. Joshua Asks Ebola Victims to Stay in Their Countries," Allafrica.com (August 4, 2014), http://allafrica.com/stories/201408050164.html.

unprecedented fever pitch of intolerance, thanks in large part to the rapidly growing popularity of radical forms of Evangelical Christianity and Islam."[39] I have described this intolerance elsewhere as simply toxic.[40] This intolerance is found not only between Christians and non-Christians but especially among Christians. In fact, churches that emphasize the presence of the Spirit describe those churches that do not appear to do so as "dead churches," sometimes creating tension among Christians. How can pneumatological reflections speak to this situation? I cannot go into any depth in dealing with this matter here. However, as the Pentecostal theologian Amos Yong has shown, one of the most fruitful theological loci for dealing with questions of interreligious conflicts is pneumatology because the Holy Spirit resists domestication in the Christian faith and forces Christians to see that the Spirit blows where it pleases, including contexts of Christian and non-Christian religions.[41] From this perspective, it makes sense to take seriously the idea, found in the Hebrew Bible, that it is the Spirit of God infused in all human beings that animates us all (Gen. 2:7). If the Spirit of God (*ruah adonai*) is present in all human beings, how is this related to the gift of the Spirit of Jesus Christ to Christians? C. René Padilla's contribution in this volume touches on this question, but it needs to be fleshed out from an interreligious perspective.

The question of how the *ruah adonai* in the Hebrew Bible relates to the Spirit of Jesus Christ in the New Testament leads us to the need to reflect on the person of the Holy Spirit in Trinitarian life. Since the Holy Spirit is understood to be the Spirit of Jesus Christ, how is the Spirit distinct from Jesus Christ? In the history of the development of Christian doctrine, it was strenuously argued, especially in the fourth century, that the members of the Trinity—Father, Son, and Holy Spirit—should be regarded as one but three, as united but distinct. The question of how the Spirit is the same as but distinct from the Father and the Son is not irrelevant because what we say about the place of the Spirit in the Trinity has important implications for the Christian life.

---

39. Jacob K. Olupona, *African Religions: A Very Short Introduction* (Oxford: Oxford University Press, 2014), 33.

40. David Ngong, "African Pentecostalism and Religious Pluralism," in *Pentecostal Theology in Africa*, ed. Clifton Clarke (Eugene: Wipf and Stock, 2014), 193.

41. Besides Yong's chapter in this volume, see also "The Spirit of Hospitality: Pentecostal Perspectives toward a Performative Theology of Interreligious Encounter," *Missiology* 35, no. 1 (January 2007): 55–73.

Perhaps it is at this point that African Christians may borrow from one of the significant ancestors of the faith, Augustine of Hippo, who put considerable thought into this matter and came up with the idea that the Spirit could be understood as a gift from the Father and the Son and as the love that unites them.[42] According to Augustine, the Holy Spirit is the eternal, non-identical self-giving of the Father and the Son. This self-giving is eternal and non-identical because the Father, as source of the Son, has always begotten the Son so that the way the Son gives himself back to the Father is as Son. Here the eternal reciprocity of non-identical (similar but different ways of) self-giving is understood as the Spirit. However, the Spirit is not only what the Father and the Son give to each other; the Spirit is also what the Father and the Son give to Christians so that the spiritual gifts are understood not just as single gifts, such as the gift of tongues or the gift of prophecy, but rather as the gift of the Spirit itself. It is this gift of the Spirit that enables Christians to participate in divine life.

Further, Augustine sees the Spirit as the love that unites the Father and the Son so that the greatest gift of God is not a particular gift but the gift of the Spirit of love, which graces Christians and the world with divine life and enables them to participate in God. By integrating Christians and the world into divine life, it is the Spirit who guarantees eschatological consummation, thus enabling Christians not to focus only on the Spirit's role in enabling human flourishing in the present. Also, because the gift of the Spirit is beyond anything that Christians can give back to God, the idea of the Spirit as gift interrupts the narrative of prosperity theology that sometimes depicts Christians as having a transactional relationship with God.[43] Finally, because the Spirit of God is the love that unites Father and Son, the Spirit ought to be seen as a source of unity rather than disunity, as often seems to be the case where claims to charismatic gifts are made. Addressing the question of the person of the Spirit in the life of the Trinity enables Christians to speak a little more clearly about the importance of ensuring present human flourishing and our ultimate participation in divine life.

42. Augustine, *The Trinity: A Translation for the 21st Century*, trans. Edmund Hill, OP (Brooklyn: New City, 1991), 15.5.

43. For the Holy Spirit as disrupting gender and capitalistic economic discourses, see Sarah Coakley, "Why Gift? Gift, Gender and Trinitarian Relations in Milbank and Tanner," *Scottish Journal of Theology* 61, no. 2 (May 2008): 224–35, and Kotsko, "Gift and *Communio*," 1–12.

Further Reading

Anderson, Allan H. *African Reformation: African Initiated Christianity in the 20th Century.* Trenton: Africa World, 2001.

Asamoah-Gyadu, J. Kwabena. *African Charismatics: Current Development within Independent Indigenous Pentecostalism in Ghana.* Leiden: Brill, 2005.

Asamoah-Gyadu, J. Kwabena. *Contemporary Pentecostal Christianity: Interpretations from an African Context.* Regnum Studies in Global Christianity. Eugene: Wipf and Stock, 2013.

Clarke, Clifton, ed. *Pentecostal Theology in Africa.* Eugene: Pickwick, 2014.

Kalu, Ogbu. *African Pentecostalism: An Introduction.* New York: Oxford University Press, 2008.

Ngong, David Tonghou. *The Holy Spirit and Salvation in African Christian Theology: Imagining a More Hopeful Future for Africa.* New York: Peter Lang, 2010.

Uzukwu, Elochukwu Eugene. *God, Spirit, and Human Wholeness: Appropriating Faith and Culture in West African Style.* Eugene: Pickwick, 2012.

CHAPTER 7

In Search of Indigenous Pneumatologies in the Americas

Oscar García-Johnson

ABSTRACT

This chapter seeks to uncover and recover important elements in ancestral traditions of the Americas with an eye on discerning pneumatological continuity between the pre-Columbian and post-Columbian
communities. My basic question was, what are we Christians to make
of God's occasional encounters with cultures and religions of the Americas before the European conquest and beyond their occidentalized socioreligious representations, given the fact that God's wider revelatory
presence has also been present in the Americas? By using an alternative theological approach, I proceed to disarticulate over-Westernized
categories to open up a path for a contextual pneumatology from the
Americas.

Robert Johnston begins his book *God's Wider Presence* with the following:

> What are we as Christians to make of those occasional encounters
> with God in our everyday lives that seem more real than everyday
> reality . . . ? Whether observing a sunset, . . . feeling awe as we have
> joined others and the Other in communal acts of justice, or being
> ushered into the divine Presence by a work of art, music, or liter-
> ature, such experiences are . . . more than mere deductions based
> on the footprint of God's act of creation. They are more than mere

echoes or traces of his handiwork, though that is sometimes how they are described by Christian theologians.[1]

These lines carry on the centuries-old tension between general and special revelation (and theology and culture) in traditional Western theology's effort to make sense of how God is present and operates in the world. Johnston, however, situates this tension in "the disconnection between the church and the world" and the "irrelevancy of the church in the culture of the West."[2] Hence, "if God has indeed revealed himself through creation, conscience, and culture then we ourselves are impoverishing ourselves in our relationship with and knowledge of God to the degree we are insensitive to that divine Presence in others."[3] How then do we Christians cope with these issues in our postmodern (Western) and postcolonial (non-Western) worlds? Johnston argues that the gifts of new theological questions (Elizabeth Johnson) and the interlacing of various disciplines-approaches (Cecilia Gonzalez-Andrieu) are indispensable tools for a constructive theological task. Furthermore, the Spirit has persistently operated outside the walls of the church, and "Christians are called to witness to the fact that God has been and continues to be active throughout creation and history, . . . active apart from Jesus Christ through the Spirit who remains the Spirit of Christ."[4]

In response to Johnston's challenge to elaborate a constructive theology informed by a wider revelatory presence of God, I confess that my first impulse, as a Latino/a theologian born in Honduras, is to hide behind the Western layer of my existence, to let those ancestral voices be guided by traditional Western questions. My second impulse, on the other hand, tends to resist such Western hegemony and seeks vindication by appealing solely to my indigenous legacy, although I have difficulty recognizing it. Fortunately, living in the Latino/a US diaspora has taught me a third impulse: a way of asking questions about God, community, life, and the world at the border of my existence. This way of interrelating ideas, experiences, theories, and traditions represents an alternative theological approach seeking to avoid gathering and or-

1. Robert K. Johnston, *God's Wider Presence: Reconsidering General Revelation* (Grand Rapids: Baker Academic, 2014), xiii.

2. Johnston, *God's Wider Presence*, xvi–vii.

3. Johnston, *God's Wider Presence*, xvii.

4. Johnston, *God's Wider Presence*, 214.

ganizing knowledge in either a Western or an anti-Western way. I call this approach transoccidentalism, which means that the interpreter positions herself beyond Westernized descriptions and categories that define one's identity and reality.

Transoccidentalism is a way of sensing, thinking about reality, and relating to God, creation, community, Scripture, and everyday life (*lo cotidiano*) at the exteriority of those ideas, categories, traditions, and institutions that Western culture has deemed essential and primary for modern thinking and Western Christianity. Transoccidentalism is a way of reaching beyond the shell of Western conceptual dependency toward a new horizon where original thought and independent research are possible by trespassing the totalizing categorizations built by traditional theologies and paradigms that have organized the world into first, second, third, and fourth worlds. So we ask, If God's wider revelatory presence has also been present in the Americas, what are we Christians to make of God's encounters with cultures and religions in the Americas before the European conquest and beyond their Western representations?

This chapter does not offer a theology of religions from the Americas because my first task is to repair the false Western assumption that the originating cultures of the Americas had no religion of their own, only mythology. In the same breath, the idea of Christianity in the Americas as merely a Western implant needs serious revision.[5] The broad picture shows God's wider revelatory presence also in the religions of the Americas. In particular, I argue that the West and the Americas should be considered two incarnational spaces (without hegemony) where the Sprit of the triune God freely reveals himself at the exteriority (prior to and beyond) the logic of Western coloniality-modernity. Correspondingly, I endeavor to uncover and recover important elements in ancestral traditions of the Americas in order to discern a pneumatological continuity between the preconquest and the postconquest communities.

The reader should be aware that my transoccidental approach does not follow the normative historical or systematic theological methodology or present a comprehensive view of all that the Western category of pneumatology implies in all the main religious expressions of the

---

5. See José Rabasa, "Thinking Europe in Indian Categories, or, Tell Me the Story of How I Conquered You," in *Coloniality at Large: Latin America and the Postcolonial Debate*, ed. Mabel Moraña, Enrique D. Dussel, and Carlos A. Jáuregui (Durham: Duke University Press, 2008), 48.

Americas. It will keep an eye on potential activities of the Spirit at the exteriority of coloniality-modernity—in those places, symbols, and peoples previously neglected and negated by Western methodologies. Hence, this chapter begins with the invention of the colonial project of the Americas and its Christian tradition upon the encounter of Europe and the New World inhabited by its originating cultures. The first section takes apart the hegemonic Western frameworks that justify the covering of indigenous knowledge at the expense of potential pneumatological contributions. The second part articulates a constructive theological-cultural framework where we can see an indigenous pneumatology.

Geopolitics of Christian Knowledge

The place where theology is formed matters.[6] Place matters because language, culture, and traditions are never neutral carriers of ideas; they always shape what they convey. Theology develops in a particular place out of the interaction, not between Scripture and culture, but between some version of the Christian tradition and the indigenous traditions of that place—both cultural and religious. We then must understand theological differences at the fundamental level of how we come to know about God, or in our case, the Spirit of God and his work in and with creation. In this new theological process, we must face the geopolitics of knowledge—the way race, geography, ethnicity, politics, economics, gender, and so forth play into the construction and transmission of knowledge in the form of ideas, categories, and narratives. This critical aspect becomes especially important when a wealth of disciplines claim epistemic hegemony over others. Then we must uncover the epistemic dominance hidden under the assumption that such a wealth of knowledge—situated in a particular culture, history, race, and ethnicity—is fundamental, universal, and inescapable. This has been the case with Western theology in respect to non-Western–minority theologies.

According to Paul Borthwick, a missionary and educator in contact with Africa, Western Christianity in the majority world faces the challenge of pluralism, globalization, and territorialism, which a Zim-

---

6. We argued this in William Dyrness and Oscar García-Johnson, *Theology without Borders: Introduction to Global Conversations* (Grand Rapids: Baker Academic, 2015), chap. 3.

babwean brother sums up like this: "What you in the West call 'global-ization' we call 'Americanization.'"[7] In the same vein, William Dyrness notes how the Western tradition is a special mix of influences: Greek philosophy, European paganism, medieval scholasticism, the Reforma-tion, and the Enlightenment.[8] This tradition currently comes under the charge of Orientalism (Edward Said) and Occidentalism (Walter Mi-gnolo) in its ethnocentric self-representation in relation to the Major-ity World, instrumentalized through Christianity, colonial-neocolonial projects, philanthropy, education, science, technology, and the like.

Occidentalism in Theological Studies

In an article titled "Retheologizing the Americas,"[9] I present two theo-logical orientations correlated with Occidentalism that have domi-nated theological thinking in Latin America and its diaspora for five centuries. The first I label the pro-occidentalist orientation. In this ori-entation, scholars and practitioners tend to limit themselves to mim-icking Western methodologies and transplanting Western ideas, mod-els, and ambitions into Latin America or its global diaspora. Obviously, the identifier "Western" is invisibilized or disguised under universal categorizations. The theological canon here revolves around "master" figures of the West—Augustine, Aquinas, Luther, Calvin, John Wesley, Edwards, and so on.[10] This orientation assumes that European theol-ogy and history are the *locus theologicus*, the universal norm, the seat of orthodox faith. Orthodoxy and original scholarship, in the Majority World, are presented as finished products of the Western Christian tradition. As a result, all that is left for Latino/a scholars and ministers to do is to contextualize, which is misunderstood as making Western ideas and practices work for the Americas.

7. Paul Borthwick, *Western Christians in Global Mission: What's the Role of the North American Church?* (Downers Grove: InterVarsity, 2012), Kindle ed. #75 (69–76).

8. Dyrness and García-Johnson, *Theology without Borders*, chap. 3.

9. Oscar García-Johnson, "Retheologizing las Américas: A Transoccidental Ap-proach," *Journal of Hispanic/Latino Theology* 10, no. 2 (2014): 9–24.

10. For a review of significant Western theologians and how their theologies con-tribute to colonizing uses of theology, see Don H. Compier, Kwok Pui-lan, and Joerg Rieger, *Empire and the Christian Tradition: New Readings of Classical Theologians* (Minneap-olis: Fortress, 2007).

The second orientation I call counter-occidentalist, which raises questions rooted in particular local contexts that are generally antagonistic to hegemonic Western ideas, structures, and patterns of action that perpetuate injustice and dependency. Orthodoxy is dethroned by orthopraxis, and Western-rooted scholarship is bypassed in attempts to do original contextual research. Represented here are theories and traditions from the progressive liberal schools of the West as well as their Latin American counterparts, liberationist movements, and critical evangelical factions (e.g., the Latin American Theological Fellowship).

Both orientations have informed reflection and practice in the Americas and have played into the logic of coloniality-modernity—one promoting Occidentalism and the other opposing it. The result is a deficit in autonomous Christian thinking and independent research. The point of gravity for autonomous thinking, Mignolo and the decolonial school argue, is Western epistemologies. Until one disengages or delinks from the epistemic dialectic vested in Western coloniality-modernity, one cannot offer a truly autonomous and liberating option.[11] I illustrate next how both orientations have been present in predominant theological traditions since the birth of Latin America, in both Roman Catholicism and Protestantism.

The Idea of Christian Tradition in the Americas

A number of significant Latin American–Latino/a intellectuals have come to the consensus that the idea of Latin America cannot be understood without the idea of coloniality, as well as the history of the expansion of Western Christianity across the Americas, as a key element in the Euro-American self-understanding as a civilizing force. Mignolo's manifesto, *The Idea of Latin America,* points this out:

> From the sixteenth-century Spanish missionary Bartolomé De Las Casas to . . . the twentieth-century British historian A. J. Toynbee, all we can read (or see in maps) about the place of the Americas in the world order is historically located from an European perspec-

11. See this argument articulated in Walter D. Mignolo, *Desobediencia Epistémica: Retórica de la Modernidad, Lógica de la Colonialidad y Gramática de la Descolonización* (Buenos Aires: Ediciones del Signo, 2010).

tive that passes as universal. . . . History is a privilege of European modernity and in order to have History you have to let yourself be colonized. . . . Perspectives from coloniality, however, emerge out of the conditions of the "colonial wound," the feeling of inferiority imposed on human beings who do not fit the predetermined model in Euro-American narratives.[12]

Western Christianity in the Invention of America

At the beginning of the Americas there were two crosses:[13] the historical event of the conquest and the theological meaning of that event in light of the Jesus of Christendom. Whether one stands in the Protestant faction (e.g., liberals, *evangélicos*, Pentecostals)[14] or in the Roman Catholic faction (e.g., official religion, popular religion, liberationist movements), excavating the origins of Christianity in the Americas will take us right to the conquest and back to deal with the historical consequences in our time.

The cross and the sword arrived in the New World as inseparable pieces of a shock-and-awe Spanish campaign intending to appropriate the natural resources of the newly discovered land in order to fund the Crusades in the Holy Land. The acquisition of the West Indies marked the land with a cross. In a letter to the Spanish royalty, Columbus writes: "And in every land where your Highness' ships arrive, and in every cape, I send out the order to place a high cross."[15] With this distinctive practice, comments the Puerto Rican theologian Luis Rivera-Pagán, "Columbus placed crosses in strategic spaces as a symbol of [his] taking of possession."[16]

12. Walter Mignolo, *The Idea of Latin America*, Blackwell Manifestos (Malden: Blackwell, 2005), xii.

13. A reworking of Jürgen Moltmann's famous quote: "At the beginning of Christianity there are two crosses"; see "The Cross as Military Symbol for Sacrifice," in *Cross Examinations: Readings on the Meaning of the Cross Today*, ed. Marit A. Trelstad (Minneapolis: Fortress, 2006), 259.

14. See the four descriptions, or faces according to José Míguez Bonino, in Bonino, *Faces of Latin American Protestantism: 1993 Carnahan Lectures* (Grand Rapids: Eerdmans, 1997).

15. Christopher Columbus and Consuelo Varela, *Los Cuatro Viajes: Testamento*, El Libro de Bolsillo (Madrid: Alianza Editorial, 1986), 245.

16. Luis Rivera-Pagán, *Evangelización y Violencia: La Conquista de América* (San Juan: Editorial Cemi, 1991), 15; my translation.

Violence, invasion, and Christian faith are historically united under the symbol of the cross, explains Rivera-Pagán, marking the Americas as a possession of the Church and the Spanish kings. "Behind the evangelizing cross," he concludes, "hides the not-so-veiled conquering sword."[17] This account, without denying some of the great contributions of Western culture, sees the process of colonization, evangelization, possession of the land, and history making also as a tragedy marked by invasion and violence. The traditional Western history, however, sees the Americas as having been discovered and civilized by Europeans, something the natives are expected to be thankful for and proud about. "Discovery" and "invention-invasion" are not merely two different terms, argues Mignolo, but refer to two very different paradigms for interpreting Latin American history.[18]

Western Tradition against Pre-Columbian Traditions

A case in point is the scholarship produced by the Spanish Jesuit José de Acosta in his *Historia Natural y Moral de las Indias*, published in 1590:

> In many ways the light of truth and reason works in them to some small degree; and so most of them acknowledge and confess a supreme Lord and Maker of all, whom the Peruvians called Virachocha, adding a very excellent name such as Pachacamac or Pachayachachic, which means the creator of heaven and earth, and Usapu, which means admirable, and other similar names. They worship him, and he was the chief god that they venerated, gazing heavenward. And the same belief exists, after their fashion, in the Mexicans. . . . Yet it has greatly astonished me that even though they do have the knowledge that I mention, *they have no word of their own with which to name God.* . . . So those who preach or write for the Indians use our Spanish *Dios.* . . . *This shows what a weak and incomplete knowledge they have of God, for they do not even know how to name him except by using our word.*[19]

17. Rivera-Pagán, *Evangelización y Violencia*, 15; my translation.
18. See Mignolo, *Idea of Latin America*.
19. José de Acosta, *Natural and Moral History of the Indies*, trans. Frances López-Morillas (Durham: Duke University Press, 2002), 256–57; emphasis added.

Acosta was, by all contemporary standards, one of the finest Christian scholars to set foot in the Americas at the beginning of the colonial era. Yet this great scholarship that brought together an appetite for objective truth, the classical disciplines of Greece and Rome, and the willingness to rigorously investigate the New World was plagued with Eurocentricism, historiographic neglect, and epistemic misrepresentation. On the one hand, Acosta's scholarship sought to give visibility and stature to the natives of the New World by conceptualizing them under a more universal history—the European. On the other hand, "its feebleness lies in its assumption that Amerindian knowledge did not count in the same way that the Greco-Latin tradition did."[20] While Acosta's account affirms certain Amerindian elements, it does so within a preconceived and neglecting historiography. This is, indeed, a Western hermeneutical pattern that has marked scholarship, church mission, and ministry since the beginning of the Americas.

Assuming that history is the horizon of epistemology, it follows that a neglecting historiography is the horizon of a demeaning epistemology. Certainly, Acosta acknowledged in Amerindian theology the categories that resembled his own tradition: "the light of truth and reason," "a supreme God," "the creator of heavens and earth." This resemblance is what made natives worthy of evangelism and Christianization. But the "recorded information in the form of pictographic images on paper, stone, and pottery, hieroglyphics, temples and pyramids used to pass down oral histories of their beliefs" was ignored, neglected, or in many cases vigorously destroyed.[21]

In short, Acosta can be identified as a proto-occidentalist theologian, perhaps the first in the Americas. Acosta's self-understanding of the Christian tradition worked against an understanding of the indigenous-local traditions. Scholarship and Christian mission that negated the indigenous-local traditions hindered the possibility of discerning how the Spirit of God was present and active in ways that were different than in the West and yet not inferior. This negation played

20. Walter Mignolo, "Introduction" to Acosta, *Natural and Moral History of the Indies*, xviii. See also Mignolo's "Introduction" to Acosta and Ivonne del Valle, "José de Acosta: Colonial Regimes for a Globalized Christian World," in *Coloniality, Religion and the Law in the Early Iberian World*, ed. Santa Arias and Raúl Marrero Fente (Nashville: Vanderbilt University, 2014).

21. See Lee M. Penyak and Walter J. Petry, *Religion in Latin America: A Documentary History* (Maryknoll: Orbis, 2006), 1–2.

into how deeply Christianity penetrated the Amerindian religious imagination (evangelism, discipleship, and mission). Indeed, to see indigenous religious practices as demonic activities has been a common assumption among Western missionaries and their disciples.

Enrique Dussel concludes that Christianity did not go deep enough into the religious imagination of the originating cultures. In his classic work, *A History of the Church in Latin America*, one of Dussel's conclusions is that a significant portion of the native population of the Americas still "longs for complete evangelization," and hence supplements the official religion with folk Catholicism. This form of Catholicism has always been present and nowadays is the majority in the Americas.[22]

Protestantism against Traditioned Catholicism in Latin America

Would these preconceived hegemonic frameworks change with the incursion of Protestantism? The short answer is not much, for at least two main reasons. First, Western Christianity never developed a functional theology of religions able to consider a wider revelatory presence of God outside Western culture:[23] (1) the apologists during early Christianity borrowed from Hellenistic sources, yet paganism was judged or ignored; (2) Augustine used Plato, but subjected every epistemology to the knowledge of Christ as the standard epistemic system; (3) Aquinas learned Aristotle through the Arabs, yet had little patience with nonbelievers and "infidels"; (4) Luther focused on purifying and reforming the church, and his anti-Semitic impulses are well documented in the last period of his life; (5) Calvin showed no desire to dialogue with or learn from other faiths; (6) John Wesley came the closest to a theology of religions by focusing on the "inward voice" (initial revelation) and

22. Dussel combats here the reductionistic concept of "mixed religions," or syncretism, by arguing that not all the layers of understanding of the indigenous people surrendered to Christian knowledge as presented by the Christendom preaching of that epoch. See Enrique D. Dussel, *A History of the Church in Latin America: Colonialism to Liberation (1492–1979)* (Grand Rapids: Eerdmans, 1981), 62–71. Adding to this, Orlando O. Espín argues that popular Catholicism is the "least invaded cultural creation of our people and the locus for the most authentic self-disclosure" ("Grace and Humanness: A Latino/a Perspective," in *We Are a People! Initiatives in Hispanic American Theology*, ed. Roberto S. Goizueta [Minneapolis: Fortress, 1992], 148).

23. Johnston, *God's Wider Presence*, 201–5.

"spiritual senses," but ended up subjecting general revelation to special revelation (Christ).

Second, the incursion of Protestantism and the political independence of the Latin American nations in the nineteenth century delayed the progress of autonomous theological thinking by bringing new imperial powers into its intellectual landscape. The political independence weakened significantly the influence of Iberian Catholicism over Latin American civic and political life, while Western Protestantism was used to build the layers of knowledge and power that yoked Latin America to a new superpower, the United States of America. After all, Latin America was ready for a different theological tone and emphasis, one able to offer progress as an exit from three centuries of colonialism, which historically had imposed tragedy, poverty, and spiritual emptiness. Consequently, a glorious theology with a triumphalist Christ—one we can find in selected biblical narratives, some aspects of creedal formulations, and Pentecostal hymnology—was passionately embraced and conceptualized as the living Christ of the *evangélicos* in diametrical opposition to the "other Christs" of the Americas, particularly the Spanish-Catholic crucified Christ. Christ has reached Latin America! (Protestants did shout).

The epistemological and ecclesiastical shift that had characterized the Protestant Reformation in Europe three centuries earlier had now set foot in the Americas—along with the excesses accumulated by the post-Reformer thinkers: to be Protestant was to be anti-Catholic and fight against all forms of popular piety that attempted to give meaning to the Roman Catholic faith by means of "idolatrous" rituals. A new epistemic element was added as well: that Christ was mediated through the Holy Spirit in the personal experience of *el culto Pentecostal* (the Pentecostal worship service). Interestingly, although there is evidence of indigenous Pentecostal revivals in South America before and at the same time as the so-called Azusa Street Revival of 1906–10, such happenings have been neglected in the normative historical accounts of Western Pentecostal Christianity.

The Spirit outside the Gate:
Uncovering an Indigenous Theology of the Spirit

A shared assumption among US Latino/a theologians holds that culture is an elemental locus of human and divine action in the theological process. What needs discernment, however, is how culture should be perceived and used as a category able to embrace both the transcendence of God's Spirit and the complexity and diversity of people's identities. Thus, we must avoid as much as possible the assumption that our modern anthropological and theological tools can objectively interpret culture or cultural practices as reflecting God's activity and character, or even human essence and purpose without conditions. We find this oversight in most modern Western theological processes— and in non-Western theologies depending on Western methods.

Un-gating the Spirit from the Western Canonical Imagination

The colonial-imperial legacy orienting modern theology begs for an understanding of tradition that is able to see the Spirit's activity prior to and beyond the Western hegemonic theological categorizations. Scripture accounts for a wider revelatory presence of God in other cultures and religions. Key biblical scenes containing non-Israelite religious sources shape the Judeo-Christian biblical imagination of the people of God: the high priest of Salem, Melchizedek, commissioning Abraham (Genesis 14); the Transjordan diviner Balaam blessing Israel (Numbers 22); Paul speaking at Mars Hill about one of the Athenians' altars referring to "an unknown god" and alluding to the words of the Greek poet Epimenides (Acts 17).[24]

Later on, early Christian believers struggled to discern the signs of the Spirit of God in the created realm. Creedal formulations attest to this discerning process, recorded, for example, in the Nicene Creed, with phrases such as *Spiritum Sanctum, Dominum et vivificatium* (the Holy Spirit, the Lord, the Giver of Life). Early Christian teachers emphasized the Spirit as a Revealer and Giver of Life. They learned and communicated this insight with fear and trembling. This insight, in itself, challenges any attempt to gate the Spirit within specific formulas, conceptualizations, or practices. Yet the threats of gnosticism, Eunomianism, the Pneumatomachi, and other traditions declared "heretical" by the religious-political establishment of the time led to a gating of the Spirit of God within confessional statements, such as the Nicene-Constantinopolitan Creed, and these statements were deemed untouchable.

24. I follow here Johnston's basic listing (*God's Wider Presence*, 203).

However, while creedal formulations were being constructed in the main cities of the empire, thousands of Christians in the deserts of Egypt and Palestine and missionary movements elsewhere were testifying to the revealing and powerful presence of the Holy Spirit, the Revealer and Giver of Life. In addition, very early in Christian history the Syriac tradition associated the Holy Spirit with the femininity of God, due in part to the Hebrew word *ruah*. This traditioning of the Spirit as "she" was subsequently replaced (or subsumed) by devotion to Mary.[25] This is to say that while creeds and conceptualizations registered important aspects of the interaction of the Spirit of God with local cultures, other traces of the Spirit were challenging the epistemic gates being constructed in the centers of imperial and ecclesial power. Thus, it is inappropriate to regard creeds and canonical artifacts as gated revelations whose keys were given only to a handful of clergy, politicians, and theologians of the Western church. It goes without saying that the so-called *filioque* clause controversy left an unhealed wound in the body of Christ precisely because of an imperial gating decision of the Latin Church. Global Christianity requires a different paradigm of dealing with the Spirit of the triune God's interaction with creation.[26]

Re-Traditioning the Spirit outside the Gate of Coloniality-Modernity

The Spirit of God has a history, comments Joel Elowsky, that can be traced in church confession with categories such as "the Inspirer and Revealer, the Lord and Giver of Life, and the Spirit's relation to the Father and the Son."[27] How dominant factions of the Western church came to use the categories of canon, creeds, and tradition with regard to the Spirit, however, says more about the gating-imperial tendencies of the Constantinian church than about the revelation of the Spirit of God itself.

When I speak in Latin America, the Caribbean, and the United

25. Joel C. Elowsky, *We Believe in the Holy Spirit*, Ancient Christian Doctrine (Downers Grove: InterVarsity Academic, 2009), xxi.

26. This is eloquently argued by Amos Yong in his contribution to this volume. See also his *Beyond the Impasse: Toward a Pneumatological Theology of Religions* (Grand Rapids: Baker Academic, 2003).

27. Elowsky, *We Believe in the Holy Spirit*, xv. See also Jürgen Moltmann, *The Spirit of Life: A Universal Affirmation* (Minneapolis: Fortress, 1992).

States on the subject of global Christianity, it is not uncommon for me to face some resistance on the basis that we are in danger of losing the legacy of the Christian tradition. More specifically, I perceive fear that the so-called shift of the center of Christianity from the global North to the global South might have adverse consequences after all, leading to a suspicion that global Christianity is not attending to orthodox ways of reflection and practice. Simultaneously, I also face a warmhearted welcome by many who are beginning to celebrate the recovering of an early Christian spirit when doing reflection and mission in different local cultural contexts. The truth is that the shift in the center of Christianity will sooner or later end the hegemony of the Western legacy, and the logic of coloniality-modernity, but not necessarily result in losing the traces of the Spirit, the Revealer and Giver of Life, and the Christian legacy itself.

The Christian tradition has been and will continue to be territorialized and deterritorialized by the Spirit of the triune God in history, which implies understanding "tradition" as a "common Christian identity narratively construed."[28] This understanding of Christian tradition is well articulated by Dale Coulter, who argues that since the beginning,

> [tradition] became embodied in the rule of faith articulated by such second-century figures as Irenaeus of Lyons, Clement of Alexandria, and Tertullian of Carthage. It did not remove the need to negotiate between local forms of inculturated Christianity, but it implicitly called for such forms to dialogue with the whole by calling parts of the common identity into question without fundamentally altering the basic contours of the narrative that God was in Christ reconciling the world.[29]

I concur with Coulter and contend that the key to the continuity of the Christian tradition does not rest on an archival-historiographic logic rooted in Western culture, but on the incarnational power of the Spirit of the triune God who reveals truth and gives life to every culture and generation everywhere. In turn, local cultures will do well to negotiate

28. Dale M. Coulter, "On Tradition, Local Traditions, and Discernment," *Pneuma* 36 (2014): 3.
29. Coulter, "On Tradition," 2.

a common Christian identity that does not negate the gift vested in their peoples' own particularities as creatures of God bearing the *imago Dei*. According to Coulter, it was through just such negotiating that the canon and the Christian tradition emerged and reemerged in the early stages of Christian history and in the history of renewal movements.

In short, what legitimates the Christian tradition must not be understood as a gate in the form of a creed, canon, hierarchy, sacrosanct succession, or enlightened culture that sees itself as the civilizing center of the world. To understand the West as the *locus theologicus* par excellence—a particular context entrusted with the treasures of the Christian faith universal—is the result of a logic of coloniality-modernity and not of divine revelation. It is the Decolonial Spirit of God in and with creation, "conscience and culture"[30]—with traces in the West in the form of Lord, Revealer, and Giver of Life—that ultimately validates any human form of Christian tradition.

Traces of the Spirit in the Americas

In this chapter I have maintained that theology develops in a particular place out of the interaction, not between the Scripture and culture, but between some version of the Christian tradition and the indigenous traditions of that place—both cultural and religious. We then must understand theological differences at the fundamental level of how we come to know about God, or in our case, the Decolonial Spirit of God and his work in and with creation (and conscience and culture). How could we apply this argument in the particular context of the Americas? I can envision three ways.

The Pacifying Spirit in Originating Cultures

Since the beginning, a neglecting historiography and a demeaning epistemology have informed Western scholarship, church mission, and ministry in the Americas, as the case of José de Acosta illustrates. Acosta saw features of Amerindian religiosity that resembled his own tradition (e.g., the light of truth and reason, a supreme God, the Creator

---

30. Johnston, *God's Wider Presence*, 190–99.

of heavens and earth), which made natives worthy of Christianization. Yet the indigenous records and oral traditions were generally ignored or destroyed. Peter and Roberta Markman observe that, throughout the development of Mesoamerican religion, "the primary meaning" of reality "is consistently expressed through the central metaphor of the mask. As Octavio Paz realized, art 'serves to open doors to the other side of reality,' and the mask through its dynamic linking of external reality to that other side of reality, the inner world of the numinous, consistently 'opened the door' from the literal to the spiritual for the peoples of Mesoamerica."[31] The logic of coloniality-modernity requires a concrete and manageable category able to define, manipulate, and represent the other in literature and research in ways that facilitate the production of knowledge, history, and the exercise of power. But a mask, Paz rightly observes, functions only as a door (not a gate) "to the other side of reality."[32]

In Mesoamerica, for instance, in the Náhuatl language, this God was called Quetzalcóatl ("Feathered Serpent"). Latin American theologian Elsa Tamez has reflected on this indigenous faith in the light of God's revelation in Scripture.[33] Quetzalcóatl, she notes, was worshiped in all the stages of Mexican history and is the supreme source of all the other, lesser powers and spirits. Especially interesting is the consistent characterization of this God as acting always on behalf of humanity, creating them, providing them corn to grow, and giving them wisdom to build homes, invent the calendar, and create art. Most surprising is the way Quetzalcóatl is shown struggling against the lord of death, even injuring himself in order to give humanity life.[34]

According to this narrative, the blood from this injury is mixed with human bones and rescues humans from the world of death. Those who have told this story across the generations confess that their continued life is due to this self-sacrifice of Quetzalcóatl. (In one version of the story other gods realize they have to model the self-sacrifice

31. Peter T. Markman and Roberta H. Markman, *Masks of the Spirit: Image and Metaphor in Mesoamerica* (Berkeley: University of California Press, 1994), xx.

32. See Octavio Paz, *El Laberinto de la Soledad y Otras Obras* (New York: Penguin, 1997), chap. 2.

33. See Elsa Tamez, "Reliving Our Histories: Racial and Cultural Revelations of God," in *New Visions for the Americas: Religious Engagement and Social Transformation*, ed. David B. Batstone (Minneapolis: Fortress, 1993), 33–56.

34. Tamez, "Reliving Our Histories," 37.

of Quetzalcóatl so that life in the universe can continue.) Tamez concludes: "these are the revelations of the God of life, the God who understands, a compassionate being who gives life to God's creatures."[35] It may well be that the Spirit of God, Giver of Life, was masked in local expressions of Quetzalcóatl for the natives of this context. Jojo Fung makes a similar case for a comparative pneumatology by focusing on the parallels between the *ruah-elohim* conception of the Christian tradition and those of the Creator Spirit–Grand Spirit found in ancestral spiritualities of Latin America, the United States, Australia, New Zealand, and Canada.[36]

Theological attention to these masks might be the key to understanding how certain indigenous cultures in the preconquest period were able to assimilate important elements of Western Christianity after the European conquest and give them local meanings that fit their epistemic universe. If I can support this claim, then I can establish my case for a pneumatological continuity, rather than rupture, where we can discern the traces of the Spirit in the Americas outside the gate of coloniality-modernity. A notable case in favor of this argument comes from the colonial history of the *Tira de Tepechpan*, a minor *altepetl* (city-state) in central Mexico.

This pictographic artifact is the result of two hundred years of artistic interpretation of history, whose main goal was to "establish the antiquity, autonomy, prestige" of the political, religious, and intellectual traditions of the patron city.[37] Lori Boornazian Diel, working through the interpretation of the *Tira de Tepechpan*, describes the historical, political, and religious implications of Painter A's work:

> The entrance of the Spaniards into Tepechpan is depicted with a symbolic representation revealing the new entanglement of indigenous and European art forms. Above the year 1 Reed (1519), Painter A drew a cross and dove floating towards the time line. . . . As European conventions for Christianity, the cross and dove easily transferred to Aztec pictorial writings as a hieroglyphic construction signifying Catholicism and the Holy Spirit. . . . The message is that Christian-

35. Tamez, "Reliving Our Histories," 39.

36. See Jojo M. Fung, "A Post Colonial-Mission-Territorial Hermeneutics for a Liberation Shamanic Pneumatology," *Voices* 36 (April–September 2013): 123–47.

37. See Lori Boornazian Diel, *The Tira de Tepechpan: Negotiating Place under Aztec and Spanish Rule* (Austin: University of Texas Press, 2008), 1.

ity arrived quickly and peacefully in Tepechpan. Meanwhile, a bru-
tal military conquest was unfolding in Tenochtitlan and would last
much longer.[38]

Let us avoid unnecessary technicalities here and pay attention to how
history and meaning are produced by indigenous intellectuals in preconquest and colonial times. To begin, the preconceived Western idea
that originating cultures lacked aesthetic capacities, intellectual traditions, and critical thinking is immediately challenged.

The fact that Christian traditional symbols, such as the dove and
the cross, are incorporated into local narratives, not innocently, but
exercising a degree of historical manipulation in order to provide an
account of what happened in Tepechpan in contrast to Tenochtitlan
is of theological interest. Obviously, the history of Tepechpan takes
precedence over that of Tenochtitlan in this representation. Second, a
peaceful encounter between this indigenous community and the Span-
iards is suggested, while Tenochtitlan is portrayed as a place of chaos
and destruction.

Independently of the accuracy of this historical interpretation, just
as in early Christian contexts, we can see how indigenous intellectuals
are negotiating epistemic meanings with a particular version of Christian tradition (Iberian Roman Catholicism), hence facilitating a new
version of indigenous Christianity. The dove symbolizes peace in European Christian history, and Painter A knows it and incorporates it into
the new historical narrative of the *Mexica* community immediately after the conquest. The dove represents the Spirit of God, Revealer and
Giver of Life, who territorializes as the Pacifier Spirit.

Traditional Christian rationalities in the West reduced the understanding of the Spirit to the invocation of the Spirit (epiclesis) in the
Eucharist (Roman Catholicism) and illumination in biblical interpretation and proclamation (Protestantism). This resulted in an epistemic
and pneumatological rupture or discontinuity with regard to the religious imaginations of the originating cultures, which included alternative rationalities for understanding spirits and rituals.[39] Consequently,
a different paradigm is discerned in Amerindian cultures and hybrid

38. Diel, *The Tira de Tepechpan*, 73.
39. I elaborate more on these Western rationalities in my article "Eucaristía de
Comunión: Sacramento de la Iglesia Glocal," *Vida y Pensamiento* 33, no. 1 (2013): 125–59.

communities. Once we take this "outside the gate" approach, the Spirit of God, the Revealer and Giver of Life, can be recognized through the masks of local spiritual powers such as Quetzalcóatl. This might be the door to understanding other masks and discerning a pneumatological correlation among different traditions within and outside the Americas.

The Decolonial Spirit in Popular Religiosity: Folk Catholicism

We have always known in the Americas that there are two churches: the official and the popular. While the official version of Roman Catholicism has promoted epistemic rupture with indigenous traditions, the popular (folk) version of Latin American Catholicism has sought continuity. This is true not just of Roman Catholicism but of Western Protestantism as well. I address Pentecostalism next. For now, let us remember Enrique Dussel's conclusion that a significant portion of the native population of the Americas still "longs for complete evangelization," hence supplementing the official religion with folk Catholicism that has always been present. Popular Catholicism maintained a degree of continuity with indigenous traditions through devotion to Mary, in many local forms. The most significant is Our Lady of Guadalupe, "la Emperatriz de las Américas" (the Empress of the Americas).

Virgilio Elizondo, considered the father of US Catholic Latino/a theology, interprets the significance of Our Lady of Guadalupe in the Americas. Our Lady of Guadalupe arguably appeared in 1531 on a rural hillside in Tepeyac (Mexico) to a native by the name of Juan Diego, and asked him to be her messenger to the Holy Church. In the words of Elizondo: "The apparition marked a spiritual beginning in America. Out of the chaos of the moment, a new people would emerge through the process of *mestizaje*, the mixing of people, biologically, culturally and religiously. In the midst of chaos, darkness and suffering, the Word became our flesh and dwelt among us through the appearance of the *Mestiza* Virgin of Guadalupe."[40] It is lamentable that for almost two centuries Protestants in Latin America and the US diaspora have not

40. Virgilio Elizondo, "Our Lady of Guadalupe, Gift of a Loving God," Duke University, http://www.faithandleadership.com-content-virgilio-elizondo-our-lady-guadalupe-gift-loving-god, accessed October 30, 2014.

been able to figure out what to do with Our Lady of Guadalupe—apart from demonizing her devotion. Elizondo, a popular speaker in US Protestant settings, usually corrects some of the Protestant misunderstandings by pointing out that Our Lady of Guadalupe is not a soteriological artifact to substitute for Jesus Christ, but "a precious gift of the infinite love of our heavenly Father."[41] We notice here a pneumatological resonance with the Pentecost event (Acts 2), where the Decolonial Spirit is the gift of love from the heavenly Father through which the church, a new creation in Christ, is born.

The Healing Spirit in Popular Religiosity: Pentecostalism

We also find traces of the Spirit in the continuities between the originating cultures and Pentecostalism. For instance, we find the gift of prophecy to be a central component of ancient Mayan religion. Munro Edmonson tells us that Mayan religious symbolism was readily accessible to all Mayans. Yet within this mystical religion Mayans needed "faith in the specialists who are trained to interpret its complexities," and the Mayan peoples "shared a genuine prophetic tradition."[42] This prophetic tradition had a deep impact on how society functioned. Prophecies could be used to confirm old traditions or establish new ones. Marcelino Tapia reports that among the Guaranies and Tainos a chief could maintain his status as long as he continued to serve the community. Part of his service included prophesying, interpreting dreams, and singing.[43] Edmonson makes clear that the Mayans did not practice some sort of blind faith, for "beyond the priests lies the final test of their knowledge: the test of time."[44] Like the Guarani, the Mayans would not hesitate to replace priests and prophets found to be a sham.

When referring to Pentecostalism per se, Samuel Solivan makes

41. Elizondo, "Our Lady of Guadalupe."

42. Munro S. Edmonson, "The Mayan Faith," in *South and Meso-American Native Spirituality*, ed. Gary H. Gossen (New York: Crossroad, 1993), 73, 74.

43. Marcelino Tapia R., "La Antropología, la Espiritualidad Indígena y los Desafíos para la Misión de la Iglesia en el Siglo 21," in *Espiritualidades Indígenas, Interculturalidad y Misión Integral*, ed. Lourdes Cordero and Marcelo Vargas (Buenos Aires: Kairos, 2010), 47.

44. Tapia R., "La Antropología," 73.

an important observation: one of the sources of Pentecostal theology is the "discerning witness of the community of faith." In addition, when an individual acts unethically or claims to have received revelation from the Spirit, observes Solivan, the community immediately acts to protect its integrity by quickly correcting "the individual in light of the Word and the tradition of that community."[45] It appears that Mayas, Guaranies, Tainos, and Pentecostals all hold to the scriptural instruction to test the spirits (1 John 4:1).

A form of the gift of divine healing was also present in preconquest communities. Ancient Andean religions practiced divine healing rituals using native herbs, part of an understanding of *Pachamama* (mother earth), who provided sustenance and health, as long as natives remained grateful to and in harmony with nature.[46] Mayan faith included a strong belief in the healing powers of the priest, although it was always tested. There were Mayans who helped cure ailments with herbs, and midwives attended to pregnant women, but the priest was the one with the power to heal serious illnesses. The ability to cure the ill gave evidence of the priest's personal power, a power given by the gods.[47] The same approach to the health and well-being of the tribe is seen in the Amazon, where normal ailments such as the common cold and coughs could be treated with herbs and home remedies; serious or abnormal illnesses could only be tackled by the *pajé*—an Amazonian healer.[48] The correlation between ancestral healers and Pentecostal healers is hard to miss here.

The shamans in the Mapuche religion had similar healing rituals and understood illness as attacks from evil spirits. In order to achieve healing the Mapuche shaman often had to perform special rituals that required singing, trances, and divination. While the Mapuche shaman underwent rigorous training under a respected shaman, power was only given by the supernatural world, and it

45. Samuel Solivan, *The Spirit, Pathos and Liberation* (Sheffield: Sheffield Academic, 1998), 106.

46. Darío López, "Interculturalidad y Misión Integral," in *Espiritualidades Indígenas, Interculturalidad y Misión Integral,* ed. Cordero and Vargas, 73.

47. Edmonson, "The Mayan Faith," 79.

48. R. Andrew Chestnut, "Exorcising the Demons of Deprivation: Divine Healing and Conversion in Brazilian Pentecostalism," in *Global Pentecostal and Charismatic Healing,* ed. Candy Gunther Brown (New York: Oxford University Press, 2011), 179.

was confirmed through dreams, visions, or omens.[49] Again we see parallels between the Mapuche shamanic traditions of Chile and the prophetic Pentecostal movement.

The Latino Pentecostal theologian Eldin Villafañe, in his *Introducción al Pentecostalismo: Manda Fuego, Señor,* describes Pentecostalism in the Americas as a complex, multifaceted religious movement with multiracial, multicultural, and multiethnic dimensions.[50] In addition to its Western emphasis on the Fourfold Gospel (Christ saves, baptizes, heals, and is coming soon), Pentecostalism implicitly considers the worship service as the *locus theologicus* (the worship service is the theology, and the theology is the worship service). This socioreligious configuration, among other things, has enabled Pentecostalism to offer indigenous-local communities in the Americas a degree of continuity in their experience of the Spirit as Creator Spirit–Grand Spirit and the Spirit of the Christian God, the Revealer and Giver of Life—worshiped in community. We also see clear correlations between significant religious institutions: healers and shamans (Amerindians) and apostles and prophets (Pentecostalism).

Further Reading

Batstone, David B. *New Visions for the Americas: Religious Engagement and Social Transformation.* Minneapolis: Fortress, 1993.

Cordero, Lourdes, and Marcelo Vargas, eds. *Espiritualidades Indígenas: Interculturalidad Y Misión Integral.* Consulta Teológica 2008. La Paz: Ediciones Kairos, 2010.

Dyrness, William C., and Oscar García-Johnson. *Theology without Borders: Introduction to Global Conversations.* Grand Rapids: Baker, 2015.

Dussel, Enrique D. *A History of the Church in Latin America: Colonialism to Liberation (1492–1979).* Grand Rapids: Eerdmans, 1981.

Gossen, Gary H., and Miguel León Portilla. *South and Meso-American Native Spirituality: From the Cult of the Feathered Serpent to the Theology of Liberation.* World Spirituality. New York: Crossroad, 1993.

49. Louis C. Faron, "The Mapuche of Chile: Their Religious Beliefs and Rituals," in *South and Meso-American Native Spirituality,* ed. Gossen, 361, 362.

50. See Eldin Villafañe, *Introducción al Pentecostalismo: Manda Fuego, Señor* (Nashville: Abingdon, 2012).

Johnston, Robert K. *God's Wider Presence: Reconsidering General Revelation.* Grand Rapids: Baker, 2014.

Mignolo, Walter. *The Idea of Latin America.* Blackwell Manifestos. Malden: Blackwell, 2005.

Penyak, Lee M., and Walter J. Petry. *Religion in Latin America: A Documentary History.* Maryknoll: Orbis, 2006.

CHAPTER 8

The Holy Spirit: Power for Life and Hope

C. René Padilla

ABSTRACT

Until fairly recently, theological reflection on the person and work of the Holy Spirit was never given much attention on the part of evangelical theologians. There was, of course, a sort of implicit theology present especially in the Pentecostal movement, strongly influenced by North American fundamentalism. This chapter attempts to show that this situation has significantly changed in the past few decades with the emergence of new voices (mainly but not exclusively Pentecostal) that are exploring the subject in depth. The basic focus in Latin American pneumatology is on the Holy Spirit as the source of power for practical life (including the mission of the church) and of hope, especially in the context of poverty and oppression.

At the second global conference of the International Fellowship of Mission Theologians (INFEMIT),[1] held in Tlayacapan, Mexico, from May 28 to June 1, 1984, thirty-seven theologians from the Majority World dealt with a subject that they regarded as central to the life and mission of the church all over the world: life in the Spirit. The words with which

1. INFEMIT is an international network of evangelical mission theologians representing the Latin American Theological Fellowship, the African Theological Fellowship, and Partnership in Mission Asia. The first INFEMIT conference was held in Bangkok, Thailand, on March 22–25, 1982. The proceedings, edited by Vinay Samuel and Chris Sugden, were published under the title *Sharing Jesus in the Two-Thirds World* (Grand Rapids: Eerdmans, 1985).

C. René Padilla

Orlando Costas introduced one of the plenary papers read at that conference are as relevant today as they were at that time:

> In the Two-thirds World—that part of contemporary life representing a religious and cultural mosaic of very poor, very weak and very oppressed people—the most significant trait of Christian experience is life in the Spirit. Wherever one goes in the Two-thirds World, one finds signs of the Spirit: a growing number of Christians and of new churches . . . joy in the midst of suffering, and a challenging hope in a context of death.[2]

Power for life and hope are made possible by the presence of the Holy Spirit in the Christian experience of people living in a world deeply affected by powerlessness and hopelessness. Costas's statement synthesizes the basic thrust of the official *Tlayacapan Declaration* that emerged from that INFEMIT conference and especially underlines the Spirit's ministry among people living in "contexts of massive poverty, feudal oppression, bureaucratic corruption, and ethnic and class discrimination."[3]

Like the *Tlayacapan Declaration*, I acknowledge that the work of the Spirit is present and visible in the new life that he imparts to every person living under the lordship of Jesus Christ regardless of socioeconomic status. For two reasons, however, I have chosen to deal in this chapter with the work of the Spirit as the source of power for life and hope, especially among the poor. The first reason is that, although there is plenty of material on this subject,[4] this perspective is oftentimes neglected in favor of other perspectives that are commonly regarded as more closely related to the work of the Spirit, such as his work of sanctification and charismatic gifts.

2. Orlando E. Costas, "La vida en el Espíritu," *Boletín Teológico* 18, nos. 21–22 (June 1986): 7; my translation.

3. *Tlayacapan Declaration*, *Boletin Teológico* 18, nos. 21–22 (June 1986) 110; my translation.

4. See, for instance, the full treatment of this subject by Gordon D. Fee, *God's Empowering Presence: The Holy Spirit in the Letters of Paul* (Peabody: Hendrickson, 1994), esp. 864–95; Clark H. Pinnock, *Flame of Love: A Theology of the Holy Spirit* (Downers Grove: InterVarsity, 1996), esp. 185–214. For a Roman Catholic perspective, see Carlos I. González, *El Espíritu del Señor que da la vida: Teología del Espíritu Santo* (México City: Conferencia del Episcopado Mexicano, 1998), and José Comblin, *O Espiritu no mundo* (Petrópolis: Voces, 1978).

The second reason is that, at least in Latin America, the large majority of people who vividly experience the presence of the Spirit (most of them Pentecostal) as the source of power for life and hope in the midst of dire poverty and oppression are not the sort of people who reflect and write on this subject. As José Míguez-Bonino has put it, "The Latin American evangelical tradition is strongly pneumatic. As expressed in the 'revivals' or the 'holiness movement' in the nineteenth century and in Pentecostalism in the twentieth century, the adscription to 'the work of the Spirit' has been very basic. And yet, none of these movements has developed a true theology of the Spirit."[5]

As we move into the proposed subject, we need to take into account that the work of the Spirit is inseparable from the work of God the Father and the work of God the Son. In the God that was revealed in Jesus Christ unity and diversity are combined in such a way that in all that the Spirit does there is a perfect correlation and interpenetration derived from the *perichoretic*[6] communion that characterizes the trinitarian unity of Father, Son, and Holy Spirit. This does not deny the distinctive action of the Holy Spirit, but it points to the fact that such action is properly understood when seen as action of the triune God. Taking this into account, we focus first on the work of the Spirit of God in creation and history, then on his role in Jesus's mission, and finally on his work in the life and mission of the church.

5. José Míguez-Bonino, *Rostros del Protestantismo latinoamericano* (Buenos Aires: Nueva Creación, 1995), 121; my translation. This book was translated into English and published under the title *Faces of Latin American Protestantism* (Grand Rapids: Eerdmans, 1997). It must be added, however, that since that book was published, a few Latin American Pentecostal theologians have at least in part filled the gap with commendable theological works on the Spirit. See, for instance, Bernardo Campos, *De la Reforma protestante a la pentecostalidad de la Iglesia: Debate sobre el Pentecostalismo en América Latina* (Quito: Ediciones CLAI, 1997); Leopoldo Sánchez, *Pneumatología: El Espíritu Santo y la espiritualidad de la Iglesia* (St. Louis, MO: Editorial Concordia, 2005); Darío López R., *La fiesta del Espíritu: Espiritualidad y celebración Pentecostal* (Lima: Ediciones Puma, 2006), and *Pentecostalismo y misión integral: Teología del Espíritu, teología de la vida* (Lima: Ediciones Puma, 2008); Daniel Chiquete and Luis Orellana, eds., *Voces del Pentecostalismo Latinoamericano III: Identidad, teología, historia* (Concepción: Red Latinoamericana de Estudios Pentecostales, 2009).

6. This adjective is derived from *perichorēsis*, a Greek term coined in theology in the sixth century to refer to the union of the Father with the Son and the Spirit.

C. René Padilla

The Spirit of God in Creation and History

The first reference to God's *ruah* is in Genesis 1:2, which the NIV renders: "Now the earth was formless and empty, darkness was over the surface of the deep, and the Spirit of God was hovering over the waters." Both the translation of *ruah* by "Spirit" and the use of a capital S at the beginning of the term suggest that the translators opted for a reading of the text in which the word *ruah* refers to the Spirit of God, the third person of the Trinity. This interpretation may be rejected as an anachronism because it attributes to the author of the text a trinitarian concept of God without taking into account that the concept of God as the triune God did not take shape before the coming of Jesus Christ. The least that can be said in response to that objection is that the reality of the Trinity precedes the human experience of it, concerning which the New Testament bears witness. This experience broadens the horizon for the interpretation of *ruah* in the Old Testament and thus contributes to the construction of the basis for the Christian doctrine of God as the triune God, a doctrine whose essential ingredients are found in the New Testament.[7]

If the NIV interpretation of *ruah* in Genesis 1:2 as referring to the Spirit of God is accepted, this is the first reference in Scripture to the Spirit's role in relation to creation. The verb that the NIV translates as "hovering" connotes the idea of flying round about—the action that, according to Deuteronomy 32:11, God performs in order to protect his people in the desert "like an eagle that stirs up its nest and hovers over its young." The image points to the Spirit of God spreading his wings over the surface of the water and escorting the whole process of creation through which the chaos is transformed into the cosmos (order) and out of the darkness emerge the multiple forms of existence that constitute the universe. Thus, right from the first chapter of the Bible it becomes clear that the Spirit's action is not limited to the "spiritual" sphere but includes material reality, the stage for human history. The whole of creation, both material and immaterial, is the result of God's action, in the power of the Holy Spirit, through his Word—the same Word that later on will become flesh and make his dwelling among us in the person of Jesus Christ (John 1:14). There is no basis here for a

7. Cf. Matt. 28:19; 1 Cor. 12:4–6; 2 Cor. 13:14; 2 Thess. 2:13–14; Titus 3:4–6; 1 Peter 1:2; Heb. 6:4; Jude 20–21; Rev. 1:4–5.

Manichean dualism that places spiritual reality over against material reality and relates the former with Good—Light—and the latter with Evil—Darkness. According to Scripture, when God's creative work was finished "God saw that all that he had made [including material reality], and it was very good" (Gen. 1:31).

All of created reality has the purpose of reflecting God's glory, and the work of the Spirit is oriented toward the fulfillment of that purpose. In both the original as well as in the new creation—the topic of the history of salvation—everything proceeds from the Father through the Son in the power of the Spirit, and everything returns to the Father in glory through the Son in the power of the Spirit. The Spirit who was "hovering over the waters" during the first creation was the same Spirit of holiness through whom Jesus Christ our Lord was "declared with power to be the Son of God by his resurrection from the dead" (Rom. 1:4) and will also be the Spirit through whom, in the final stage of creation, God will give life to the mortal bodies of those in whom he lives (Rom. 8:11). As in the case of Jesus Christ's ministry, the Spirit's ministry has cosmic dimensions.

This biblical perspective on the work of the Spirit in connection with creation raises a number of questions with regard to Christian involvement in society in relation to issues that the majority of Christian believers everywhere generally regard as merely "secular." If the work of the Spirit of God is limited to the sphere of redemption and the church, those "worldly" issues have no place in the Christian agenda. If, on the contrary, the intermediary God is present in creation and history, all issues that affect human beings, regardless of race, sex, or socioeconomic status in the present world, become a matter of Christian concern. The *Tlayacapan Declaration* on this subject is quite relevant:

> The Spirit's creative work can be seen in all the spheres of life— social, political, economic, cultural, ecological, biological, and religious. It can be seen in anything that awakens sensitivity to the needs of people—a sensitivity that builds more just and peaceful communities and societies and that makes possible for people to live with more freedom to make responsible choices for the sake of a more abundant life. It can be seen in anything that leads people to sacrifice on behalf of the common good and for the ecological wellbeing of the Earth; to opt for the poor, the ostracized, and the oppressed, by living in solidarity with them for the sake of their

uplift and liberation; and to build love relationships and institutions that reflect the values of the Kingdom of God. These are "life sacraments" that glorify God and are made possible only by the power of the Holy Spirit.[8]

An outstanding value of this statement is that, at a time when ecological topics were almost completely ignored by evangelical Christians, it included ecology and "the ecological wellbeing of the Earth" among the spheres of life in which "the Spirit's creative work can be seen." Since the *Tlayacapan Declaration* was issued, what Bob Goudzwaard[9] called "ecological vulnerability" has increased to such a degree that the very survival of planet Earth is under threat. The damaging effects that corporate capitalism has produced on a global scale can hardly be exaggerated. Among these effects are the depletion of the ozone layer, acid rain, loss of biological diversity, toxic chemical wastes, deterioration of agriculture, destruction of human health, deforestation, the problem of energy supply, and the one effect that perhaps more than any other places a big question mark regarding the future of life on planet Earth: global climate change.

Space does not allow a detailed discussion of the huge impact that climate change is having on the poor. Suffice it to say that, beyond doubt, the sector of the population most deeply affected by the present ecological collapse consists of the people at the bottom of the social scale, commonly regarded as nonpersons. As Pope Francis in his encyclical *Laudate si: On Care for Our Common Home* has rightly stated, "Today . . . we have to realize that a true ecological approach *always* becomes a social debate on the environment, so as to hear both *the cry of the earth and the cry of the poor*."[10] In light of this dreadful double cry, one of the greatest challenges that we Christians face today is a rediscovery of the ecological dimension of God's mission in which we are called to participate on the basis of the recognition that the Spirit of God is active in creation and history. As John Taylor has put it, "The Spirit of God is

8. *Tlayacapan Declaration*, 106; my translation. Cf. John Taylor, *The Go-Between God: The Holy Spirit and the Christian Mission* (London: SCM, 1972), 16–17.

9. Bob Goudzwaard, *Capitalism and Progress: Diagnosis of Western Society* (Toronto: Wedge, 1979), 136.

10. *Laudate Si: On Care for Our Common Home*, chap. V, sec. 49. On this subject, see my chapter entitled "Globalization, Ecology and Poverty," in *Creation in Crisis: Christian Perspectives on Sustainability*, ed. Robert S. White (London: SPCK, 2009).

ever at work in nature, in history and in human living, and wherever there is a flagging or corruption or self-destruction of God's handiwork, he is present to renew and energize and create again. Whenever faith in the Holy Spirit is strong, creation and redemption are seen as one continuous process."[11]

The Spirit of God in Jesus's Mission

From the perspective of the Synoptic Gospels, Jesus is the archetype of the man who has been anointed by the Spirit of God in order to fulfill the mission that God has committed to him. Several New Testament passages explicitly refer to the close relation between the Spirit's action and the events through which Jesus accomplished redemption: his incarnation (Matt. 1:18; Luke 1:35), his earthly ministry (Luke 4:18), his crucifixion (Heb. 9:14), his resurrection (Rom. 1:4), and his ascension (Eph. 1:19b–23).

Before the initiation of his earthly ministry, when Jesus was baptized by John the Baptist, the Spirit descended on him "in bodily form like a dove. And a voice came from heaven: 'You are my Son, whom I love; with you I am well pleased'" (Luke 3:22; cf. Matt. 3:17; Mark 1:11). This narrative is followed by the description of the temptation in the desert. The Synoptic Gospels mention that "Jesus was led into the desert to be tempted by the devil" (Matt. 4:1; Mark 1:12; Luke 4:1). Both the baptism and the temptation are part of Jesus's preparation for his earthly ministry. Both events are explicitly related to the Spirit's action, and the Gospel of Luke mentions the Spirit again with reference to the initiation of that ministry: "Jesus returned to Galilee in the power of the Spirit, and news about him spread through the whole countryside" (4:14). Note the connection that this text establishes between the Holy Spirit and Jesus's Galilean option[12]—the option for the marginalized sector of the population living in Palestine at the time. Jesus, who has been anointed as the Son of God and a prophet, goes

---

11. Taylor, *The Go-Between God*, 27.

12. Cf. Orlando Costas, "The Evangelistic Legacy of Jesus: A Perspective from the Galilean Periphery," chap. 4 of *Liberating News: A Theology of Contextual Evangelization* (Grand Rapids: Eerdmans, 1989), 49–70. According to Costas, "Galilee is the place where Jesus established his messianic credentials, built the base of the messianic community, and began to experience his messianic sufferings for the world" (55).

from town to town throughout Galilee, "teaching in their synagogues, preaching the good news of the kingdom, and healing every disease and sickness among the people" (Matt. 4:23; cf. 9:35). Clearly, in Jesus's case the anointing of the Spirit is not a subjective or ecstatic experience, but an experience of the Spirit of power for life and hope related to his public ministry, much of which is dedicated to the most vulnerable sector of the population. This observation is ratified by Jesus's manifesto at the synagogue of Nazareth, at the beginning of his ministry, according to Luke 4:18–19:

> The Spirit of the Lord is on me,
> because he has anointed me
>   to preach good news to the poor.
> He has sent me to proclaim freedom for the prisoners
>   and recovery of sight for the blind,
> to release the oppressed,
> to proclaim the year of the Lord's favor.

Space does not allow a full analysis of this passage, but the following observations are relevant here. In the first place, the opening reference to the Spirit must be viewed in light of the definition of Jesus's mission: the purpose of the anointing of the Spirit is the fulfillment of Jesus's messianic mission. An important antecedent of New Testament pneumatology is the relation of God's *ruah* with two Old Testament figures: the Messiah and the suffering Servant of the Lord. The prophet Isaiah foresees the coming of David's descendant, "from the stump of Jesse," on whom the *ruah* of the Lord—"the Spirit of wisdom and of understanding, the Spirit of counsel and of power, the Spirit of knowledge and of the fear of the Lord"—will rest (Isa. 11:1–2). In line with this prophetic vision of the suffering Servant of the Lord, Jesus is anointed by the Spirit in order to fulfill his messianic role. For him, the Spirit's anointing and the mission are inseparable.

In the second place, the mission of the Messiah in the power of the Spirit is oriented toward the most vulnerable persons in society: the poor, the prisoners, the blind, the oppressed. The passage read at the synagogue in Nazareth is Isaiah 61:1–2, in which the prophet addresses a group of disappointed Jews shortly after the exile. The quotation, however, includes an additional phrase taken from Isaiah 58:6, "to release the oppressed," which in its original context has definite social connotations. Israel's oppressed are those who, feeling totally unable to cover their basic needs, have sold themselves as slaves. The only hope for them, as for all who are in positions of disadvantage in society, is the cancellation of their debts and their liberation from oppression. As Brueggemann has pointed out in relation to this passage, "the verbs of deliverance refuse to accept as a given any circumstance of oppression."[13]

In the third place, Jesus was convinced that his ministry was to promote radical socioeconomic changes big enough to be regarded as signs of the coming of a new era of justice and peace—"the year of the Lord's favor," the Jubilee year (cf. Leviticus 25)—a metaphor of the messianic era initiated in history by Jesus Christ,[14] in other words, the kingdom of God. Both the reference to Isaiah 61:1–2—one of the songs of the Servant of the Lord in Isaiah—and the arrival of the year of the Lord's favor give to Jesus's ministry an eschatological note. In fact, Jesus's claim is that in his own person and work the Old Testament messianic promises are being fulfilled. What Jesus is announcing is nothing less than the arrival of a new age in human history. Anointed by the Spirit of God, the Messiah is the agent of eschatology in the process of fulfillment. According to Judaism at that time, the Spirit of God had departed from this world and his return would bring in the fulfillment of messianic expectations. Jesus's announcement, therefore, must be understood as the affirmation of the beginning of a new age of justice by the power of the Spirit manifested in his own person and work.

Jesus's own ministry, synthetically described throughout the Gospels, provides elements for understanding his programmatic Nazareth manifesto: he focuses his ministry on the needy not only from a physical and economic perspective but also from a social and spiritual dimension, according to the will of God. It is evident that his mission includes the restoration of harmony of people with God, with each other, and with creation. It is, in one word, a *shalom* mission. His presence, his actions, and his words are signs of the kingdom of God, concrete manifestations of the work of the Holy Spirit in the age of fulfillment. His words in Matthew 12:28 point in that direction: "[If] I drive

---

13. Walter Brueggemann, *Theology of the Old Testament: Testimony, Dispute, Advocacy* (Minneapolis: Fortress, 1997), 208.

14. Cf. Robert B. Sloan Jr., *The Favorite Year of the Lord: A Study of Jubilee Theology in the Gospel of Luke* (Austin: Scholars, 1977).

out demons by the Spirit of God, then the kingdom of God has come upon you."[15] The Spirit is God's eschatological gift that makes "the year of the Lord's favor" a present reality through the person and work of Jesus Christ—the embodiment of the prophetic hope not just for his disciples, but for the multitudes that are attracted by his ministry.

In fact, although much of Jesus's ministry is dedicated to his disciples, especially to the twelve that he chose to train as his apostles,[16] it is by no means restricted to them. At times he is so pressed by the crowds who gather around him that "he and his disciples were not even able to eat" (Mark 3:20). The Gospel of Matthew provides the key to understanding Jesus's unwanted popularity: "When he saw the crowds, *he had compassion on them*, because they were harassed and helpless, like sheep without a shepherd" (Matt. 9:36; emphasis added). Already in Old Testament times God had revealed himself as a God full of compassion for the poor and the oppressed, "a parent of the orphan, the widows' champion . . . [who] gives the friendless a home and brings the prisoner safe and sound" (Ps. 68:5, 6). The God who reveals himself through Jesus as God's Messiah is this God-man of boundless compassion who was anointed by the Spirit to be the source of power for life and hope, especially among the poor. As Gustavo Gutiérrez has put it, "The works on behalf of the poor and the needy identify Jesus as the Messiah."[17]

The Spirit of God in the Mission of the Church

The Promise of the Holy Spirit

The Holy Spirit who is active in Jesus's mission is also active in the life and mission of the church. Already in the Old Testament there are traces of God's promise that at the end of times the Holy Spirit's ministry will not be limited to a select group (i.e., Israel) but will be extended

15. Note that in the parallel passage in Luke 11:20 "the Spirit of God" is replaced by "the finger of God."

16. A classical work on this subject is one that was originally published in 1871 but has endured the test of time as is the case of few theological works in the history of the church: A. B. Bruce, *The Training of the Twelve* (Grand Rapids: Kregel, 1971).

17. Gustavo Gutiérrez, *Beber en su propio pozo* (Salamanca: Ediciones Sígueme, 1984), 60; my translation.

to the whole people of God regardless of ethnic background. Ezekiel 36:26–27 and Joel 2:18–32 deserve special mention as two passages that are in the background of New Testament teaching on this subject. The prophet Ezekiel foresees a new era in which Israel will receive a heart inclined to obey God's commandments, that is, "a new heart," "a heart of flesh" in place of their "heart of stone," a heart that will open the way for the enactment of a "new covenant" and God's promise: "you will be my people, and I will be your God" (36:26–29). The fulfillment of this promise, reiterated by Jeremiah (chaps. 31–33), will be mediated by God's *ruah*. According to the prophet Joel, the messianic outpouring of God's *ruah* will not be limited to Israel. God's promise is embracing: "And afterward, I will pour out my Spirit on all people. Your sons and daughters will prophesy, your old men will dream dreams, your young men will see visions. Even on my servants, both men and women, I will pour out my Spirit in those days" (2:28–29). The sphere of action of God's *ruah* includes men and women, young and old. No one is excluded. This promise is the climax of a whole series of elements that, beginning with verse 18, are combined in order to give a vision of the salvation that God will bring into effect for his people. Joel brings together all the basic elements of the spirituality that result from the Spirit's action in human life and can be synthesized in love for God and love for one's neighbor. This is the spirituality that Jesus Christ confirms in his ministry and his teaching as well as in his lifestyle. It is also the spirituality that the church needs for its life and mission.

This promise becomes clearer in the preaching of John the Baptist, the forerunner of the Messiah, who defines the difference between his own ministry and that of Jesus in the following terms: "I baptize you with water. But one more powerful than I will come, the thongs of whose sandals I am not worthy to untie. He will baptize you with the Holy Spirit and with fire" (Luke 3:16; cf. Matt. 3:11; Mark 1:8). In the final chapter of his Gospel, Luke returns to John the Baptist's announcement by quoting Jesus's words to his disciples right before his ascension: "I am going to send you what my Father has promised; but stay in the city until you have been clothed with power from on high" (24:49). The reference to the Spirit is not explicit, but it seems clear that the content of the Father's promise to which these words refer is the outpouring of the Spirit with which the disciples will be "clothed with power from on high." The same promise made by Jesus to his followers appears again at the beginning of the book of Acts, this time with an explicit reference to the Holy Spirit: "Do not leave Jerusalem, but wait for the gift my Father promised, which you have heard me speak about. For John baptized with water, but in a few days you will be baptized with the Holy Spirit" (1:4b–5). God's promises are many, but this one is the Father's promise par excellence.

As we will see further on, Pentecost marks the fulfillment of this promise of Jesus to his disciples. On the basis of the two passages that have been quoted, however, it is clear that this promise has implications for God's mission: it is closely related to the extension of the gospel to all nations. This is made evident by several expressions that are repeated in the context of the two passages and suggest a missiology that takes as its starting point the outpouring of the Spirit: "witnesses" (Luke 24:48 and Acts 1:8), "power" (Luke 24:49 and Acts 1:8), and "to all nations" and "to the ends of the earth" (Luke 24:47; Acts 1:8).

Jesus's words in Acts 1:8 are of special importance with regard to the role of the Spirit in relation to God's mission through the church: "But you will receive power when the Holy Spirit comes on you; and you will be my witnesses in Jerusalem, and in all Judea and Samaria, and to the ends of the earth." This is Jesus's response to a question that his disciples have asked him: "Lord, are you at this time going to restore the kingdom to Israel?" (1:6)—a question that shows that the disciples have not given up the nationalistic messianic aspirations that apparently encouraged them to follow Jesus from the beginning. Jesus's project, however, is not the reestablishment of Israel's kingdom, but the formation of a new humanity in which God's purpose for human life and for all of creation will be fulfilled. His disciples will participate in that project as "witnesses" who, beginning in Jerusalem, will spread the good news of the kingdom "to the ends of the earth." And for that purpose they will receive the power of the Holy Spirit.

Therefore, what we have in Acts 1:8 is not a missionary mandate, but the ratification of the risen Lord's promise to send his Holy Spirit to his disciples (cf. Luke 24:49; John 20:21) in order to empower them for the fulfillment of God's mission "to the ends of the earth." The Lord's premise is that this mission cannot be carried out merely on the basis of human effort, but in the power of the Spirit. When that premise has been forgotten, the cost that throughout history the church has had to pay in terms of failures and frustrations has been exceedingly high. "The Lord of the harvest" has so designed the crop that the gleaning of it does not depend on sophisticated techniques, or on human strategies, or on financial resources, but on the Resource that he himself provides for that purpose.

Pentecost and the Church

From a Christian perspective, Pentecost and the church of Jesus Christ are inseparable realities and both of them jointly point to the presence and action of the Holy Spirit. In order to understand them, however, they need to be approached in light of Jesus's purpose in sending his Spirit. To speak of Pentecost is to speak of the power of the Holy Spirit that, in fulfillment of Jesus's promise, God gives to his people for the spread of the good news of the kingdom in all nations. The church that emerges out of Pentecost is by nature a missionary community.

At the same time, to speak of Pentecost is to speak of the church as a pneumatic community—the community of the Spirit. At the beginning of the first volume of his two-volume work, Luke relates the Holy Spirit with Jesus's baptism (Luke 3:21–22) and with his messianic ministry (4:18). At the beginning of the second volume of his work, he relates the Holy Spirit with the church. Pentecost is the baptism of the church through which God enables it to continue Jesus's mission to the very end of time.

We now turn our attention to what may be regarded as the key passage for understanding the Holy Spirit's role in the life and mission of the church in Acts 2, which may be divided into three parts: the Pentecost event (vv. 1–13), the meaning of Pentecost (vv. 14–39), and the results of Pentecost (vv. 40–47).

The Pentecost Event (Acts 2:1–13) The feast of Pentecost was one of the three annual festivals with which the Jewish people used to celebrate the harvest, and it was held for fifty days (hence the reference to *pentekoste*, meaning "fifty" in Greek) after the Passover—the beginning of the harvest. Luke simply mentions that the outpouring of the Holy Spirit took place "when the day of Pentecost came" (v. 1), without drawing any conclusions from this fact. The important issue is what follows: the Spirit of God descended upon the 120 disciples of Jesus Christ gathered in Jerusalem. As we have already stated, this is the baptism of the church, an event concerning which three observations are relevant here.

First, it was both a personal and a social experience. The author seems to make an effort to communicate this idea when he states, on the one hand, that the disciples "saw what seemed to be tongues of fire that separated and came to rest *on each of them*" (v. 3) and, on the other hand, that "they were *all together* in one place" (v. 1) and that "*all of them* were filled with the Holy Spirit" (v. 4; emphasis added in each case). The experience of the Spirit is not a private experience, but an experience in which the personal and the social dimensions are brought together.

Second, it was an experience in which the Holy Spirit manifested his presence through apparently "natural" phenomena, namely, "a sound like the blowing of a violent wind" (v. 2) and "what seemed to be tongues of fire" (v. 3). They are elements probably taken from the theophanies, or visible manifestations of God, in the Old Testament: wind, a symbol of power; fire, a symbol of purification. The reference to them is clearly related to John the Baptist's announcement: "He [Jesus] will baptize you with the Holy Spirit [*pneuma* = wind] and with fire" (Luke 3:16).

Third, it was an experience that made possible the proclamation of the gospel to "all nations," an anticipation of the evangelization that, beginning in Jerusalem, was to reach "the ends of the earth" (Acts 1:8). Luke leaves no room for doubts about the international character of the multitude that was present in Jerusalem for the celebration of Pentecost. He states that the city of Jerusalem was full of God-fearing Jews who had come from the diaspora, "from every nation under heaven" (2:5). Then he includes a long list of the nationalities represented (vv. 9–11a), a list that puzzles New Testament scholars because of its apparent lack of coherence. What Luke seems to want to bring into relief, however, is that on the Day of Pentecost, by the Spirit of God's action, "the wonders of God" (v. 11) were proclaimed to people from many nations, a symbol of the whole inhabited world (the *oikoumene*).

The purpose of glossolalia (speaking in tongues, v. 4) on the Day of Pentecost can only be understood in light of God's intention that the gospel be proclaimed to all nations of the world. It was not an ecstatic or mystical experience, but a resource for mission. This conclusion is supported by the statement that each of the people present "heard them speaking in his own language" (v. 6), and by the comments made by the listeners: "Then how is it that each of us hears them in his own native language?" (v. 8), "we hear them declaring the wonders of God in our own tongues!" (v. 11). On the Day of Pentecost God gives the church the power it needs to communicate his Word to all the nations. By the action of the Spirit all nations are recognized as part of the one human race and placed within the context where the gospel is announced in order to give shape to a new humanity with members "from every nation, tribe, people, and language" (Rev. 7:9). As Peter Goodwin Heltzel has put it, "Pentecost provides a template for the Christian movement as a Spirit-empowered, transnational, multilinguistic, intercultural movement for justice."[18]

A piece of information that should not be overlooked is that the first messengers of the gospel were Galileans (Acts 2:7), that is, people whom the inhabitants of Jerusalem generally regarded as inferior. Is this not a sign of how oftentimes throughout the history of the church the Spirit of God manifests his power and humility?

The Meaning of Pentecost (Acts 2:14–39) Despite the diversity of the languages represented at Pentecost, all the people can hear the proclamation of the gospel in their own language, and that provokes great amazement (v. 12). There are, however, "others," a minority, that do not understand what is going on and make fun of those speaking in tongues, saying that the messengers are drunk (v. 13). That induces Peter to present an interpretation of the meaning of Pentecost, on which we can make the following observations.

First, Peter explains the Pentecost experience in light of Scripture. The quotation of Joel 2:28–32 is an open window that enables us to see the use of the Old Testament in the New Testament. I cannot analyze this subject in detail, but I can point out that the quotation resembles what in the Dead Sea Scrolls is called a *pesher*, that is, an interpretation of the Old Testament in light of a contemporary event that is understood as the fulfillment of an eschatological prophecy. From this perspective, with the coming of Jesus, the Messiah, the new age has arrived and God is fulfilling his promises and carrying out his purpose in history. From this eschatological perspective, what has just happened is what the prophet Joel predicted—"the day of the Lord" has arrived and God has poured out his Spirit on all people, including sons and daughters, young and

---

18. Peter Goodwin Heltzel, "The Holy Spirit of Justice," in *The Justice Project*, ed. Brian McLaren, Elisa Padilla, and Ashley Bunting Seeber (Grand Rapids: Baker, 2009), 48.

old, men servants and women servants, without making distinctions. Pentecost means the creation of a new humanity in which God "democratizes" the experience of the Spirit and consequently makes possible that all the members of the church prophesy. All of them participate in the proclamation of the good news of salvation in Jesus Christ. Beyond doubt, this is the key to understanding the evangelization process that has taken place since the earliest history of the Christian church. They become active "amateur" missionaries anxious to spontaneously share the gospel with others. As Orlando Costas has put it: "The early church interpreted the ministry of evangelization as a communal mission. The traditions of the New Testament, which interpret both Jesus' evangelizing ministry and the various apostolic missions of the early church, affirm categorically that evangelization is not the private property of gifted individuals but rather the responsibility of the whole people of God."[19]

Second, Peter explains the Pentecost experience from a Christological perspective. According to him, the sender of the Spirit is Jesus of Nazareth, "a man accredited by God" by miracles, wonders, and signs that God did through him (v. 22), who was crucified (v. 23), raised from the dead (vv. 24–32), and "exalted to the right hand of God" as Lord and King (vv. 33–36). From that position of universal authority to which he has been exalted by the Father, he has sent the Spirit and invested the church with power to be his witness "to the ends of the earth." As is made clear by Matthew 28:16–20, this universal lordship of Jesus Christ is the basis for the mission of the church to all nations.

Third, Peter links the Pentecost experience with the call to repent and to be baptized "in the name of Jesus Christ" as well as with the promise of forgiveness of sins and the gift of the Holy Spirit (vv. 37–39). Any person who responds to the call receives the promise. The gifts of the Spirit have the same outreach as his call. Therefore, the church is open to receive any person willing to change his attitude, to place his life under the lordship of Jesus Christ, and to share with others the good news of salvation in Jesus Christ.

The Results of Pentecost (Acts 2:40–47) The results of the Pentecost experience are amazing. In a sense, they point to what the church can

19. Costas, "The Evangelistic Legacy of Jesus," 134. Cf. Michael Green, *Evangelism in the Early Church* (London: Hodder & Stoughton, 1984).

expect throughout the centuries as a result of the work of the Holy Spirit in it and through it. These results may be synthesized as follows.

First, there is *evangelization*. The small community of disciples is unexpectedly transformed into a church that even today would be considered large. Note that this growth is the direct result of the preaching of the gospel in the power of the Spirit: "Those who accepted his [Peter's] message were baptized, and about three thousand were added to them that day" (v. 41). Further on, however, another important datum, closely related to this growth, is added: "And the Lord added to their number daily those who were being saved" (v. 47). There is no doubt with regard to the subject of the action, but it is also clear that the Lord uses several means to accomplish his purpose: the proclamation of the gospel (v. 41), "many wonders and miraculous signs . . . done by the apostles" (v. 43), love expressed in terms of mutual sharing and communion among the believers (vv. 44–46), a worship spirit (v. 47a), and "the favor of all the people" (v. 17b). Today there is plenty of evidence to show the dangers of a unilateral emphasis on "church growth" defined in terms of numeral growth accomplished mainly, and sometimes even exclusively, through the oral communication of the gospel.

Second, there is *apostolic teaching*.[20] The presence of the Spirit is made evident through a theological awakening in all the community: "They devoted themselves to the apostles' teaching" (v. 42a). It is not a sterile intellectualism, but a genuine search for a deep understanding of God's truth revealed in Jesus Christ and mediated through the apostles, so as "to call people . . . to the obedience of faith" (Rom. 1:6; cf. 16:26). The apostolic teaching (the *didachē*) is at the center of every church that is open to the work of the Spirit.

Third, there is *fellowship*. The Spirit creates new relationships in the body of Christ. In the case of the church in Jerusalem, because of his presence the believers "devoted themselves . . . to the fellowship" (v. 42b). The extent of this fellowship is clarified in the following verses, which refer to the believers' mutual sharing of material things (vv. 44–45; cf. 4:32–37). The same Spirit who sends "what seemed to be tongues of fire" (2:3) motivates the believers to sell their possessions

20. For a valuable essay on the apostolic teaching, see Oscar Cullmann, "The Tradition," in *The Early Church*, ed. A. J. B. Higgins (London: SCM, 1956), 55–99.

and goods and to give "to anyone as he [or she] had need" (v. 45).[21] Although this passage is descriptive rather than prescriptive, it clearly illustrates how the Christian community created by the Spirit affects personal relationships to such an extent that it includes radical change in the economic field—a field in which, perhaps more than in any other, the authenticity of both our trust in God as the only true sustainer of our lives and our concern for our neighbors, especially the poor and needy, is tested.

Fourth, there is *celebration*. Luke points to this ingredient of the communion created by the Spirit as he affirms that the believers in the church of Jerusalem "devoted themselves . . . to the breaking of bread and to prayer" (v. 42c). This is apparently a reference to the celebration of the Lord's Supper (probably as part of a community meal) and to joint prayer at community meetings. Other data that are added further on enrich the picture: "Every day they continued to meet together in the temple courts. They broke bread in their homes and ate together with glad and sincere hearts, praising God and enjoying the favor of all the people" (vv. 46–47). Clearly, the community that results from Pentecost is a concrete manifestation of the power of the Spirit and a hopeful sign of the fulfillment of God's purpose for humankind.

The picture would not be complete, however, without the words with which the passage closes: "And the Lord added to their number daily those who were being saved" (v. 47b). The preaching of the gospel and the community life that the believers experience as a result of Pentecost are the means that the Spirit of God uses to accomplish a purpose that transcends the Jerusalem church: the creation of a new humanity that confesses Jesus as Lord of history and lives in light of that confession. As in Jesus's case—the purpose of whose anointing he himself defined in the synagogue of Nazareth—the experience of the church in Jerusalem resulted in a mission oriented toward the transformation of every aspect of human life including, as we have seen, its material basis.

---

21. These words echo Deuteronomy 15:4: "there should be no poor among you." "Both the gift of the Spirit and the gift of sharing in community are essential and belong together. Spiritual life cannot be genuine without solidarity with all God's people, particularly those in need." Ross Kinsler and Gloria Kinsler, *The Biblical Jubilee and the Struggle for Life* (Maryknoll: Orbis, 2000), 143.

Conclusion

A brief analysis of the book of Acts throws into relief the spread of the gospel in Jerusalem, Judea, and Samaria, and to "the ends of the earth." As we move from Acts to the epistles, however, we are surprised that the emphasis shifts from the Spirit's action in relation to the mission of the church to the Spirit's power in other areas of the Christian life such as the gifts that he provides for the building up of the church (1 Corinthians 12), love (Rom. 5:5), the Christian character (Gal. 5:19–26), holiness (1 Peter 1:2), Christian unity (Eph. 4:3), and so on. It becomes evident that the same Spirit who empowers the church for mission is also the Spirit who empowers the church to confess Jesus Christ as the Lord of the totality of life and to experience the kingdom of God as a present reality. This is, in fact, God's call to the church between the times of Christ: to live by the power of the Holy Spirit according to the values of the kingdom of God inserted into history in the person and work of Jesus Christ, in the hope that he who began a good work in the church will in the end carry it on to completion to the glory and praise of God.

Further Reading

Corrie, John, and Cathy Ross, eds. *Mission in Context: Explorations Inspired by J. Andrew Kirk.* Burlington, VT: Ashgate, 2012.

Darko, Daniel K., and Beth Snodderly, eds. *First the Kingdom of God: Global Voices on Global Mission.* Pasadena, CA: William Carey International University, 2014.

Padilla, C. René, "Globalization and Christian Mission," "Globalization and Greed," and "The Globalization of Solidarity." *Journal of Latin American Theology: Christian Reflections from the Latino South* 9, no. 2 (2014): 17–90.

Padilla, C. René. *Mission between the Times: Essays on the Kingdom.* Rev. ed. Carlisle: Langham Monographs, 2010.

Contributors

OSCAR GARCÍA-JOHNSON (PhD, Fuller Theological Seminary) is associate professor of theology and Latino/a studies and associate dean for the Center for the Study of Hispanic Church and Community at Fuller Seminary in California. Born in Honduras, he is an ordained minister with the American Baptist Churches, planted four churches, and worked as a Regional Minister for the American Baptist Churches of Los Angeles for eleven years prior to coming to Fuller. He is the author of *Jesús, Hazme Como Tú: Cuarenta Maneras de Imitar a Cristo* (Wipf and Stock, 2014) and *The Mestizo/a Community of the Spirit* (Pickwick, 2009) and coauthor of *Theology without Borders: Introduction to Global Conversations* (Baker Academic, 2015). His current research focuses on critical ecclesiology, de-colonial theology, and intercultural/global religious conversations from the South.

GENE L. GREEN (PhD, University of Aberdeen) is professor of New Testament at Wheaton College in Illinois. Previously he taught New Testament and served as academic dean and rector of the Seminario ESEPA in San José, Costa Rica. He is the author of four biblical commentaries written in Spanish and English, coauthor of *The New Testament in Antiquity* (Zondervan, 2009), and coeditor of *Global Theology in Evangelical Perspective* (IVP Academic, 2012). His current research focuses on the intersection of the Christian faith and cultures, both ancient and contemporary, and the theology of Peter.

WEI HUA (PhD, Peking University) is associate professor of philosophy and Christian studies at Huaqiao University, Xiamen, China. He has published several articles on biblical and Augustinian studies, including "A Brief Investigation of Sarx and Sōma in *Romans*" (*Biblical Literature Studies* 6 [February 2012]), "On the Rise of Augustine's Concept of *Voluntas*" (*Sino-Christian Studies* 15 [June 2013]), and "*Galatians* 2:11–14 and the Exegetical Controversy between Augustine and Jerome" (*Logos & Pneuma: Chinese Journal of Theology* 42 [Spring 2015]).

SAMUEL M. NGEWA (PhD, Westminster Theological Seminary) is professor of New Testament at Africa International University, Nairobi, Kenya. He is the author of *The Gospel of John for Pastors and Teachers* (2003) and several commentaries in the Africa Bible Commentary Series, including *1 & 2 Timothy and Titus* (2009). He also serves as a pastor with Africa Inland Church, Kenya.

DAVID TONGHOU NGONG (PhD, Baylor University) is associate professor of religion and theology at Stillman College in Tuscaloosa, Alabama. He is originally from Cameroon, Africa. In addition to many articles, he is the author of *The Holy Spirit and Salvation in African Christian Theology* (Peter Lang, 2010) and *Theology as Construction of Piety: An African Perspective* (Wipf and Stock, 2013).

C. RENÉ PADILLA (PhD, University of Manchester) is executive director of Ediciones Kairos and president emeritus of the Kairos Foundation of Buenos Aires, Argentina. In addition to many articles, he has authored or edited more than twenty books, most of them on the subject of integral mission. His main book, *Mission between the Times: Essays on the Kingdom* (Langham Monographs, 2nd ed., 2010), has been published in English, Spanish, Portuguese, Korean, German, and Swedish.

IVAN SATYAVRATA (PhD, Oxford Centre for Mission Studies) has spent more than twenty years in Christian leadership training, but presently serves as senior pastor of the Assembly of God Church in Kolkata, a multilingual congregation, with a weekly attendance of more than four thousand people and a social outreach that provides education and basic nutrition for several thousand underprivileged children. He has authored two books: *Holy Spirit, Lord and Life Giver* (IVF, 2009) and *God Has Not Left Himself without Witness* (Regnum, 2011).

ZAKALI SHOHE is associate professor of New Testament and academic dean at Trinity Theological College (affiliated with the Senate of Serampore College [University]) in Dimapur, Nagaland, India. She has contributed chapters to several monographs and is the coeditor of *Theology-In Context* (2010). Her upcoming monograph is *Acceptance Motif in Paul: Revisiting Romans 15:7–13* (Peter Lang).

AMOS YONG (PhD, Boston University) is professor of theology and mission and director of the Center for Missiological Research at Fuller Theological Seminary in Pasadena, California. He has authored or edited more than forty books, including, most recently, *Renewing Christian Theology: Systematics for a Global Christianity* (Baylor University Press, 2014).

Index of Names

Abhishiktananda, Swami, 45, 47–48, 50, 51
Achtemeier, Paul J., 59n
Acosta, José de, 149–50, 156
Alexander, Estrelda Y., 131n
Alfaro, Sammy, 31n
Anderson, Allan H., 21n, 23n, 127n, 135n
Anderson, Jonathan A., 31n
Appasamy, Aiyadurai Jesudasen, 19, 42, 43, 51, 53, 55n
Aquinas, Thomas, 3, 42, 146, 151
Asamoah-Gyadu, J. Kwabena, 127n, 129n, 133
Athanasius of Alexandria, 2, 123, 124
Atkinson, William P., 32n
Attanasi, Katherine, 25n
Augustine of Hippo, 6, 20–21, 87n, 123, 124, 140, 146, 151
Aurobindo, Sri, 43
Axelson, Sigbert, 125

Bailey, G. M., 53
Bao, Huiyuan, 80
Barclay, John M. G., 88n
Barrett, C. K., 111n
Barth, Karl, 6
Basil of Caesarea, 2, 16

Beare, F. W., 105n
Bebawi, George, 127n
Bernard of Clairvaux, 3
Borthwick, Paul, 145, 146n
Bortolot, Alexander Ives, 126n
Boyd, Robin, 39n, 40, 43, 53n
Braybrooke, M., 37n
Brock, Sebastian P., 16n, 17n
Bromiley, Geoffrey W., 64n
Bruce, F. F., 105n, 115n, 174n
Brueggemann, Walter, 173
Bruner, Frederick Dale, 14n
Bulgakov, Sergei, 17
Burgess, Stanley M., 18n
Burke, Trevor J., 64n

Calvin, John, 6, 146, 151
Campbell, W. S., 59n
Campos, Bernardo, 167n
Chakkarai, Vengal, 19, 44–45, 50, 51
Chalassery, Joseph, 16n
Chenchiah, Pandipeddi, 19, 36, 43–44, 51, 71
Chestnut, R. Andrew, 162n
Chettimattam, J. B., 48n
Chhattopadhyay, Gouranga, 70n
Chiquete, Daniel, 167n
Church, Joe, 101–2

Index of Subjects

Index of Scripture References